THE BOOK OF GARLIC

This book has been approved and hand-stamped by the authorized represent- ative of LOVERS of the STINKING ROSE ©

D1122691

ABOUT THE BOOK

Everything . . . you ever wanted to know about Allium Sativum, and then some . . .
—Christopher Lehmann-Haupt,
New York Times

A lively and scholarly labor of love . . .
—*High Times*

One of the most delightful, entertaining texts we have seen in a long time.
—*Medical Newsmagazine*

. . . a delightful romp of folklore, legends, comedy, historical fact and recipes.
—*The Des Moines Register*

Mr. Harris, a publisher, has produced his own authoritative work . . . Its ultimate ac- colade was a French translation.
—*The Manchester Guardian*

ABOUT LSR'S NEWSLETTER, GARLIC TIMES

Under the kindly, mischievous and tal- ented auspices of L. J. Harris—champion of garlic—the *Garlic Times* newsletter is a stim- ulating blend of healthful fact and frolic.
—*Health Quarterly*

The *Garlic Times* is a wonderful publica- tion.
—*The New Orleans Times-Picayune*

ABOUT THE AUTHOR

32-year-old L. J. Harris is a resident of Berkeley, CA where he administers his gar- lic club and newsletter. Mr. Harris is also the publisher of Aris Books, and is working on several new books of his own.

Line drawings by
    Licita Fernandez

Collages by
    Lloyd J. Harris

Typography, production and design by
    Martin Ilian, Dennis Koran,
    Bob Sibley and L. J. Harris

New contributions by
    Lovers of the
    Stinking Rose
    and the editors of
    Garlic Times

Cover design by
    Seymour Chwast

Title page drawing by
    Jane Veeder

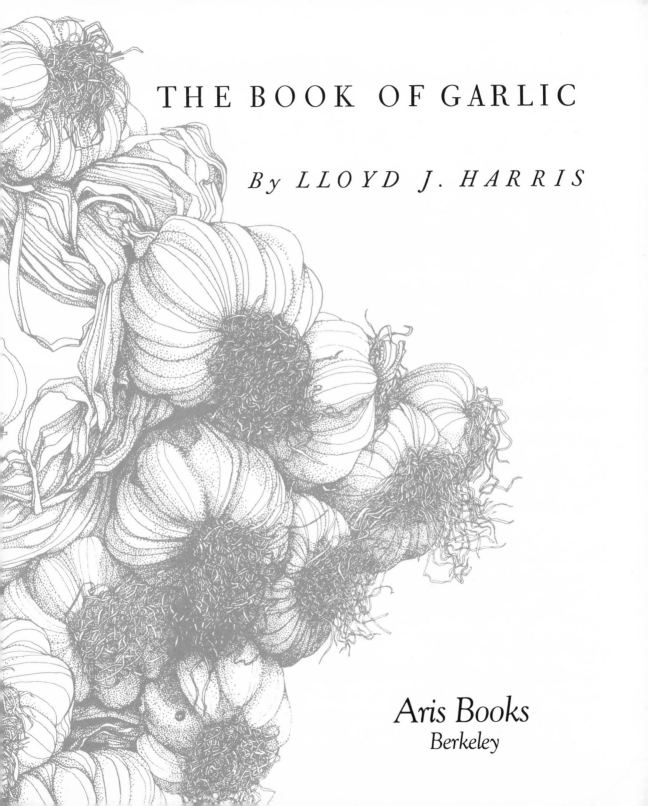

THE BOOK OF GARLIC

By LLOYD J. HARRIS

Aris Books
Berkeley

Library of Congress Cataloging in Publication Data

Harris, Lloyd J. 1947–
      The book of garlic.

      Bibliography: p. 279
      1. Garlic. 2. Garlic (in cooking, folklore, etc.).
3. Garlic—Therapeutic use. I. Title.
GR790.G3H37 1980   615'.324'324   79-20972
ISBN 0-943186-00-5
(Formerly published by Panjandrum/Aris Books,
ISBN 0-915572-29-X)

Tenth Printing, April 1984
Third, Revised Edition
Acknowledgments and permissions on page 286 constitute an extension of this copyright page.

Manufactured in the United States of America for Aris Books by Thomson-Shore, Inc.

Aris Books/Harris Publishing Company, Inc.
1621 Fifth St.
Berkeley, CA 94710

For my mother and father and for Linda

Photo by Roy Williams. Used by permission of the *Oakland Tribune*.

"When people ask me if I take garlic seriously, I answer 'No' to those who take me seriously, and 'Yes' to those who don't. But the real question is not whether I take garlic seriously, but whether I take it. And the answer is 'Yes; every chance I get.'"

—*L. J. Harris*
Reprinted from Garlic Times

CONTENTS

PART ONE: A SERIOUS HISTORY

In Which the Author Elucidates the Use of Garlic as Food, Medicine and Magic in Many Lands, and the Argument For and Against Garlic

RECIPE INDEX

11

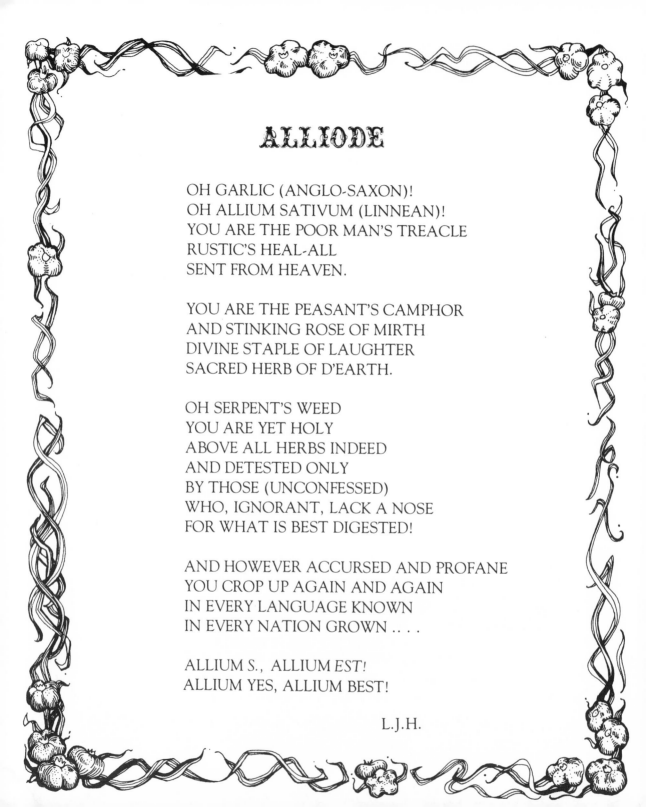

ALLIODE

OH GARLIC (ANGLO-SAXON)!
OH ALLIUM SATIVUM (LINNEAN)!
YOU ARE THE POOR MAN'S TREACLE
RUSTIC'S HEAL-ALL
SENT FROM HEAVEN.

YOU ARE THE PEASANT'S CAMPHOR
AND STINKING ROSE OF MIRTH
DIVINE STAPLE OF LAUGHTER
SACRED HERB OF D'EARTH.

OH SERPENT'S WEED
YOU ARE YET HOLY
ABOVE ALL HERBS INDEED
AND DETESTED ONLY
BY THOSE (UNCONFESSED)
WHO, IGNORANT, LACK A NOSE
FOR WHAT IS BEST DIGESTED!

AND HOWEVER ACCURSED AND PROFANE
YOU CROP UP AGAIN AND AGAIN
IN EVERY LANGUAGE KNOWN
IN EVERY NATION GROWN .. . .

ALLIUM S., ALLIUM *EST!*
ALLIUM YES, ALLIUM BEST!

L.J.H.

INTRODUCTION

To The Third Edition

WELCOME TO *The Book of Garlic;* or should I say the *world* of
garlic? Since publication of the first edition in 1974, world consumption of
garlic has skyrocketed, world interest in garlic has reached fan and fad proportions, and my own personal "world" has been overthrown by forces of the
Garlic Revolution. The first-time reader may already get the picture that
there is more to garlic than meets the eye. True. Since the first edition, there
has been the growth of Lovers of the Stinking Rose, a garlic fan club, and a
club newsletter called *Garlic Times.* The most universally notable success of
these garlic organs has been to raise garlic consciousness through our national
boycott of mouthwash products. So if this book works and your garlic consciousness is raised sufficiently, you might want to follow the instructions for
joining LSR on page 103.

Getting back to the book at hand, I'd like to thank those stinking souls
who have helped me to revise, expand and update this new edition. Most of
these human cloves are either officers or members of LSR: Charles Perry
(gastrojournalist, Associate Editor of *Rolling Stone* and Contributing Editor to
New West), Bruce Aidells (Chef at Berkeley's *Poulet* and Recipe Editor of
Garlic Times), Robert and Amora Charles (legendary proprietors of La Vieille
Maison, the garlic/French restaurant in Truckee, CA), Jeanne Rose (LSR's
herb consultant and author of *Kitchen Cosmetics* and other herbals) and Les
Blank and his assistant Maureen Gosling (makers of the film "Garlic is as
Good as Ten Mothers").

If it were not for the following folks, there would be no LSR, GT or
"revised edition:" Dennis Koran, Martin Ilian, Beau Beausoleil and Leslie
Carr—all of Panjandrum/Aris Books; Nanou Stark of LSR; Don Christopher
and Caryl Saunders of the Garlic Growers Association in Gilroy, CA; Alice

Waters and all the folks at Chez Panisse, the home of Berkeley's annual garlic festival; The Cheeseboard Collective in Berkeley, CA; and last but not least, the wonderful members of Lovers of the Stinking Rose whose letters, recipes, anecdotes, tips, art work, etc. have kept me going.

For those of you who have used previous editions of *The Book of Garlic,* I'd like to explain what's new in this edition. First, some of the new material is in the form of *Garlic Times* updates. These are recognizable by their two-column format. Most of the changes in this edition will be found in: A Garlic Times Recipe Supplement, page 263; a new chapter called In Defense of the Stinking Rose, page 101; an expanded Appendix, page 212; a recipe index, page 10; and new recipes, folklore, medical/herbal data, jokes and graphics throughout. Some material from previous editions has been deleted to make room for the new material.

As for the future of *The Book of Garlic,* it rests with you, the reader. Your contributions to *Garlic Times* (recipes, letters, jokes, art work, poems, ideas, remedies, etc.) will form future editions. So please stay in touch with us either by joining LSR, subscribing to *Garlic Times* or just sending in your material. The manuscript title of this book, changed for a variety of reasons, was "The Peoples' Book of Garlic." As the years and cloves squeeze by, it is becoming just that.

—L. J. Harris
1980

FOREWORD

To The Second Edition

IT IS PERHAPS rare that one allows himself the luxury of devoting almost two years of his life to something so personal and perhaps irrelevant that in the very act of this devotion, the object of the private passion becomes itself invested (magically or absurdly) with a new power and relevance of its own. After two years of my private garlic inspiration (If I can *perspire* garlic, then can't I also *inspire* it?), not only am I in a real sense changed, but so also is garlic; and I don't seem to tire, as you will see, of explaining and analyzing this strange conversion experience.

It is as if a poor slovenly bum were whisked off by some legendary benefactor, given new clothes and an allowance, and taken to the finest night spots. The bum may not adjust to this miracle and may stick out like a sore thumb despite his formal dress, accruing insults and cries of "fraud" and "impostor." Even so, the benefactor did effect a change in the fellow's circumstances, and this former derelict does have, at least, a new set of clothes. Well, poor humble eccentric garlic, eternal victim of vile insults and slanders (enumerated in the pages to come), has a new set of attire as well: earthy, smelly garlic is now elegantly covered by it's very own treatise, this book.

This transformation has worked both ways. I have changed garlic, and garlic has, I now see, changed me—yes, into garlic. Proof? Simply read this book and make a list of garlic's contradictory qualities, e.g., sweetness/pungency, popularity/disrepute, complexity/simplicity; this list could be the story of my own cleaved existence. Unconsciously, I have been drawn to garlic by an irrational *affinity*.

The amazing thing is that I, garlic's brazen benefactor, am not alone in my garlic infusion. I have unwittingly found myself thrown in with a whole

15

throng of garlic benefactors, fans, worshippers, and assorted other alliophiles. The evidence for what I call a Garlic Revolution is simply self-evident. During the months of work on this book I became aware of an upsurge of enthusiasm for garlic in the press and in publishing and journalistic circles. Garlic, traditionally déclassé in Victorian America, is now "in." Books, articles, medical findings, and news stories seem to appear daily, blessing garlic with new interest and energy. And if the gourmets writing in sophisticated cookbooks and magazines generally dismiss the findings of doctors and researchers writing in sophisticated medical and health journals about garlic's health value, this is all for the good: garlic thrives on controversy. One noted newspaper man, Charles McCabe of the San Francisco *Chronicle,* is perhaps the only journalist in America who has actually accepted this garlic controversy as a phenomenon of national significance (see his stories, pages 184-188)

What it all boils down to is that garlic, according to a large producer in California, is now the second most consumed spice in America after pepper; it is being incorporated into our evermore cuisine-conscious culture as a veritable *staple.* Thus, although anti-garlic powers are still rampant in the land, the Aristocrats of the Palate (those who celebrate food as "art" and can afford to do so) and the Peasants of the Palate (who like garlic in anything and everything in great amounts and regardless of the "rules" of haute cuisine) are consuming garlic in ever-greater quantities and varieties. Understandably, the domestic garlic growing and processing industry is having a field day with this Americanization of allium: powders, granules, flakes, chips, dips, purées, concentrates, etc. Most of these products rely on the booming processing/dehydrating industry, and we are told that over 60% of the garlic consumed in the United States is in the dehydrated form. Still, the use of fresh garlic is also, despite its minor inconveniences, becoming a national pastime. If 200 million pounds of garlic are being produced annually in the U.S. (compared to the pre-mechanized garlic industry of 1956 with 36 million pounds) then we should be hearing "please pass the garlic" about as often as we hear "please pass the salt and pepper."

The variety of garlic products is the telltale sign of Americanization. In France, Spain, and Japan, for example, garlic *is* simply garlic. In the U.S., garlic is an endless array of nifty consumer miracles. Along with foreign imports, the U.S. has all the raw materials it needs to support the garlic habits of all citizens from the most fastidious connoisseurs (where often "just a pinch" is sufficient to explode their sensitive tastes) to the most humble of clove-chomping neo-agrarian hipsters and ethnic oldsters. Even our dogs and cats have shown a marked preference for the *je ne sais quoi* hints of garlic in their canned foods (check the label!).

As if this "irrelevant" garlic-mania were indeed more than of trivial concern in our anxiety- and violence-crazed world, the scales of justice have been set in motion over the Garlic Dilemma (every revolution is caused by a *dilemma*), a dilemma confronting humans since the Romans passed laws limiting the use of garlic (see page 53). That is, what do garlic-haters do about the sometimes devastating fallout from garlic-lovers? And conversely, what do the garlic-eaters do when confronted with the outraged (albeit refined or *processed*) sensitivities of alliophobes. It may be that the definition of the Pursuit of Happiness will have to include, ultimately, a resolution of this issue. A first step was taken recently by a New York State Supreme Court judge, in a case involving the "garlicky odors" wafting from a French restaurant in Manhattan; the judge ruled that garlic odors were not a public nuisance. The party (an English professor) seeking the injunction against the restaurant was told by the judge that the pleasures of French cuisine are as important to civilization for some as pollution-free air is to others (*Sourian* vs. *Saleh, N.Y. Law Journal,* Jan 2, 1975). The judge ordered the restaurant to take more precautions, but would not shut down this obviously thriving establishment. In other words, the vicissitudes of garlic are legal!

We see here a possible solution to more than the Garlic Dilemma. Beyond certain reasonable limits, we all live in the same world, breath the same air, sniff the same aromas. So, if you will excuse the simplistic moralizing, to survive each other (Hell is other people), we must learn to tolerate the very things we *cannot* tolerate. Join the Garlic Revolution, a revolution with *breath!*

L.J. Harris
1975

PREFACE
To The First Edition

I LOVE garlic, hence this book. I love garlic *a lot,* and hence this rather thick book on garlic. And since until recently I knew almost nothing about garlic (except that I loved it a lot), hence a book that has to do with everything (more or less) that has to do with garlic. In fact, this book contains just about everything I could dig up about garlic in my crash program to "find myself" through the mysteries of the Great Garlic.

> It takes a heap a' heaping to make a heap a' heap.
> — Fred Holtby
> The Author's Favorite High School Teacher

In the creation of the heap that is this book, I did find myself a bona fide Alliomaniac (from Allium or garlic) of the first order: And whatever befalls this book, nothing can shake my loyalty to that pungent little creature, Allium Sativum (botanical name for the most widely used of the garlics). Indeed, this is not a book about garlic but a tribute to this amazing phenomenon of the vegetable kingdom, and not a half-baked tribute, but one worthy I hope, of the phenomenal richness of garlic; because for some irrational reason, the world appears on closer scrutiny to be revolving not around the sun, but viewed mystically — from the *inside* — around the sublime garlic, Lily Extraordinaire, Stinking Rose, Camphor of the Poor, Rustic's Treacle (heal-all) and Balm and Nectar of the Gods. It is my hope that with this book, I will have helped restore garlic to its Universal position at the hub of man's preoccupation with Existence. And if not, well so much the worse for Existence, because it may be that garlic could, in its own special way, mean the difference between the survival or extinction of Natural Humanity, a humanity still immersed in the natural environment.

My own involvement with garlic began as a love of its taste, but my daily consumption of garlic became more of a ritual than a dietary practice, and I became fascinated by the idea of exploring the meaning, if any, behind this obsession with a simple but perhaps eccentric food. To my great surprise, I had involved myself with the most passionately beloved, and yet at the same time, the most viciously attacked of herbs in history. This book, then, is an attempt to come to the roots of this passionate ambivalence regarding garlic, and to present the information compiled in almost a year of research. I must apologize if some of the text (especially the historical data) seems a bit undigested: I am neither an expert in the history of garlic, nor in the history of History, and thus do not have the tools needed to present a "definitive" work (but then most definitive works are definitely boring). I feel it important, however, to get the story of garlic and its potential value for the human future in front of the public now. Others can, if they are interested, sift through this material and determine where its greatest value lies. There is enough garliciana—technical and entertaining—lying untapped to fill a second volume of *The Book of Garlic*, and perhaps along with the inevitable corrections in this volume, I may attempt this task. For more on my personal and life-long love of garlic, I call your attention to the Afterword.

Perhaps by the end of this book, the reader will be able to judge for himself just exactly what there is about garlic that explains its confused, passionate and eccentric history. My own ideas are sprinkled throughout, and if I happen to wax pedantic and wander off into nebulous realms, relevant perhaps only to my own sense of relevance, it is because I always wanted to be a philosopher when I grew up. Well, I am grown up and I find myself involved with garlic. I hope my philosopher's approach to the simple garlic and the sometimes too shimmering gauze of my prose do not detract from a clear vision of Allium Sativum. It is as if the potent lily had the power to loosen one's tongue and feather one's cap. So, in this I blame garlic and not any rambunctiousness on my part.

There is, though, no avoiding the fact that however clearly one may wish to see garlic, this vision must be built of complex and involuted layers of meaning. Garlic is like a crystal ball that collects the mysterious and complex relationships of life and reflects them back as a single unmistakable entity—a Garlic! One could spend a life-time reflecting on the ways in which garlic suggests the Cosmos and all the "mechanics" contained therein.

My primary focus, though, is on *garlic* and not on these technical and esoteric matters. In touching on all areas that touch upon garlic, I run the risk of being merely *exhausting* and not *exhaustive*. But in my own defense I can say that I have tried to stop short of making grandiose and conclusive statements about the Miracle of Garlic. Rather, I have presented possibilities which have always excited me more than most actualities. Perhaps garlic has been a means for presenting the underlying philosophy — In any thing, Everything — the assumption that if one looks carefully and penetratingly at any *thing* in existence, *everything* will become visible through it. This attitude (common to so-called mystical ways of thinking) allows one to perceive Existence as a hall of mirrors, and within this "structure" infinite connections are possible. Add a Christian morality or hierarchy to this perception and you have the old herbalist philosophy that life, from top to bottom, is connected and good — each part, no matter how ugly or evil, serving the whole of Life (discussed in The Herbalist Tradition — Part One).

I personally stop short of seeing existence as both connected and good: Things are indeed connected, but they are good-bad or bad-good. Garlic is, again, a wonderful representative for this idea of merging opposites, for there is hardly a food on Earth that can lay claim to tasting as *good* as garlic, and at the same time (after the fact) to smelling as *bad*. I do not, then, want to overstate Good Garlic at the expense of Bad Garlic. I have tried to state the case for both sides of the garlic Passion. My own loyalty and positive passion for garlic will show through, but I feel, however, that my personal involvement with Allium Sativum includes or absorbs the negative Alliumphobic position. After all, it is precisely this controversy concerning garlic that makes it a Universal phenomenon.

WARNING

This book is in part a compilation of current and historical data and in no way should the various garlic remedies and regimens herein contained, be considered a medical prescription for the reader. Any garlic treatments should be taken with the consultation of a medical doctor, or nutritionist; and if they won't prescribe it, try your local herbalist, automechanic, Rabbi, or other ethnic representative.

Berkeley, 1974

INTRODUCTION TO
THE BOOK OF GARLIC

> Garlic has been used for so long, for so
> many illnesses, by so many different
> people and is so effective that pages
> could be devoted to rhapsodizing about
> its wonders.
>
> Jeanne Rose, Herbalist

A SERIOUS HISTORY

Part One of this book deals with the popular use of garlic throughout
ancient, medieval and modern times. There is no doubt but that garlic has
received as much or more attention in the lives and literature of people in all
cultures, East and West, than any other herb, as food, as magical charm, and
as medical specific.

As if to balance this passion *for* garlic, an equally strong passion *against*
garlic has been evident as well: Precisely to the degree that garlic is loved, an
equal hatred for garlic arises. We will see this especially in the Egyptian,
Greek and Roman cultures. The chapter on the historical Argument
Against Garlic will trace the underlying issues in this almost universal antagonism between Alliumphiles and Alliumphobes.

GARLIC AS A MEDICAL SPECIFIC

Although this book is not a medical herbal as such, the value of garlic as
a medical specific cannot be ignored. Part Two — Garlic the Super Herb —
focuses on this aspect of the wonderous Allium Sativum. Doctors and re-

searchers have discovered in the last 50 years that indeed, garlic is a valuable anti-microbial agent. Although these findings remain controversial, it is my hope that *The Book of Garlic* may at least stimulate interest in the claims for this natural, inexpensive and easily grown antibiotic.

I invite the scientific-medical community to evaluate the material presented in Part Two — Garlic the Super Herb. I do not want to be a fanatic about garlic, but I am impressed with the quantity and quality of data from Europe, Asia and America regarding garlic's medical values, and I would like to see more American research done to clarify these studies so that the public will know specifically what garlic can and cannot do. It is incredible that so much research has been carried out on garlic, and yet so few Americans are aware that garlic is good for more than a "hint" of flavor in pasta and lamb stew. If garlic is ultimately found to be less than a Panacea, as the ancients viewed it, well then we can settle back and enjoy that garlicky pasta and that lamb stew — not a bad consolation prize. But I predict that garlic will become an important nutritional and therapeutic staple in the American diet in years to come.

EXCURSIONS INTO GARLICIANA

As a by-product of this most ignored of world-wide wars, The War of the Garlics, humor arises (black, white, green, absurd, silly, surreal) in its role as adaptive and integrative mechanism. Part Three will take the reader on various excursions into these fun-filled realms where garlic serves as nothing less than a Primal Comic agent. In Lawrence Durrell's short story, "If Garlic Be the Food of Love", garlic wreaks havoc in the British Diplomatic Corps. Charles McCabe, in "Garlic Country", relates various trials and tribulations of Garlic Lovers. Other areas explored in Part Three include garlic in political history, a fascinating account of Alburria, a garlic nation unknown to the world until now, and in a Special Appendix you will find material from the *Garlic Times Scrapbook*.

A GARLIC GALA GASTRONOMIQUE

Perhaps an explanation for garlic's universal use is in the truism that the human stomach, midway between feet and head, is at the center of history as well; and what could be more connected to humanity's stomach than garlic, the king of herbs, seasonings and spices. Part Four will serve as a compendium of loved garlic recipes from international cuisine — haute and popular. It is hoped that this garlic gourmet cookbook will not only whet the appetites of the most timid of garlic eaters, but will serve also as a valuable reference tool by presenting important tips and hints.

I

A SERIOUS HISTORY

*In Which the
Author Elucidates the
Use of Garlic as
Food, Medicine & Magic
In Many Lands*

AND

*The Argument
Against
Garlic*

à z'ails ! à z'aulx !...

From l'Artiste Douaisien Ad. Robaut, 19th century, reproduced in the Arleux Garlic Festival magazine.

INTRODUCTION

GARLIC is a central character in the history of diet, folk medicine, and in the ritual and beliefs of early religion. There is evidence that garlic was worshipped as a God and even within the same culture, scorned as an agent of the devil. These extreme attitudes concerning a simple little herb may appear naive or primitive to our modern rational vision, but it would be wrong to assume that what has come down to us concerning garlic, or any of the herbs, from ancient and medieval times is merely magic and superstition compared to our modern "facts". Superstition and fact are relative. Franz Strung in his history on medieval natural science points out that "all superstition is ancient science, all science is new, modern superstition . . . what is superstition today was once science." (1) It is a rather common attitude today that the scope of our modern science is only now beginning to re-incorporate (and confirm) some of the insights of ancient and medieval science—insights that have been swept under the rugs of history. The ancient and "old" worlds knew well the value of garlic, and it wasn't just "belief" or faith, as our new understanding of garlic indicates.

Admittedly, it would be nearly impossible to return to a day when garlic was literally worshipped as a God. I cannot imagine the English (and their soul mates in America) overcoming their almost natural disdain for garlic and its alliacious odors. But then it would be hard for any people, even the garlic-loving peoples of Europe and Asia to live up to the ancient enthusiasm for a simple herb such as garlic in which even the "winds" it produced after consumption were seen as *divine*. The sacred "burp" and the divine "fart" are no more. The worship of these necessary bodily functions is at best a fanciful antique custom that may never re-emerge in our increasingly sterile (deodorized) societies.* But all is not lost! Garlic lovers can rejoice in the knowledge that one need not worship garlic to Enjoy it, and to benefit from it. And if we must concede to the manners that tell us to excuse ourselves from the table to release the once holy "ill wind behind" to use Dr. Johnson's expression (Dr. Samuel Johnson, *Dictionary* London, 1755), then this is not too great a price for the pleasure and health received from the divine little Allium Sativum.

In the course of garlic's history, in certain cases, the enthusiasm for garlic reached a point of balance or refinement, before garlic began its voyage into relative obscurity in the modern age, due in part to the development of chemical or synthetic medicines. In the following letter from Beatrice d'Este, Duchess of Milan, to Isabella d'Este, Duchess of Mantua in March of 1491, this refined yet enthusiastic Alliumphilia is evident:

> I cannot enjoy any pleasure or happiness unless I share it with you. And I must tell you that I have had a whole field of garlic planted for your benefit, so that when you come, we may be able to have plenty of your favorite dishes! (2)

*There are signs that a minor excremental re-awakening is in progress, particularly in the cinema. Two recent films *Le Grand Bouffe* and *Blazing Saddles* celebrate the fart in true Rabelaisian style with absurd-slapstick undertones. A brief survey of girlie magazines (*Playboy, Oui, Penthouse, etc.*) will also reveal a growing fascination with the female behind and sex associated with that area. Is this an example of Freud's "return of the repressed"?

  I don't mean to give the impression that garlic consumption leads irrevocably to "ill winds". Garlic is strong, and if overdone—especially raw—can upset the stomach. Also, if one has an affinity for gas, garlic will promote this activity. In fact, garlic was used in traditional folk medicine as a treatment for flatulence, i.e., as a gas expeller.

The Serious History of garlic contains on the other side, as I have said, the Garlic Haters or Alliumphobes, who have fought the Peoples' garlic with a viciousness uncommon to matters of diet.

As we move into the 21st Century, it is not inconceivable that in some sense the world will divide itself into two warring factions—those who see in garlic an aspect of Divine Nectar, and those who equate the pungent bulb of Allium Sativum with Filthy Lucre. This possible future world will be in essence a continuous struggle between the powers of the Natural world versus those of the Technological world. Garlic is a pretty good means of sizing up where people stand on the scale between these extremes.

ACCORDING TO WEBSTER

When we speak of garlic, we mean a particular member of the Allium genus within the family of lilies known as Liliaceæ.

> Garlic (gárlic), ne. (Me. garlek; AS. garleac; gar, a spear +leac, a leek: From spearlike leaves).
>   1. a bulbous plant of the lily family (Allium Sativum)
>   2. a strong smelling bulb of this plant, made up of small sections called cloves, used as seasoning in meats, salads, etc.

It is strange to think of garlic, the smelly herb, as a cousin of the Easter Lily—symbol of fragility and virginity. The fact of the relatedness of garlics and lilies proves one of the more interesting facets in the lore of the plant kingdom, reflecting as it does on the level of Botany, the same ambiguity that re-occurs throughout the social history of garlic as both a sacred (loved) and profane (hated) food.

GARLIC LINGUISTICS

All the Turkic languages from Singkiang Province of China (the Uighurs) to Turkey, from the Tatar Autonomous Soviet Republic (the Kazan or Volga Tatars) 500 miles east of Moscow to the Uzbeks of Afghanistan (and including such oddball tongues as Qaraim, the Turkish dialect of certain Jewish communities in Poland and the Crimea), have a word for garlic. It is *sarimsaq* (sarmisaq, sarimsok, samsaq).

On the other hand, there is no universal Turkic word for onion. In Turkey they say *soğan,* and similar words are used by the Kirgiz and Uighur peoples (suğan), but many of the Turkic tongues use the Persian word *piyaz.* This may indicate that onion culture was later or less deep in the Turkic or Altaic peoples, or that when Turks came in contact with the onion-loving Iranian peoples they adopted the more highly developed Persian onion culture; the corollary would be that the Turks were relatively more garlic-loving than the Iranians.

In Arabic there are a number of garlic puns. Garlic is *thum* (pronounced toom or thoom) and an example would be "Ya 'aib el-thum"—"Ya 'aib el-shum" means "mercy me what a shame," but changing the last word to "thum" makes it mean "O shame of the garlic." This pun gets big laughs among the six-year-olds.

—*Charles Perry*

If you find yourself in any of the following countries, ask for garlic with the correct word.

Iceland	knapplaukur
Moscow	chesnok
Albania	hudhrë
Prague	chesnak, or chesnek
Lithuania	chesnakas
Spain	ajo
France	ail
Italy	aglio
Croatia	cheshnyak or biyeli luk
Japan	niniku
Davos, Switz.	agl (this is Romansch, or Ladinic)
Wales	garlleg
Malta	tewm
Arabia	tūm (varies with location)
Holland	knoflook
Germany	Knoblauch
Basque land	berakatz
Estonia	küüskauk
Ukraine	chasnik
Finland	laukka (or sipulitävä)
Norway	løk
Malaysia	bawang poetih (means "white bulb"
Slovenia	chesen
Budapest	foghagyma
So. Africa	knoffel
Sweden	vitlök
Latvia	kiploki
Flanders	knoflook
Esperanto	ajlo

—*Bill Harmon*
Esperanto League of
North America
San Francisco

ALLIUM SATIVUM

Linguists derive the "al" of allium from the Celtic "al" meaning "burning." Garlic shares the allium genus with onions, leeks, chives, shallots and others. In the ancient days of language, the "leek" meant in Hebrew "herb" or "grass" and was known as the herb *par excellence* (3). In the language of Celts and Slavs "leek" had the meaning of "succulent herb." Leek is also related to the German "lauch" (knoblauch<garlic<cloven leek). So garlic then is that lily which is related to the burning bulbs of the Allium genus, and which is made up of several sections called cloves. Of course there are many species of garlic, but here we are concerned with Allium Sativum, sativum meaning to harvest or cultivate. Allium Sativum is the garlic that is most often used in diet and medicine. Wild Garlic or Ransoms are extremely pungent and little used for food, and Giant or Elephant Garlic is not technically garlic, but more closely related to the leek. Its cloves are about three times the size of Allium sativum cloves, and the flavor is mild. Another near garlic is Rocambole, not yet widely used in the U.S. Slightly smaller than sativum, and slightly less potent, Rocambole develops bulblets at the top of its flower stalk. Both Rocambole and Elephant Garlic seed can be obtained from selected nurseries. See Part Four, Growing Your Own, for more information on these and other Alliums.

CHAPTER ONE

GARLIC IN OLDEN DAYS

DE CANDOLE in his *Origin of Cultivated Plants*, places garlic as a native to the Kirgiz desert region of Siberia. Since its origins in western Asia, garlic has been naturalized all over the world. De Candole explains that garlic was brought via Asia Minor to Egypt by nomadic tribes and from there back up through India via the trade routes to eastern Asia, and westward to Europe.

The fact of garlic's significance in the diet and pharmacy of civilizations past is incontestable. The Babylonians of 4500 years ago were great lovers of garlic, and it is noted by K. Hintze in his history of nutrition that garlic took a special place at the table of one Babylonian God-king. It is said that some 395,000 bushels garlic were delivered to the court at one time (4). The sea-faring Phœnicians and Vikings took garlic with them on long voyages as both a nutritious food, and a valuable remedy for the various ailments common to sailors.

Later, the Romans came to call the Egyptians garlic—and onion—eaters in reference to their more primitive society, and the Hebrews were called the "stinking ones" because of their characteristic garlic smell. We will discuss this possible source of anti-semitism in the Argument Against Garlic.

The Chinese, the Indians, the Russians, and indeed most civilizations in both the old and new world were intimately involved with Allium Sativum on one side of the Garlic Dilemma, or the other.

ANCIENT EGYPT

In 450 B.C., Herodotus, the Greek historian, in his work *Euterpe–Concerning the History of Egypt* speaks of an inscription inside the Cheops pyramid at Gisa built around 2900 B.C.:

> There is an inscription inside the pyramid which is written in Egyptian characters. It tells us of the quantity of radishes, onions and garlic that were consumed by the workers building the pyramids. I remember most exactly that the interpreter who deciphered the inscription for me remarked that the sum of money spent on these items would amount to 1,600 talents of silver (5).

Converted to dollars this would be about $2,000,000 spent over a period of 20 years during which time hundreds of thousands of workers built the pyramid. The onions, radishes, and garlic were more than dietary staples; they were magical-medical agents responsible for the physical and spiritual survival of the workers.

The garlic was so valued that it was used as a medium of exchange: 15 pounds of the herb could buy a "healthy" male slave. It is noted also that when the shipments of the garlic and other foods began to slacken off, the pyramid builders went on strike, which may be the earliest recorded workers' strike in history (6).

Garlic as Cosmic Symbol

The garlic, as were all the bulbs of the Allium genus, was held to be symbolic of the Universe; the series of successive layers of skin forming the bulb and clove represented the concentrically layered heavens and hells of the ancient Egyptian Cosmogeny. But one aspect of the garlic separating it from the other allium bulbs is the clove structure which when revealed by cutting away the superficial skins resembles the design of the solar system, with smaller bodies rotating around a central larger hub. The seriousness with which the people took the garlic as food, medicine and religious symbol is seen in their habit of swearing by Garlic when taking oaths (7).

Available from LSR.

Garlic-to-go: around the neck, on a fob, to one you care for. Hinged container 1-1/8″ h. 5/8″ w. Can hold solid perfume, whatever. In 18K Gold $250, 14K $230, Sterling $45. With captured and leashed 18K Bat add $35. Please include $2 shipping cost. Cal. residents add Sales Tax. Personal checks accepted.

Prices subject to change without notice.

© Carrie Adell 1978

Tut Mania and Garlic Mania

The Egyptian mania for garlic is demonstrated quite conclusively by Tackholm and Drar in their "Flora of Egypt" (1954). It is well known that garlic and onion were involved in the mummification process, but few know that six bulbs of garlic were found in the tomb of King Tut. Since garlic and onion were medical and magical as well as culinary plants, one can assume that the garlic was meant to insure health, and ward off evil spirits.

Tackholm and Drar also described clay models of garlic bulbs that were found in predynastic cemeteries in Egypt:

> In making these, a core of clay was first formed, probably globular in shape, and on this were pressed about nine long sausage-like rolls of clay, the tips being firmly pressed until they adhered to the core. The whole was then white-washed, and presents a very natural appearance.

These early garlic-shaped models, dating from before 3000 B.C., are followed by tomb finds of actual bulbs dating some 1,500 years later.

Egyptian Spring Festival

Garlic Times editor Charles Perry found the following material in Practiques Rituelles et Alimentaires des Coptes, by Ceres Wissa Wassef, published in Cairo.

This festival, "Shamm al-Nasim" (Sniffing the Breezes), falls on Easter Monday, but Moslems as well as Coptic Christians celebrate it. Needless to say, it is an old pagan festival. The customs differ from place to place, but Shamm al-Nasim is celebrated from one end of Egypt to the other.

> In Cairo, people get up at dawn, and old and young alike breathe a green onion crushed in vinegar. That day all the Cairenes, without distinction of age, sex or religion, go out to "sniff the breezes" in the public gardens, in the countryside or on Nile boats. An immense throng moves through the streets and invades all the green spaces; they chant, dance, light firecrackers, wear hats of bright-colored paper or crowd onto carts known as "karro", made of wooden boards mounted on wheels and drawn by a donkey; wandering merchants sell branches of green chickpeas, lettuce, lupins and other snacks; lunch is usually a picnic outdoors. The gardens most frequented are around the Cairo dam. There they eat lots of colored hard-boiled eggs, stuffed grape leaves (the leaves are particularly tender in this season), *molokheyya* (mallow soup) made with goose or duck broth, filets of *fesikh* (dried fish) accompanied by green onions. . . . The traditional foods of this day are eggs, fruits, salt fish and above all onion and garlic.
>
> The day of Cham-en-nessim or spring festival, they cut up onions on the doorsill so that one soaks it with their juice, always with the aim of turning away from the house every kind of illness and evil during the year; they hang over the door a bundle of onions linked together; this usage was observed by myself in the (remote and mostly Coptic) province of Fayoum, by Mr. Ascherson in the small oasis (presumably the even more remote oasis of Siwa).
>
> —*Schweinfurth, 1886*

Garlic and onion are uniquely associated with this festival, but there is no way to determine which Pharaonic festival it descends from. We know of the importance of these bulbs in ancient Egypt—onions are very frequently represented in tomb paintings. Packets of garlic were found in the Theban tombs. The Hieroglyphic name for garlic, *khizan,* was found by V. Loret in the Harris papyrus (no relation to L. J. Harris) and in the Coptic version of the Bible. Ramses III distributed it (garlic) to the temples in great quantities. And Loret mentions that the onion was one of the most highly regarded foods to be offered to the dead.

The Egyptians have long experimented with "les qualites eminentes de l'oignon": to fresh, calm, ease, soften, excite the appetite, serve as an aphrodisiac or stimulant of menstrual flow . . . it cures dog bite, scorpion sting and the attacks of other venomous animals.

It also played a role in mummification:

> Onions are found inside the cadaver (pelvis, epigastric region or upper part of the thorax); in the hand of the deceased, along his legs or attached to the bottom of his feet, near his left armpit, in his outer ear, or in the eyesocket in place of the eye. Sometimes onion skins, carefully cut in the shape of the parts which should recover, were glued on the mouth or the eyes of the mummies.

> —Christophe,
> *"Gerard Nerval au Caire,"*
> *Revue de Caire*

Modern fellahs are great onion lovers as well. It is essential to their eating; usually they eat their bread seasoned only with green onions. Their curative powers are much solicited; onion juice is squeezed in the eyes of the newborn seven days after birth or in the eyes of ophthalmia victims (NB: under British colonial rule, the Nile was dammed so that three cotton crops a year could be raised, resulting in endemic bilharziasis—Egypt had the highest rate of blindness and eye disease in the world, because onion juice in the eye doesn't kill liver flukes). Onions are all-powerful against the Evil Eye—they are hung around the necks of infants, exactly as they are around the necks of the dead in the Theban tombs; an onion and, usually, also a clove of garlic, to protect against various ills, above all the Eye. Onions and garlic also have a magical power (after burning with other ingredients) of rendering an enemy unconscious.

—*Charles Perry*

Egyptian Pharmacy

Religion and pharmacy were nowhere more linked than in the lands of the pyramids. The pyramids themselves are great examples of this dual function of religion and science in Egypt; the pyramid was not only a tomb for the dead Pharaohs, but an elaborately designed mechanism in which mummification (the means for attaining immortality) was enhanced; astrological calculations were also made possible by the complex symmetry of the pyramids. The uncontested merit of the Egyptians is to have been the first civilization to practice *medicine* as we know it today; they had developed pharmaco-therapy to a very high degree. The priests, the official healing practitioners were trained in special boarding schools, and joined a temple community after an examination where they would swear an oath by the holy books kept in the temple (8).

The Ebers Codex

One of these holy books is the Codex Ebers, a medical papyrus first discovered by the German Egyptologist George Ebers and published in 1878. This is the best preserved and most comprehensive medical work of early antiquity dating to around 1550 B.C. The papyrus contains more than eight hundred therapeutic formulas, 22 of which mention garlic for a variety of ailments including headache, heart problems, body weakness, human bites, worms, throat tumors and problems of childbirth and menstrual cycle.

Table 33 of the papyrus mentions garlic in an enema for inflammation of the anus in a mixture of wine, bile of a fat ox, opium and honey. Table 37 is a remedy for disorders of the pit of the stomach: make a wheat bread, large amounts of absinthe, a small container of garlic with beer and fat ox meat. This being eaten, the patient's eyes and nose open, leading him to a bowel movement. For gynecological problems, a ball would be formed from garlic and other ingredients and inserted into the vulva, or injected into the vulva in a wine solution. For menstrual disturbances, a plaster made of crushed garlic, unleavened wheat bread and shearings of cedar trees would be placed on the abdomen (9).

Egyptian Pregnancy Test

In two Egyptian texts, the Papyrus Carlsberg VIII and Papyrus Kahun, there is a fascinating example of ancient understanding of hormones. To determine whether a woman is pregnant, here is the procedure:

> You shall let a clove of garlic remain the whole night in her womb until dawn. If the smell is present in her mouth, then she will conceive; if not, she will not conceive.

This procedure was later used in Greek medicine. The above "recipe" is found almost word for word in a Hippocratic work *On Sterility.* This primitive pregnancy test depends on the stimulation of seedlings by pregnancy urine, and may be among the earliest observations on hormonal effects. In the Greek version, it is advised to cut off the tip of the clove of garlic first. This exposes the sprout. It is well known, it should be added, that the odor of garlic permeates the whole body within hours of ingestion. Hence modern medical reports of the odor of garlic coming from newborn infants whose mothers had ingested garlic soon before delivery.

(Egyptian and Greek material from "The Transitions from Ancient Egyptian to Greek Medicine" *by J. B. de C. M. Saunders, M.D., University of Kansas Press, 1963.)*

The ancient Egyptians were not at the point of having a theory of bacteria but the Ebers papyrus leads one to think that along with the doctors of Babylon and Ur, the Egyptian doctors had the notion that some disease (those not inflicted by the gods) was in part due to a substance of earthly origin; that is, to some causative agent *below* the level of the gods. The Babylonians called the agent "the worm" and the Egyptians took the term from them. In this respect these ancient doctors were on the level of the thinking of the European doctors of the Middle Ages before the discovery of the microscope. They believed that by eating garlic and onions and radishes as well as many other plants in their pharmacopea, these "worms" and the diseases caused by them could be cured (10). Obviously, any substance that could do this was elevated to the level of the gods and worshipped.

The fact that the people worshipped the garlic had an interesting effect on the priests who came to detest this foul-smelling "god" of the people. It is suggested that the mere association of garlic with the masses of subjugated peoples in Egypt was enough to turn the priests "off." An example of this split in Egypt over garlic occurs in the movie *The Ten Commandments:* Moses (Charleton Heston) has returned to Egypt after wandering with his new-found people, the Hebrews. The Egyptian Princess who has loved Moses throughout the movie confesses to him her still ardent love, and tantalizes him with her sweet smell. She compares her smell to the garlicky smell of Moses' new shepherd girl friend.

THE ANCIENT ISRAELITES

Under the bondage of the Egyptians, the Israelites were copious garlic consumers, and as the Bible illustrates, when the Jews left Egypt to wander in the wilderness of Sinai they cried out for the life they left behind:

> We remember the fish which we did eat in Egypt
> so freely, and the pumpkins and melons, and the
> leeks, onions and garlic. (11)

Wherever the Jews found themselves, garlic was cultivated as a dietary staple along with onions and leeks. But of course Garlic was more than just a food, and indeed, diet was more than eating enough food to stay alive. For the ancient Jew the garlic was a very particular substance capable of stimulating the organism; it was even held in high esteem as an aphrodisiac (later, the Romans would also worship the aphrodisiacal powers of garlic).

In the Jews' understanding of food and chemistry, certain foods were believed to stimulate or depress the body's humors, those cardinal fluids—blood, phlegm, choler (yellow bile) and melancholy (black bile). Popular physiology held that garlic had generative powers, and could even inflame sexual desire. Garlic was, in this view, a "hot" food. The use of "cold" foods such as melons, legumes, salted fish, etc. would chill or cool desire (12). This hot-cold system can be traced in many societies where the understanding of the human organism is based on concepts of vital fluids which must be kept in balance to achieve health and long life. Thus the affects of food on this system of fluids were studied very closely by the old physicians, and out of this early science emerged the principles of herbalism which we will discuss below as the precursor to our modern fields of physiology, botany and pharmacology.

Garlic for the ancient Jew was put in the same category as wine, and there were specific steps one could take to counter an unwanted attack of sexual desire. One could either devour large quantities of the cold foods, or immerse oneself in cold baths until the lust abated. If both of these steps were not possible, one could conquer the lust in the following manner:

> . . . by pressing his big toes firmly into the ground and resting the entire weight of his body upon them without leaning against a wall; this will banish all sensual thoughts (13).

These kinds of rituals cross the line from Science into Magic, and thus it is that many beliefs concerning such ordinary things as garlic may seem to us to be "superstition". But superstition is a kind of logic, although logic based on limited or wrong information. For instance, if garlic was peeled or cut and left overnight it would turn black. This was explained as contamination by spirits and demons (Mazzikim, Lilin, Lutins, and Faes) (14). We simply would say, based on our knowledge of bacteria, that the garlic was rotting. Ancient peoples did not have this concept of germs, and theories such as that of the "worm" in Egyptian pharmacy had not been incorporated into popular knowledge.

Epidemics and plagues, then, presented an interesting problem for the ancient and medieval mind. One could only account for this kind of apocalypse of disease and death by attributing it to Evil Spirits and Angry Gods. We know today that garlic is an effective antibacterial agent and may indeed protect one from certain infections and diseases, but it was easier for the ancient Jew to interpret this effect of garlic as Magic, as a charm against evil spirits. Indeed, the medieval Jew would walk about during a plague with garlic in a pocket (15). This garlic then would be later disposed of along with any black "evil-infected" garlics left exposed, which were, of course, never to be directly touched.

The Talmud

This later prescription—not to touch the contaminated garlic—reveals a very early awareness of hygiene in the Jewish culture. The Talmud, the repository of Jewish civil and religious law, gave explicit directions to the doctor to wash his hands before touching a wound: "It is the hand that causes the inflammation." Once the inflammation had taken hold, it was to be treated by the application of garlic or onion skin (16).

The Talmud seems also to have sanctioned the use of garlic as an aphrodisiac. During the rebuilding of the Temple and resettlement in Palestine, Ezra originated the institution of "The Ten Regulations of Ezra." Number 5 told the people:

To eat garlic on Friday on account of its salutary action (17).

41

The Rabbis felt that the night of the Sabbath should be devoted to conjugal pleasures, and garlic of course would "spice up" that conjugality.

In later writings of the Talmud, a number of remedies using garlic and onions are given, particularly for gynecological and menstrual disturbances. For excessive menstrual bleeding, an onion stew was prescribed: ". . . take three measures of Persian (large) onions. Stew them in wine and let the woman drink it, and say to her at the time, 'Get up from the flood'" (18).

It was obviously known by the Jews, even if they did not understand the principles involved as we know them now, that antibiotics (anti-devils) need not come only from microbes (penicillin), but can be manufactured by higher plants such as the garlic and other allium plants. And to this day, in Russia and Poland, old and poor Jews interrupt their religious practices to break their fast on bread and raw garlic. Nutritionists and doctors have found that among these pious garlic-eating Jews, cancer is relatively unknown. This is not to say that garlic is the only factor responsible for the low incidence of cancer. More on this in Part Two.

ANCIENT PALESTINE

In the ancient world garlic was a sign not only of sexuality through its powers as an aphrodisiac, but a sign also of fecundity in general. One legend told in Palestine connects garlic with the Garden of Eden and the Tree of Life:

> Once, ladies, long ago the Garlic grew very tall, so tall that the top of it could not be seen. Then this blessing became a curse, for there were too many people in the world—there was no room in the world for them all. So God in His Mercy shortened the Garlic and it has been small ever since. But it is still good to eat for health and long life and good, too, against the "Eye"...Those must have been strange days you say, when the Garlic was tall? (19)

THE TREE OF KNOWLEDGE: Was it an apple tree or an Allium tree?

Another expression of garlic's fertility powers was for a groom to wear garlic in his buttonhole as a sign of successful marriage. The reference to the "Eye" is of course the Evil Eye, the mark of the Demonic transferred through the eye of a possessed soul to his victim. Garlic served as a protective charm against the Eye in all cultures of antiquity.

Mohammed Speaks

Mohammed had the following to say about garlic:

> In cases of stings and bites by poisonous animals, garlic acts as a theriac. Applied to the spot bitten by the viper, or sting of scorpion it produces successful results.

But despite this medical approval of garlic, the Moslem people did not much fancy the foul-smelling garlic. Below, in an excerpt from Sir Richard F. Burton's book, *Pilgrimage to Al-Madinah and Meccah,* note is taken of the Moslem disdain for garlic:

> So the Pilgrim squatted apart, smoking perpetually, with occasional interruptions to say his prayers and to tell his beads upon the mighty rosary; and he drank the muddy water of the canal out of a leathern bucket, and he munched his bread and garlic with a desperate sanctimoniousness.

Sir Richard footnotes this reference to garlic in his travel diary and speaks of its use throughout the Nile Delta area.

> Those skilled in simples, Eastern as well as Western, praise garlic highly, declaring that it "strengthens the body, prepares the constitution for fatigue, brightens the sight, and by increasing the digestive power, obviates the ill-effects arising from sudden change of air and water." The traveller inserts it into his dietary in some pleasant form, as "Provence-butter" because he observes that wherever fever and ague abound, the people, ignorant of cause but observant of effect, make it a common article of food. The old Egyptians highly esteemed this vegetable, which, with onions and leeks, enters the list of articles so much regretted (missed) by the Hebrews (Numbers xi. 5; Koran, chapter 2). The modern people of the Nile, like the Spaniards, delight in onions which, as they contain between 25% and 30% of gluten, are highly nutritive. In Arabia, however, the stranger must use this vegetable sparingly. The city people despise it as the food of a Fellah—a boor. The Wahhabis have a prejudice against onions, leeks, and garlic, because the Prophet disliked their strong smell, and all strict Moslems refuse to eat them immediately before visiting the mosque, or meeting for public prayer. (20)

We see here another example of the pious and the city people looking down upon the garlic and the garlic-eaters because of its strong odor. This implied link between the pious and the sophisticated city dwellers, and a certain over-sensitivity to strong *earthy* odors, reads as a virtual refrain in the politico-social history of almost every major civilization from antiquity to present.

ANCIENT GREECE

Garlic was used by ancient Greeks as much for magic and medicine as it was for food. One magical use was to place garlic on piles of stones at cross-roads as a supper for Hecate, the under-world goddess of magic, charms, and enchantment. Another magical or quasi-medical use of garlic (as there may be some evidence to support this claim) was to take garlic for strength before a battle. The following line is from the play, *Knights*, by Aristophanes, the Greek satirical playright:

> Now bolt down these cloves of garlic. Well primed with garlic you will
> have greater mettle for the fight.

The metabolic effects of garlic may explain this belief in garlic's strength-giving powers: Garlic stimulates gastric secretions, perspiration, and is held by many modern herbalists to be a tonifying substance. It has also been observed by zoologists and anthropologists that the powerful primate Gorilla generally situates his home where wild garlic flourishes which he eats most eagerly. But this is merely circumstantial evidence for garlic's powerful effects.

While the people were feeding garlic to gamecocks to fuel their tempers before a fight (21), Homer was saving Ulysses with its magical powers in one of the most widely known references to garlic in classical literature.

Moly, the Magic Garlic

In the *Odyssey*, Ulysses' men had been turned into swine by Circe on the way back home, after the Trojan War. Ulysses came to their aid with the help of Mercury, or Hermes as he was known to the Greeks, the god of science. There is also a connection here with Hermes Trismegistus, the Greek name for the Egyptian god Thoth, god of alchemy and the occult sciences. In the *Odyssey*, Hermes delivers to Ulysses a magical protective herb called Moly:

> In vain she endeavours to transform you;
> The virtue of this medicinal plant stands
> against her . . .
>
> Its roots were black and milky white
> flowered the blossom.
> Moly it is named by the gods.

So when Circe tried to turn Ulysses into a pig, nothing happened. She was so astounded by Ulysses' power to resist her magic that she fell head-over-heels in love with him and let all his men go. Here, garlic seems to be acting as both protective herb and aphrodisiac. The controversy continues as to what specific allium Moly really was, or whether it was a mixture of herbs. Today, certain wild species of garlic have the botanical name Allium Moly.

The Evil Eye

Garlic was used throughout antiquity to counter-act the Evil Eye. The use of the "Eye" could threaten the welfare of new-born infants, brides and grooms, and just about anyone else who happened to contact it. In Greece, a midwife would do her job with an ample supply of garlic on hand. The room

47

would be reeking of it and a few cloves would be fastened about the baby's neck after baptism, if not directly after birth. If no garlic was available in a moment of impending danger, one could voice with great drama, "garlic in your eyes!" (22) This would banish the "Eye."

The Neriades, Malicious Nymphs

Another danger encountered by the ancient Greeks was the jealous and malicious Nymphs or Neriades. These beautiful half-divine, half-human creatures envied the joys of wedlock and childbirth and their jealous behavior could mean the ruin of an unprotected wife or mother-to-be. Protection consisted of wearing amulets, garlic being a popular ingredient, or one could place bunches of garlic over the door of the homes where women were kept confined during the 40-day period before marriage. To this day, these same precautions are taken by Greek women, as Neriades are still seen by the peasants (although they often "vanish" in thin air) in the forests and hills of Greece. Some folk even boast of having had a grandparent who actually married a Neriade, and tradition has it that these ancient Playboy-esque fantasy women make very fickle wives, and the marriages do not last (23).

There is an interesting Scandinavian mythic female, the Huldra, who is very much like the Neriades, and likewise is said to be invisible when viewed from the back. One story tells of the Huldra Talle-Maja whose powers captured a husband. Every night this husband went to her in the forest to make love. His wife had no power to keep him in the house once the Huldra knocked on the door. One night the wife went out and met the Huldra before she reached the house, and asked the Huldra how one could keep a bull from wandering off at night. The Huldra told her to give the bull garlic, grass from the north side of the chimney and other ingredients. The wife gave this to her man-bull, and he stopped going out at night (24).

48

THE NERIADES in ancient Greece, who worshipped a phallic-serpent god, could be guarded against by displaying garlic. Here, near the Parthenon, a giant garlic protects the gates of Athens from the malicious nymphs.

GREEK MEDICINE

Hippocrates (460 B.C.), known as the Father of Medicine, and creator of the tradition in western medicine of the Hippocratic Oath, used garlic for a variety of infections and intestinal disorders as well as for wounds, toothaches, leprosy, epilepsy and chest pains.

Aristotle (384 B.C.) said of garlic, "It is a cure for hydrophobia and tonic, is hot, laxative, but bad for the eyes." I have yet to find evidence that garlic is bad for the eyes, but it does seem to be the one objection to garlic in early writings, second only to complaints about its smell. The wealthy Greeks detested the garlic, feeling that it betrayed the man of the lower classes. The attitude concerning garlic's ill-effects on the eye may be linked in some way to the tradition of garlic's use against the "Evil Eye". It may also be that because of garlic's, and especially onion's, effects on the lacrymal (tear) glands, ancient observers may have equated the tear-producing powers of Allium as a physical danger.*

Dioscorides

The Greek doctor Pedanios Dioscorides Anazorbaeus lived in the first century A.D. He traveled with the Roman armies and was with the Roman Emperors Claudius and Nero in the campaigns of North Africa and Britain. His written works include a *Materia Medica* and a book of *Household Remedies*. Dioscorides' descriptions of his pharmacological preparations, the precise dosages, weights, and the apparatuses and procedures used to prepare

---

*As far as this writer is concerned, a few more tears would not hurt anyone, especially the male members of our society. I have even given thought to opening an Institute for Creative Crying in which garlic and onions would be used to initiate the therapy sessions. Our motto could be: "If your life is a lie, what you need is a cry!" So much for Aristotelian Alliumphobes.

the external and internal medicines, served as a prototype in medicine up until the end of the Middle Ages. Even as late as the 19th century, his pharmacology was in use in the Turkish empire. One of Dioscorides' greatest contributions to Botany was to have recognized similarities in plant forms. Instead of listing plants alphabetically, as previously done, he began to systematize the knowledge of the plant world based on careful observation. His system, based on the external shapes of plants, suggests the Medieval Doctrine of Signatures, followed by herbalists who believed that in the design of a plant you could "read" its use as a medicine. A plant such as garlic, with a long hollow stalk, would be good for all diseases of the wind pipe, and plants with similar design would have similar effects. The following text is from the *Greek Herbal of Dioscorides*, translated by J. Berendes:

> Garlic is cultivated as a garden plant. In Egypt it is of one head, like leek, sweet, small and purple colored; another type is of many cloves and white. The cloves are called aglithes. There is a wild type called ophios-korodon (serpent's garlic) in Andros and Cypress. It is sharp, biting, wind-producing, excites the belly, dries out the stomach, creates thirst and produces growths on the body skin. If eaten, it helps eliminate the tapeworm, it drives out the urine. It is good against snake bite with wine, or when crushed in wine. It is good against the bite of a rabid dog. It makes the voice clear, soothes continuous coughing, when eaten raw or boiled. Boiled with oregano, it kills lice and bed bugs. It doth clear the arteries. Burnt and mixed with honey, it is an ointment for bloodshot eyes; in case of baldness, it helps too. Together with salt and oil, it heals eczema. Together with honey, it heals white skin spots, herpetic erruptions, liver spots, leprosy and scurvy. Boiled with pine-wood and incense, it soothes tooth ache when solution is kept in the mouth. Garlic plus fig leaves and cumin is a plaster against the bite of the shrew-mouse. Boiling the umbrel flower is good for a sitzbath (sitting bath) to help the coming of menstrua-tion and placenta. For the same purposes it can be smoked. A mush from crushed garlic and black olives is a diuretic. It is helpful in dropsy (25).

The Household Remedies of Dioscorides

These concoctions are partially based on Egyptian tradition, and the use of garlic was usually combined with other ingredients:

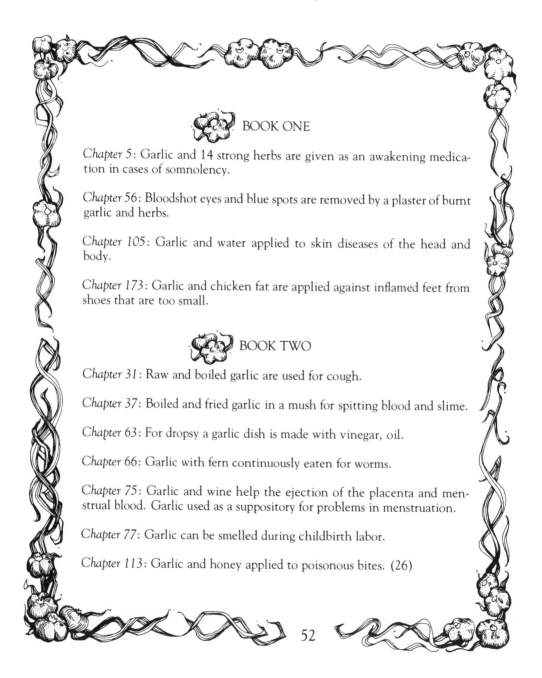

BOOK ONE

Chapter 5: Garlic and 14 strong herbs are given as an awakening medication in cases of somnolency.

Chapter 56: Bloodshot eyes and blue spots are removed by a plaster of burnt garlic and herbs.

Chapter 105: Garlic and water applied to skin diseases of the head and body.

Chapter 173: Garlic and chicken fat are applied against inflamed feet from shoes that are too small.

BOOK TWO

Chapter 31: Raw and boiled garlic are used for cough.

Chapter 37: Boiled and fried garlic in a mush for spitting blood and slime.

Chapter 63: For dropsy a garlic dish is made with vinegar, oil.

Chapter 66: Garlic with fern continuously eaten for worms.

Chapter 75: Garlic and wine help the ejection of the placenta and menstrual blood. Garlic used as a suppository for problems in menstruation.

Chapter 77: Garlic can be smelled during childbirth labor.

Chapter 113: Garlic and honey applied to poisonous bites. (26)

ANCIENT ROME

Like the cultures preceding it, Rome held the garlic in an ambivalent light. Again, the people enjoyed it and even worshipped the garlic, while the aristocracy rejected the foul-smelling little bulb. Although Roman Senators passed laws forbidding the use of garlic by those entering the Temple of Cybele, Mother of Zeus, they continued to feed vast amounts of the déclassé bulb to their soldiers who derived strength and courage for the athletic and battle fields (27). It was the Roman Legions that introduced garlic to the peoples of other lands, en route to conquering most of the ancient world.

The Roman people held garlic in high repute as an aphrodisiac and at the Festival of Ceres, Romans ate the garlic in vast amounts to celebrate its seminal powers. Taken with coriander, it proved an excellent Love Potion.

The Roman author and poet Virgil (70-19 B.C.) knew that garlic was "essential to maintain the strength of harvesters"; and garlic was valued as a tonic for the endurance of extreme temperatures while working in the fields. In Virgil's poem, *Moretum,* garlic is mentioned in what is perhaps the oldest literary source in Latin on the use of garlic, found in a parchment codex in the Vatican Library, dating from the 9th century.

That's what he wanted now,
he went into the garden,
he loosens up the top soil
slightly with his fingers,
pulls out the garlic,
four pieces with the root fibers,
then he picks clery leaves,
the rigid leaf of the rue, corriander,
dangling at the thread of the stem.
So he has everything together,
he sits down at the gay fire,
and asks the servant for the mortar,
then he frees the garlic cloves from the roots,
peels off the skins, the outer ones,
which he contemptuously scatters around on the floor and discards.

MORETUM

(lines 87-102)

53

He keeps the cloves, wets them and puts them in the mortar,
adds salt, and salt-hardened cheese, adds then
the mentioned herbs,
arranges with his left hand his smock,
but his right hand crushes the fragrant garlic
with the pestle.
Then he crushes everything, it is permeated
by the juice. (28)

PILGARLIC: Bald men (as well as Lepers) were called Pilgarlics in
Medieval Europe because of their use of Allium as a scalp tonic and as an
application for leprosy. Another theory is that the shape of the bald head
suggested a peeled garlic bulb.

ROMAN MEDICINE

Based on the traditions of Egypt and Greece, Roman medicine was
much aware of garlic's powers to heal. Galen (131-200 A.D.) was a physician
whose methods and teachings were prominent for one thousand years. It is
said of Galen that he did for medicine in general what Dioscorides had done
for pharmacology. It was Galen who first coined the name for garlic
"Theriaca Rusticoriam," which meant Poor Man's Treacle or Heal-all.

PLINY

Pliny, the Roman naturalist, was the most prolific writer and advocate of the wonders of garlic as medicine. Below is reprinted Pliny's 61 garlic remedies from his *Natural History:*

Garlic has very powerful properties, and is of great utility to persons on changes of water or locality. The very smell of it drives away serpents and scorpions, and, according to what some persons say it is a cure for wounds made by every kind of wild beast, whether taken with the drink or food, or applied topically. Taken in wine, it is a remedy for the sting of the haemorrhoid more particularly, acting as an emetic. We shall not be surprised too, that it acts as a powerful remedy for the bite of the shrew-mouse, when we find that it has the property of neutralizing aconite, otherwise known as "paralianches." (Pard or panther-strangle). It neutralizes henbane, also, and cures the bites of dogs when applied with honey to the wound. It is taken in drink also for the stings of serpents; and of its leaves, mixed with oil, a most valuable liniment is made for bruises on the body, even when they have swelled and formed blisters.

Hippocrates is of opinion also, that fumigarions made with garlic have the effect of bringing away the after-birth; and he used to employ the ashes of garlic, mixed with oil, for the cure of running ulcers of the head. Some persons have pre-scribed boiled garlic for asthmatic patients; while others, again, have given it raw. Diocles prescribes it, in combination with centaury, for dropsy, and to be taken in a split fig, to promote the alvine evacuations: taken fresh, however, in unmixed wine, with corian-der, it is still more efficacious for that purpose. Some persons have given it, beaten up in milk, for asthma. Praxagoras used to prescribe garlic, mixed with wine, for jaundice, and with oil and pottage for the iliac passion: he employed it also in a similar form, as a liniment for scrofulous swellings of the neck.

The ancients used to give raw garlic in cases of madness, and Diocles administered it boiled for phrenitis. Beaten up, and taken in vinegar and water, it is very useful as a gargle for quinsy. Three heads of garlic, beaten up in vinegar, give relief in toothache; and a similar result is obtained by rinsing the mouth with a decoction of garlic, and inserting pieces of it in the hollow teeth. Juice of garlic is sometimes injected into the ears with goose grease, and, taken in drink, or similarly injected, in combination with vinegar and nitre, it arrests phthiriasis (the Morbid pedicularis) and porrigo (ringworm). Boiled with milk, or else beaten up and mixed with soft cheese, it is a cure for catarrhs. Employed in a similar manner, and taken with peas or beans, it is good for hoarseness, but in general it is found to be more serviceable cooked than raw, and boiled than roasted: in this last state, however, it is more beneficial to the voice. Boiled oxymel, it has the effect of expelling tape-worm and other intestinal worms; and a pottage made of it is a cure for tenesmus. A decoction of garlic is applied topically for pains in the temples; and first boiled and then beaten up with honey, it is good for blisters. A decoction of it, with stale grease, or milk, is excellent for a cough; and where persons are troubled with spitting of blood or purulent matter, it may be roasted in hot ashes, and taken with honey in equal proportions. For convulsions and ruptures it is administered in combination with salt and oil; and, mixed with grease, it is employed for the cure of suspected tumours.

Mixed with sulphur and resin, garlic draws out the humours from fistulous sores, and employed with pitch, it will extract an arrow even from the wound. In cases of leprosy, lichen, and eruptions of the skin, it acts as a detergent, and effects a cure, in combination with wild marjoram, or else reduced to ashes, and applied as a liniment with oil and garum (an expensive kind of fish sauce). It is employed in a similar manner, too, for erysipleas; and, reduced to ashes and mixed honey, it restores contused or livid spots on the skin to their proper colour. It is generally believed, too, that taken in the food and drink, garlic is a cure for epilepsy, and that a clove of it, taken in astringent wine, with an obolus' weight of silphium, will have the effect of dispelling quartan fever. Garlic cures coughs also, and supurations of the chest, however violent they may be; to obtain which result, another method is followed, it being boiled with broken beans, and employed as a diet till the cure is fully effected. It is a soporific also, and in general imparts to the body an additional ruddiness of colour.

Garlic acts as an aphrodisiac, beaten up with fresh coriander, and taken in pure wine. The inconveniences which result from the use of it, are dimness of the sight and flatulency; and if taken in too large quantities, it does injury to the stomach, and creates thirst. In addition to these particulars, mixed with speit flour, and given to poultry in their food, it preserves them from attacks of the pip. Beasts of burden it is said, will void their urine all the more easily, and without any pain, if the genitals are rubbed with garlic. (29)

I must apologize to the reader for not providing definitions for much of the above technical language—the truth is that I could not find the definitions. It is clear, however, that much of the herbal tradition's use of garlic comes from Pliny who at that early date was treating many conditions with garlic, now treated by herbalists: Respiratory ailments, gastro-intestinal disorders, infections, wounds, etc.

ANCIENT INDIA

In ancient India it may have been that you would have to leave town to eat your garlic. Within the Brahman class, garlic was always shunned, for it was said to be "tamasic," which in Sanskrit pertains to ignorance in attaching importance to sense perceptions and a surrender to illusion. Evidently, it was thought that the taste and effects of garlic took the minds and souls of the pious away from their spiritual path. It was also held that the smell of garlic signaled the presence of evil spirits. On the other hand, another Sanskrit word for garlic means "slayer of monsters". Again we see the ambivalence towards garlic based on one's place in the social hierarchy. For the ancient Indian *people,* the people that created a dazzling tradition of erotic art, garlic (Lasan or Lasuna) was held to be a valuable food and medicinal herb.

The Bower Manuscript

Lieutenant Bower, a British officer in the colonial troops in India, bought a manuscript from an Indian who had found it in a ruins near Kichar in Kashgonia (Turkestan) in 1890. The document consisted of 56 birchbark page-leafs, 54 of which were written on both sides in Sanskrit. The following text on the origins of garlic was probably written in the 5th century, and originates from the works of ancient Indian doctors, especially Sus'ruta and Charaka:

ON THE ORIGINS OF GARLIC

On the holy mountain, where the medicinal plants grow, the Munis dwell; men with a sublime spirit . . . they test the taste, properties, shapes, powers and names of the healing plants. When Sus'ruta has found a special plant, he asks the Muni Kâsirâja. This holy man answers: "The Lord of Asuras himself drank the well-shaken nectar. The holy Ianârdana beheaded this Lord. The pharynx stayed with the head. Blood drops fell to the ground from the pharynx, and they were the origin of garlic. Ever since the Brahmans do not eat garlic since it stems from a corpse. Due to that also, its evil smell. Because garlic lacks a salty taste they call it Ras'ûna. The people know it as las'una. In taste and digestion, it is sharp and biting, but also sweet in digestion. It is easy, and as the smell shows, also difficult to digest. As to its forces, it is hot, also an aphrodisiac. Most Munis say that because of its sour, hot, and oily nature, it is likely to soothe the strength of the airy juices, and because of its sweet and bitter nature, as shown in its taste, to soothe the bilious juices. It is made to subdue the strength of the phlegmatic juices because of its sharp, hot, and biting nature. The Creator created garlic to remove the defects of these three juices so that it can heal all diseases (30).

The Garlic Festival

Another segment of the Bower Manuscript describes the circumstances in which a garlic festival should be celebrated:

Garlic corrects the phlegmatic juices; it is enticing to digestion and is excellent to restore vital energy and colour. Those who like strong drinks, meat, butter, barley and wheat should celebrate the festival of garlic in winter time, during the months of March and April. When women do not wear decorated belts to win men, when they do not wear necklaces on their breasts because of the cold, when there are no amusements on the roofs of the houses which otherwise are so pleasant because of the touch of the many rays of the moon, then the garlic festival should be celebrated. The gables of the houses, the doors, and the windows should be hung with garlic; and on the floor the members of the house should be made to wear wreaths of garlic. This is how the Svalpovanna Festival should be celebrated (31).

The Origins of Garlic and Onions

The following text is from a speech by the Venerable Kalu Rimpoche, Abbot of the Samdup Darjeeling Monastery in Darjeeling, India. The translation is by Kenneth McLeod and was forwarded by Byron Black of Vancouver, B.C. Rimpoche is a high lama of the Tibetan Buddhist tradition, and he has a wide following in the U.S. The text that follows is an abridged version of an answer to the question: "Is it wrong to eat garlic and onions?" (Used by permission)

In the beginning, the merit of human beings was almost that of the gods. So, the physical human form was much finer and more subtle than it is now. The world was filled with light shining from human forms. There was no need of any external illumination, and there was no sun or moon or star in the sky. But the merit of human beings slowly deteriorated, and so the radiance in the human form degenerated, the physical form became coarser, less subtle, and the world grew darker.

In order to alleviate this darkness, the most powerful gods, such as Indra and others, together with the Titans, stirred the waters of the ocean, and out of this the sun and moon came into existence. Also out of this came a potent elixir which was kept in a crystal vase. The gods would drink this potion much as we would drink tea now.

On one occasion, one of the great Titans thought to appropriate this elixir for himself and swooped down on the gods, stole the vase and flew away. The gods chased him, and realizing he could not escape, the Titan drank the elixir. The gods hurled their weapons at him, and one of these sliced his body in ribbons, but because he had taken the elixir his body could not die, and the blood and flesh of his body fell to the earth. Where it fell, onions and garlic now grow.

This story explains the dual nature of such as garlic and onions. The unwholesomeness of the Titan results in the odor of garlic and onions which is so powerful that it can destroy the effectiveness of some mantras and tantras. Nevertheless, because of the elixir the Titan had consumed, these plants are extremely beneficial to one's own body.

Therefore, if one is using lower tantras [meditation systems], one should not eat garlic and onions, but if using higher tantras, such as the Anatara Yoga Tantra, then it doesn't make much difference.

Drawing by Annetta Günther

Indian Herbal Medicine

In the Indian herbal system, garlic was used in the following disorders: skin diseases, loss of appetite, abdominal ulcers, cough, under-weight, leprosy, weak digestion, rheumatism, consumption, intestinal disorders, enlarged spleen, hemorrhoids, hemiplegy, sciatica, worms, difficulty in urination, physical and mental exhaustion, head colds, epilepsy.

Today in India, garlic is still used in herbal medicine, and below is a list of some of the disorders treated, along with particular garlic remedies.

HYSTERIA, FLATULENCE, SCIATICA, HEARTBURN: A decoction of boiled bulbs, water and milk. Boil until liquid is evaporated. It is given in small doses.

ASTHMA, HOARSENESS, COUGH, BRONCHITIS: A syrup is prepared by boiling one pound of freshly sliced bulbs and sugar in one quart of water until it has a syrupy consistency. Add vinegar and honey.

DYPHTHERIA, TYPHUS, TYPHOID FEVER: Constant chewing of whole cloves of garlic.

INTESTINAL PARASITES SUCH AS ASCARIDES: Garlic juice diluted with water is injected into rectum.

COLD FITS OF INTERMITTENT FEVER: Doses of the aromatic oil of garlic obtained from the seeds.

SNAKEBITE: The fresh juice is taken internally and rubbed on the wound. At the same time, a few drops of juice mixed with ox urine are dropped into the nostrils.

GREYING HAIR: Garlic diluted in water and applied as a tonic to scalp (32).

The Garlic Saint

A spokesman for the Tantric Research Institute in Oakland, California, tells the following story concerning the Sufi Saint Nirale Miyan, who is now a strong 95 and lives in Rampur.

The Saint cures tuberculosis patients by having them live in a room

61

completely filled with garlic: garlic stuffed in the mattress and pillows, garlic hanging from the ceiling and bulging out of cupboards and closets. The patient also wears a necklace of garlic. The Saint is said to have cured many people in this manner.

CHINA

In the 13th century, Marco Polo passed through Yunnan in China and found the people eating meat raw:

> The poore sort go to the Shambles and take the raw liver as soon as it is drawn from the beasts; then they chop it up small, put it in garlic sauces and eat it there and then. And then they do likewise with every other kind of flesh. The Gentry also eat their meat raw, and some believe this to be the origin of Stake Tartare (33).

Since Polo used "Tartare" as a synonym for "Chinese," it is doubtful that this Yunnan use of garlic is the origin of Steak Tartare.

The function of the garlic, besides its use as a spice, was as a preservative of the fresh meat, and indeed today, researchers have shown that the antimicrobial effect of garlic is very useful in preserving the freshness of meat, and increasing shelf-life of packaged meat two to four times (34).

Also, the potent smell and taste of garlic was used as a masking agent for meat and fish past their prime. The people of China were also aware of garlic's medicinal value to the spleen, stomach and kidneys, and its powers as a sedative and detoxicant for a variety of problems including the noxious effect of putrid meat and fish.

There are several accounts of garlic's origin in China. One account holds that although garlic was native to central Asia, it spread first to Greece and Egypt before coming to eastern Asia. Garlic was later brought back up to China through the trade routes leading through Afghanistan and India. During the reign of Wu-ti of the Han dynasty around 130 B.C., garlic is said to have entered China for the first time, but it was later discovered that a native garlic existed in Chekiang province already. Both species grew together and crossed until now there is only one discernible species.

Another account states that Allium Sativum (Suan, Hsiao) was mentioned in the Calendar of the Hsia, 2000 B.C. An ancient text, the Erh-ya, tells that when Emperor Huang-ti was ascending a mountain, certain members of the party accompanying him were poisoned by eating a certain plant. By eating the local garlic they were saved, and from this time forward garlic was cultivated. Of course, for the Buddhist priesthood, the garlic has always been tabooed.

Early Chinese Alliophobe

Li Yü (Li Liweng, "The Fisherman": 1611-1676) was the archetypal food snob of the Ching Dynasty. He made a great fuss about rare ingredients and affected simplicity. For instance, his idea of a fine dish was plain boiled rice on which was sprinkled the dew from flowers—wild roses in preference to garden roses.

"Li Liweng . . . liked bland but exotic things. He professed to shun garlic, onion and chives for juniper berries. Not many people [in China] have tasted juniper berries. They suggest eccentric refinement. . . . He never used garlic, never used onion, and cooked only with the tips of chives, not their stalks, which are more scented." (From *Chinese Gastronomy*, by Hsiang Ju Lin and Tsuifeng Lin.) Such people are apostles of stilted rhythm. They make utterly tiresome conversation. They are vampires, and garlic is our best defense.

—Charles Perry

VARIOUS PICKLED GARLIC PRODUCTS from the Orient. Pickled garlic is very mild, the pungency being absorbed by the fluid, whether it be vinegar, honey or soy.

Moxibustion

Garlic found an interesting place in the ancient Chinese materia medica in conjunction with moxibustion, or moxa treatment. Generally speaking, mugwort is applied to the skin at various points on the body, corresponding to the "points" of acupuncture.

In moxa treatment, various herbs can also be used between the burning cone and the skin. Ginger is often used, and for ailments of the respiratory system a slab of fresh garlic is placed on points where the cones are to be applied. A small hole is bored through the garlic and a moxa cone is placed over it. The heat of the moxa (traveling through the hole) in conjunction with the chemical properties of the garlic, is found beneficial in cases of asthma, bronchitis and tuberculosis (35).

CHAPTER TWO

THE HERBALIST TRADITION

DURING the Dark Ages, the earlier portion of the Middle Ages—from about 500 A.D. (the fall of the Western Roman Empire) to roughly the 10th century—garlic seems to have fallen somewhat from favor. At least, it is said that the Crusades revitalized European culture, and in the cross-currents of exchange between the Christian West and the Moslem East, garlic re-emerged from its exile in the gardens of monks and herbalists.

The invention of the printing press by Gutenberg (1450) ushered in the modern era and made possible the spread of literary, religious and scientific knowledge. In the literature of medicine in the 16th century, based on the Roman tradition of Galen and Dioscorides, garlic was held to be beneficial for a variety of diseases and ailments. What follows is a brief look at the medieval herbalist and his use of herbs, especially the garlic.

THE HERBALISTS

> Ancient traditions, when tested by the severe processes
> of modern investigations commonly enough fade
> away into mere dreams: but it is singular how often
> the dream turns out to have been a half-waking
> one, presaging a reality.
>
> T.H. Huxley

Much of what we know about the ancient and medieval uses of herbs as medicine comes to us from various treatises on plants known as herbals, which were often a re-working of earlier Roman texts. These venerable works contain observations and theories which anticipate the theories of modern botanists, biologists, chemists, zoologists, doctors, etc. The herbalists practiced their "profession" in that rather vague area between witchcraft, alchemy, and science as we know it today.

Many of the herbalists and naturalists had much to say about garlic or garleak and its remedial value. Culpepper was one of the most widely read herbalists in the English-speaking world. New editions of his herbal are still arriving on the market today.

The Doctrine of Signatures

The Herbalist philosophy, if it can be generalized, suggested that no matter what perils befell man, God the Creator of Nature has provided a remedy to be found among the herbs, animals, and other created things. This was to say that everything under the sun was connected in a meaningful, mutually beneficial relationship (36). An excerpt from Cole's *Art of Simpling* explains this attitude:

> Though sin and Sathan have plunged mankinde into an Ocean of Infirmities, yet the mercy of God, which is over all His workes, maketh Grasse to grow upon Mountaines, maketh Herbes for the use of men; and hath not only stamped upon them a distinct form, but also give them particular Signatures, whereby a man may read, even in legible characters the use of them (37).

The Doctrine of Signatures was the underlying philosophy in most of the herbal works of the late Middle Ages, and in Lauremberg's *Apparatus Plantarium*, garlic is "analyzed" according to this doctrine:

The seed of Garlic is black; it obscures the eyes with blackness and darkness. This is to be understood of healthy eyes, but those which are dull through vicious humidity, from these Garlic drives this viciousness away. The tunic of Garlic is ruddy, it expels blook . . . It has a hollow stalk, and it helps affections of the wind pipe (38).

The Doctrine of Signatures is history now, not science, but amidst the naiveté and superstition of the early pre-scientists, there was a profound response to the phenomenal world that has been lost in the age of Technology; a purity of vision that has been replaced by the materialistic, super-rational, and indeed cynical eye of the modern man of science. And although much has been gained for Man/Woman through the modern vision, it has often been at the expense of a more Human, more integrating, and in some ways, perhaps a more helpful vision of man. We are starting now, at the brink of environmental doom, to see once again the interrelationships in Nature that are essential for survival . . . not mere survival alone, but meaningful survival, a survival in harmony with our natural world as well as with our man-made technological world.

> For naught so vile upon the earth doth live
> But to the earth some special good doth give.
> —*Romeo and Juliet*

The Old-Fashioned Way

Joseph Wood Krutch in his very lovely *Herbal* explains that interest in plants as medicinal agents fell off sharply at the turn of the 19th century. The industrial-technological vision of Medicine had triumphed over Natural Medicine in the form of Chemotherapy (the synthesis of chemical medicines). Technicians in a laboratory, and not folk practitioners in the fields, were seen now as more capable of developing cures. And this is perhaps true in many respects. After all, *new* diseases caused by the *new* environment of technology needed in the short run that same technology, perhaps, to right itself. But history will tell us to what ultimate benefit the disease-oriented chemotherapeutic approach to medicine will have for humanity.

The cracks in the foundation are starting to show already. Increasingly, laymen and professionals alike are taking another look at what we threw out with the bath water of Traditional (Old-Fashioned) Healing Arts. Robert De Ropp offers an explanation of why it is that scientists fail to recognize the importance of some old tried and true remedies:

> . . . this situation results in part, at least, from the rather contemptuous attitude which certain chemists and pharmacologists in the West have developed toward folk remedies and drugs of plant origin. . . . they further fell into the error of supposing that because they had learned the trick of synthesizing certain substances, they were better chemists than Mother Nature who, besides creating compounds too numerous to mention, also synthesized the aforesaid chemists and pharmacologists (39).

The other point that is worth making concerning the old herbalists (and the new herbalists) is that aside from the issue of the relevance of their analytical or theoretical positions, they were able to remain in contact with the joyousness and beauty of the nature they were observing:

> Perhaps the chief charm of the Herbalists . . . is just that they are more likely than the modern scientist to impart a sense of beauty and wonder—both of which the scientist may feel, but considers it no part of his function to communicate (40).

The lesson that is being learned once again is that the poetic Old-Fashioned Way has its relevance even in highly technological cultures. Witness if you will the inroads made in the West by the Oriental "art" of acupuncture, which works despite the fact that nobody really knows or can show how it works. The Chinese texts that have survived for over 6000 years are still being used to teach acupuncture, and how else can one better describe the language and vision of the Oriental medical/philosophical tradition than as "poetic". The images in their texts—Chi or "life force", Yin-Yang (positive-negative), etc.—are not the "hard facts" of Western medicine, although our Western physics does yield a kind of abstract poetry. The Oriental vision of human connectedness both *within* the self and *with* nature is not unlike that of the old herbalists of Europe. The application of this kind of vision, of course, differs from culture to culture, but the wisdom reflected comes from the deepest layers of the human spirit, and this "place" is the same in all peoples.

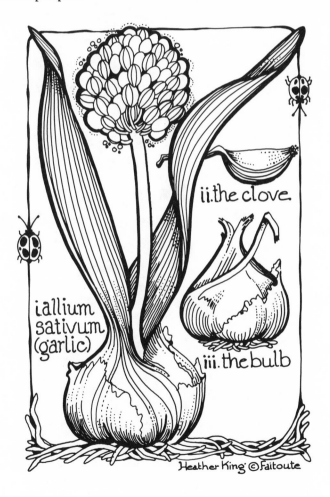

i.allium sativum (garlic)
ii. the clove.
iii. the bulb

Heather King ©Faitoute

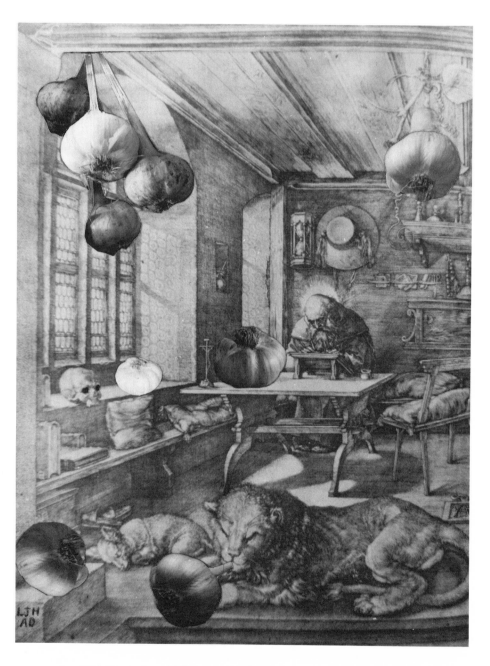

An Old Herbalist-Alchemist Studying a Giant Allium Sativum

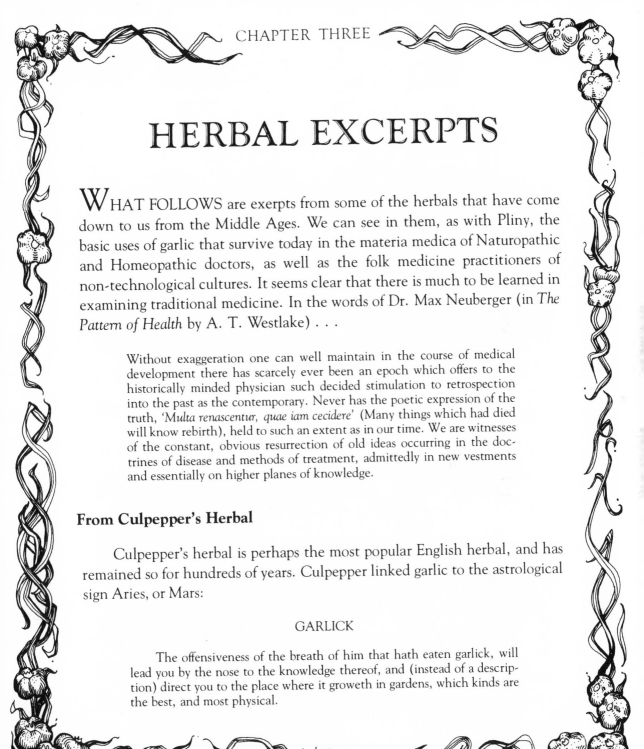

CHAPTER THREE

HERBAL EXCERPTS

WHAT FOLLOWS are exerpts from some of the herbals that have come down to us from the Middle Ages. We can see in them, as with Pliny, the basic uses of garlic that survive today in the materia medica of Naturopathic and Homeopathic doctors, as well as the folk medicine practitioners of non-technological cultures. It seems clear that there is much to be learned in examining traditional medicine. In the words of Dr. Max Neuberger (in *The Pattern of Health* by A. T. Westlake) . . .

> Without exaggeration one can well maintain in the course of medical development there has scarcely ever been an epoch which offers to the historically minded physician such decided stimulation to retrospection into the past as the contemporary. Never has the poetic expression of the truth, '*Multa renascentur, quae iam cecidere*' (Many things which had died will know rebirth), held to such an extent as in our time. We are witnesses of the constant, obvious resurrection of old ideas occurring in the doctrines of disease and methods of treatment, admittedly in new vestments and essentially on higher planes of knowledge.

From Culpepper's Herbal

Culpepper's herbal is perhaps the most popular English herbal, and has remained so for hundreds of years. Culpepper linked garlic to the astrological sign Aries, or Mars:

GARLICK

The offensiveness of the breath of him that hath eaten garlick, will lead you by the nose to the knowledge thereof, and (instead of a description) direct you to the place where it groweth in gardens, which kinds are the best, and most physical.

Government and Virtues: Mars owns this herb. This was anciently accounted the poor man's treacle, it being a remedy for all diseases and hurts (except those which itself breed). It provoketh urine and women's courses, helpeth the biting of mad dogs and other venomous creatures; killeth worms in children, cutteth and voideth tough phlegm, purgeth the head, helpeth the lethargy, is a good preservative against, and a remedy for, any plague, sore, or foul ulcer; taketh away spots and blemishes from the skin, easeth pains in the ears, ripeneth and breaketh imposthumes (abscesses), or other swellings. And for all those diseases the onions are as effectual. But the garlic hath some more peculiar virtues besides the former, viz., it hath especially quality to discuss inconveniences coming by corrupt agues or mineral vapours, or by drinking corrupt and stinking waters; as also by taking wolfbane, hen-bane, hemlock, or other poisonous and dangerous herbs. It is also held good in hydropic diseases, the jaundice, falling sickness, cramps, convulsions, the piles or hæmorrhoids, or other cold diseases. (41)

A Persian Herbal of the 10th Century
by Abu Mansur Muwaffak Bin Ali Harawi

The garlic is a means whereby the health is perpetuated because it has the power to prevent stagnation of the blood. It is at the same time a food and a useful remedy. The garlic which grows wild . . . is employed against corrupted humors . . . It acts as an antidote for deadly poisons, and snakes flee away from it. We should not be without it in any kitchen, nor leave it out of any food, nor despise it on account of its unpleasant odor . . . it drives away the toothache if you bruise it and lay it upon the tooth . . . it cures baldness by stimulating the growth of hair . . .it increases the natural heat of the body, and promotes digestion. (42)

Gerard's Herbal

With figge leaves and cumin it is laid on against the biting of the mouse.

Turner's Herbal

It is good against all venome and poyson, taken in meats or boyled in wine and drunken, for of his own nature it withstandeth all poyson: insomuch that it driveth away all venomous beasts from the place where it is.

The Herbal of Rembert Dodeus

It can be used against all poisons. Will cure coughs and toothache. Used to strengthen loose teeth. Cures all skin diseases.

Cole's Art of Simpling

Cocks are 'most stout of fight, and so are horses,' and if the garden is infected with moles, garlic will convince them to 'Leap out of the ground presently.'

The Death of Herbalism

Culpepper linked magic and astrology to herbalism, which in the long run, contributed to its demise. The dawning of the Modern Era repudiated magic and astrology and with them, herbalism, which had become more associated with planetary movements than healing ingredients. Although the mainstream of medicine turned to the Scientific method and a concentration on causes of disease rather than on health and preventative "right living", herbalism stayed alive on the fringes of Orthodox Medicine (more on Orthodox vs. Unorthodox medicine in Part Two).

GARLIC AT THE EDGE OF MODERN MEDICINE

Although Herbal Medicine was on the decline in the 19th century in England and America, herbs were still used by physicians, particularly family physicians, those gentlemanly doctors usually practicing medicine in rural or small-town areas. The following excerpts are from two popular medical books of the late 19th century.

HOME BOOK OF HEALTH by John Gunn, M.D. (1878)

 Garlic is a stimulant, diuretic and expectorant, and applied to the skin, rubefacient, that is, it will produce a blister. The medical uses of garlic are very numerous, it being recommended by some as a valuable expectorant in Consumption and all Affections of the Lungs; by some as an important diuretic in Dropsies, and again by others as a remedy for Fevers, especially of the Intermittent type. It is generally considered a good remedy for Worms, and is often given to children for that purpose. It is an excellent remedy in Nervous and Spasmodic Coughs, Hoarseness, and the like; and may be given in the form of a syrup, tincture, or in substances; but the best way to use it when fresh, is to express the juice, and mix it either with syrup or some other proper vehicle . . . (43)

HERBAL SIMPLES by W.T. Fernie, M.D. (1897)

 The bulb, consisting of several combined cloves, is stimulating, antispasmodic, expectorant, and diuretic. Its active properties depend on an essential oil which may be readily obtained by distillation. A medicinal tincture is made (H.) with spirit of wine, of which from ten to twenty drops may be taken in water several times a day. Garlic proves useful in asthma, whooping-cough and other spasmodic affections of the chest. For an adult, one or more cloves may be eaten at a time. The odour of the bulb is very diffusible. (44)

The tradition of the family physician, and the medical texts for "home use", is being revived today, and there are many such books on the market. In one, *The Well Body Book* (Random House, 1973), herbal medicine is incorporated into a general guide for care and treatment of various illnesses and disorders; nutrition is given its proper place in the maintenance of health. Another recent medical guide gives an Oriental approach to medicine and disease. This book, *Healing Ourselves* (Avon, 1973), elucidates the use of garlic in the treatment of cancer, lung disorders, and illnesses involving imbalances in the flow of "vital energy."

GARLIC AND THE LODESTONE

Brewer's Dictionary of Phrase and Fable tells us of an old superstition that garlic can destroy the magnetic power of the Lodestone. This belief carries the sanction of Pliny, Solinus, Ptolemy, Plutarch, Albertus, Mathiolus, Rulandus, Renodaeus and Languius. But this notion was later denied by Sir Thomas Browne and W. Salmon. From *The Complete English Physician* by W. Salmon (1693):

> Martin Rulandeus saith that Onions and Garlick . . . hindar the attractive power of the magnet and rob it of its virtue of drawing iron, to which Renodaeus agrees; but this is all lies.

In his *Pseudodoxia Epidemica* or *Enquiries Into Vulgar and Common Errors,* Sir T. Browne took a look at this popular belief:

> But certainly false it is what is commonly affirmed and believed, that Garlick doth hinder the attraction of the Loadstone, which is nothwithstanding delivered by grave and worthy Writers, by Pliny, Solinus, Ptolomy, Plutarch, Albertus, Mathiolus, Rueus, Langius, and many more. An effect as strange as that of Homer's Moly, and the Garlick that Mercury bestowed upon Ulysses. But that it is evidently false, many experiments declare. For an Iron wire heated red hot and quenched in the juice of Garlick, doth notwithstanding contract a verticity from the Earth, and attracteth the Southern point of the Needle. If also the tooth of a Loadstone be covered or stuck in Garlick, it will notwithstanding attract; and Needles excited and fixed in Garlick until they begin to rust, do yet retain their attractive and polary respects. (45)

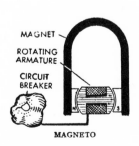

MAGNET
ROTATING ARMATURE
CIRCUIT BREAKER

MAGNETO

CHAPTER FOUR

GARLIC IN MODERN TIMES

MOVING away from ancient and medieval times, the garlic maintains its place as a favorite food and herbal medicine with the peoples of the Old and New Worlds, but the gap between the tradition of the Herbalist and that of Modern Science begins to widen: The older herbal tradition becomes Folk Medicine rather than official Science.

THE FRENCH

Raspail, the French author, called garlic "the camphor of the poor". This sounds much like the Theriaca Rusticoriam of Galen over 1500 years earlier. The peoples' fondness for garlic expressed itself in the annual consumption of Provence Butter. It is reported that in Paris of the 16th century, butter and garlic would be mixed every spring as the fresh deliveries of spring garlic and butter made their way in from the countryside. This mixture was held to be a great health concoction as well as a taste treat.

The great novelist, A. Dumas, spoke quite lovingly of garlic, and of Provence, garlic's "spiritual home". In Provence, where the people would breakfast on garlic and dark bread, Dumas noted that the air was ". . . particularly perfumed by the refined essence of this mystically attractive bulb."

One is hard-put to find any evidence at all of alliaversion or alliumphobia in France. Yet, in 1100 A.D., Robert of Normandy apologized for garlic's smell (also attributed to Nash):

Sith garlic then hath poure to save from death
Bear with it though it make unsavoure breathe. (46)

In 1609, Sir John Harrington added to these lines:

> And scorn not garlic like some that think
> It only maketh men wink and drink and stink.

Henry V, Le Roi d'Ail

This king of France was anointed at birth with wine and garlic, and he popularized the use of garlic in his court. Garlic on a baby's lips functioned as a stimulant and antiseptic.

Vinaigre des Quatres Voleurs

Perhaps the most celebrated garlic cure in history came out of the plague in Marseilles in 1721. A band of thieves, it is claimed, made great profits robbing the bodies of plague victims, and remained immune to the plague raging around them. They are said to have taken a macerate of wine and garlic which protected them from infection. Another story states that a man named Richard Forhaves sold this drink, and from For-haves came Four Thieves. This decoction became a popular folk remedy for a variety of intestinal and respiratory diseases (47).

VAMPIRES IN EASTERN EUROPE

We know that in Central and Eastern Europe, garlic was hung in doors and windows to protect against vampires. In the horror film, *Fearless Vampire Killers,* Roman Polanski spoofs this use of garlic as a protective charm against the Living Dead. But not too many years ago, vampires were taken very seriously by Europeans, and when a suspected vampire was caught, a series of tests were conducted to prove whether the suspect was indeed a vampire.

Following the tests, assuming they were affirmative, various steps were taken to not only kill the vampire, but to keep him dead. One of these procedures was to stuff garlic in his mouth before the body was buried (48). This procedure is linked to the ancient use of garlic as a disinfectant for burying the dead.

It is hard to say why the garlic became a protection against vampires. A possible explanation may be in the naive attitude towards the rash of plagues that swept over Europe. There was no way for the people to understand or explain the sudden death of whole populations in very short periods of time except to say that the phenomenon was the result of some sort of evil influences. There was no accepted theory of germs to explain the outbreak of disease, and since a scientific explanation was not available, a religious one filled the gap. Devils, Demons and Vampires were thought to be responsible for the death and disease.

For centuries, the trial-and-error method of medicine had shown garlic to be effective against plague-like diseases (Four Thieves Vinegar), and so in the popular mind, garlic became a charm against those anthropomorphic agents of plague and disease.

Vampires Were Burned or Buried with Garlic
to Ensure Death

There may also be a more specific connection between vampires and the plagues. Vampires were believed to be dependent on human blood for survival, and since the plagues were seen as massive "blood lettings", it was "logical" to conclude that vampires were responsible. Garlic, then, became a protective charm against both the plague itself and the agents of the plague.

SPAIN AND THE NEW WORLD

So many cultures have adopted the garlic into their diet, that it is difficult to say in which countries garlic is most used. One thinks, of course, of Italy or the south of France as garlic centers. Spain too makes heavy use of the garlic, and in an old lyric of Edward Robert Bulwer-Lytton (1831-1891), Spain is picked out to symbolize the "land of garlic":

> . . . The Italians have voices like peacocks;
> The Spanish smell, I fancy, of garlic.

John Minsheu, in his *The Guides Into the Tongues*, published in London in 1627 said:

> . . . The Spaniard, therefore, as it seems, having a colder stomack than other countries, doth well brooke the smell hereof, when everie day before he goeth out of his Inne, as he journieth, he causeth garlicke to be stamped, crums of bread and oile to be fried together in the manner of a hastie pudding, and so eateth thereof; and the commonsort doe live by it, so that it is the poor man's Physicke and Food. (49)

Sayings and Proverbs

Spanish proverbs and sayings strongly reflect this connection with garlic. To "*suspirar por los ajos y cebollas de Egypt*" is "to sigh for the garlic and onions of Egypt", a direct connection to the Biblical reference of the wandering Jews missing their garlic and onions. Another saying reflects the common use of garlic as Food and Physicke during long voyages and mountain crossings; "*Ajo puro y vino crudo, passan el puetro segŭro . . .*" which translates "pure garlic and rough wine help one to traverse safely the high mountain passes." (50)

San Martín of South America

The famous revolutionary San Martín, leader of the fight for the independence of Argentina, Chile and Peru in the early 19th century, made use of the garlic during his crossing of the Andes. He ordered garlic stuffed into the nostrils of horses and mules collapsed from lack of oxygen. His men also sniffed and chewed garlic to counter the symptoms of high-altitude journeys or Mountain Sickness.

Magic Charm

In the following practice introduced by the Spanish into the Americas, a connection is seen with the ancient Greek "supper for Hecate" involving the magic of garlic placed at the meeting of crossroads. The Spanish version rids a young girl of an undesirable suitor. She must choose a spot where two roads cross, and on the ground she must place two crossed pins and a piece of garlic. Then she has to get the fellow to walk over the charm (51).

Spanish Jews

The Jews in 13th-century Barcelona had the following custom. When a boy was born, an old cock would be slaughtered as a redemption, and its head would be cut off and hung with garlic over the entrance to the child's house (52). The reason behind this ritual slaughter escapes me. Perhaps the symbolism can be explained as a *rebirth* of the new child from the old cock. The garlic may act here merely as a disinfectant and protection against hostile spirits.

Official Alliaversion

The battle against garlic raged on in the court of King Alfonso XI, of Castile. It is said that he held garlic in such aversion that in 1330 he founded a Knightly Order based on this hatred of the garlic. The statutes of the order provided that a Knight who had eaten garlic would not be allowed to appear at court or communicate with other members for at least a month (in Dumas', *Dictionaire*).

In the New World

Not only did the American Indian tradition of herbal medicine help the white European explorers survive in the New World, but Europeans brought a wealth of information that influenced the native populations of the Americas. The Spanish were as we have seen no new-comers to the glory of garlic and they in turn introduced garlic as a potent medication to the areas of their exploration (and conquest).

Garlic Remedies

The American Southwest (in the Santa Fe area) was one area into which Spaniards introduced the garlic. Below are listed certain uses of garlic that became part of the folk tradition of The Upper Rio Grande.

> *AILING HORSES:* When a horse was Malo (suffering a swollen neck) garlic was crushed with twigs of mule pine and hot water was added. This

was allowed to cool and then administered to the ailing horse.

PAIN IN THE BOWEL (HUMAN) ON THE LEFT SIDE: Two garlic cloves were baked until soft, then crushed. A little cold water was added, and this mixture was taken orally.

RABIES AND WORMS: Dogs were treated for rabies and worms by mixing garlic in with their food.

FLATULENCE (HUMAN): Garlic was roasted whole on coals, cleaned, then chewed and swallowed with cold water. Gas disappears. (53)

A Cuban Jaundice Preventative

In Cuba, thirteen cloves of garlic at the end of a cord, worn around the neck for thirteen days, was considered a safeguard against jaundice. It is necessary that the wearer, in the middle of the night of the thirteenth day, should proceed to the corner of two streets, take off his garlic necklace and flinging it behind him, run home without turning around to see what has become of it.

AMERICAN INDIAN FOLK TRADITION

In the exploration of the West, the "white" man encountered Indian herbal medicine and often survived because of it. A few stories illustrate how explorers on the North American continent were saved by Indian garlic remedies.

During Stephen Long's expedition to the Rocky Mountains (1820), outbreaks of scurvy were treated successfully by a wild garlic, Allium Reticulatum. This cure can be attributed to garlic's comparatively high vitamin C content. Maximillian, Prince of Wied, was stricken some years later and doctors were at a loss. An Indian cook, who had been with Long, remembered the garlic remedy and had Indian children go out and pick garlic from fields near the fort. The cook chopped up the garlic and the Prince, having taken the garlic, recovered, to the surprise of the doctors (54).

It is also claimed that wild garlic saved Marquette's party from starvation en route to the Great Lakes. He named their campsite *Cigaga-Wunj*, which is Indian for "place of the Wild Garlic", and it is claimed that *Cigaga* later became Chicago (55).

Indian Garlic Remedies

EARACHE: Garlic was placed in wool with salt and stuck in the ear. Herbalists prescribe this same remedy today.

FLATULENCE: Roasted garlic was taken with cold water.

INJURIES TO THE FOOT: Pounded hot garlic was applied to the injury in the form of a poultice.

DIPHTHERIA: Garlic was used as a charm, worn around the neck, for diphtheria and other infectious diseases.

Legends, Rumors and Tall Tales of the Old West

There are many stories that have come down to us concerning garlic in the Americas. Typically, they involve supernatural dimensions not unlike other more popular lore such as that of Paul Bunyan. One garlic story tells of a Giant Garlic that grew in the Southwest. When the great railroad expansion began to slow up in the West, it was often rumored back in the East that the delay was due to certain bizarre hazards encountered in the rugged Western territories. One such rumor mentioned that this Giant Garlic caused at least one head-on collision between the locomotives of two competing railroad companies.

Another story told of strange tribes lurking in the lush tropics of Mexico. It was believed among polite circles that the natives ate much of the reviled garlic, and that one tribe even had garlic-shaped heads. This tall tale is obviously a merging of both a racial fear and an unconscious taboo against smell.(56) (This will be elucidated more fully in The Argument Against Garlic.)

Both of the above tales are given fanciful interpretations in the following lithographs attributed to a minor American artist.

HEAD-ON COLLISION

I Dreamed I Spied Upon a Tribe of Garlic-Heads

CHAPTER FIVE

THE ARGUMENT AGAINST GARLIC

They haven't got no noses
And goodness only knowses
The noselessness of man.
— G.K. Chesterton

IT TRULY can be stated now, and with a wealth of history to prove it, that garlic has always been a "peoples'" food and remedy (magical and medical); and where the people loved it most, the upper classes (priests, kings, aristocrats, politicians) created taboos against its use. The people worshipped it anyway. The historian Victor Hehn explains why, for instance, in ancient Egypt, the high-priests disdained the peoples' sacred herb (57). Hehn argues that since the Egyptians connected the most common things with the mysteries of religion (a kind of pantheism), it was inevitable that their favorite foods and medical plants would become sacred and worshipped as gods. The mere strength of garlic's odor was proof of its sacred and medicinal nature. The priests condemned the use of this plant and would not touch it; either because it was sacred and therefore untouchable by human hands, or because it was sacred *to the people* and, like them, smelled of the earth. The garlic was, in this latter sense, vulgar and thus beneath the level of the religious elite. Garlic's reputation as an aphrodisiac is also said to have scared off the celibate clergy. The satirical Roman poet Juvenal mirrors this upper-class disdain for the peoples' sacred garlic in the following verse:

How Egypt mad with superstition grown
Makes gods of monsters, but too well is known,

> 'Tis mortal sin an Onion to devour;
> Each clove of Garlic has a sacred power,
> Religious nation, sure, and bless'd abodes
> Where every garden is o'er-run with gods. (58)

The ancient Israelites were very much attached to their garlic — in and out of bondage in Egypt — and it has been suggested that their persecution may have in part been due to their garlic-eating habits. An anecdote has come down to us that when Marcus Aurelius, the Roman soldier-emperor, crossed Palestine after victories against the Marcomanni and Quadi, the odor of the Jews was so heavy that he exclaimed, "Oh Marcomanni, Quadi, Sarmatians! I have found a people even worse than you!" (59)

ALLIAVERSION

The pattern is obvious: Increased civilization and "manners" turned a basic infatuation with the earthy garlic into a loathing among the increasingly upward-moving citizens. Garlic became vulgar and indicative of remaining barbarism in the peoples of Egypt, Rome, and Greece. Horace, in his third Epode, said this:

> Garlic is the stomach of the reapers...to me
> garlic seems a poison given by a wicked witch!
> It scorches my limbs like the sun of Apulia, like
> the Nessus-garment of Hercules! Should ever, O Maecenas,
> the whim take thee to eat of this Herb, may thy
> mistress refuse to kiss thee, and fly from thy
> embrace to the farthest end of the couch! (60)

Hundreds of years after Horace, a Frenchman replied: "Horace if you had tasted it you had rather be crowned with Garlic than with Laurel." (61)

Plutarch relates that onions and garlics were neither food for fasters nor for feasters, for in the former they awakened desire, and in the latter they induced tears (62).

The Greek priests excluded garlic eaters from the Temple of Cybele, wife of Chronos and Mother of Zeus. The story is told that when the witty and impious philosopher, Stilpor, lay down to sleep in the sanctuary of Cybele, after indulging in large quantities of garlic, Cybele appeared to him in a dream and asked, "Art thou a philosopher, and fearest not to transgress the law?" To which he replied "Give me something else to eat and I will abstain from garlic." (63) That Stilpor gave up his garlic so easily makes one question the true dimensions of his passion, or enables one to understand the power of gods in ancient times.

It is obvious that the strength of the pungent garlic odor is the common denominator for the rejection of garlic, and the fact that people worshipped it, increased the disrepute into which it fell for those higher up in the social hierarchy. The fact that lepers (Pilgarlics) made use of garlic as an antidote to their misery added additional fuel to the abhorrence of garlic. The term "garlic-eater" came to mean "lowly fellow."

GARLIC AVERSION IN LITERATURE

Even our great friend Don Quixote, a bit of a garlic-eater himself, despite the airs and fantasies of his lost nobility, could not understand why a peasant woman he mistook for his lovely Dulcinea smelled of garlic. His explanation was that he was being tricked by magicians who wished to spoil the sweetest moment of his life. Aristophanes and Shakespeare used garlic as a comic device and symbol of vulgarity. From an Aristophanes comedy:

> Don't go near them! They've eaten garlic!

From Shakespeare's *Midsummer Night's Dream* (Act IV, scene 2), Bottom says:
> And most dear actors, eat no onions, nor garlic, for we are to utter sweet breath.

And from *Measure for Measure* (Act III, scene 2):

> The duke would mouth with a beggar, though she smelt brown bread and garlic.

More on garlic in literature in Part Three — Excursions into Garliciana.

GARLIC AND SATAN

A link between garlic and demonic evil is attributed back to the Garden of Eden in a Mohammedan legend:

> When Satan walked from the Garden of Eden
> garlic appeared from the ground where his
> left foot rested and an onion sprouted at his
> right foot. (64)

AN APPLE FOR THE TEACHER

Dr. Weiland Hand, of the Department of Folklore at the University of California at Los Angeles, explained another legend linking Satan and garlic in the Garden of Eden taken from the Dutch *Flora Diabolic* (a paraphrase):

> Gabriel brought a son to Mary which made Satan very jealous. Satan threw down his claws at the place of a sacred flower and the claws, circling the flower, turned into the cloves of the rank garlic. The sacred flower survived this attack and thrust the garlic and Satan out of the Garden.

Since garlic is related botanically to The Sacred Lily, symbol of virginity and purity, one has here an interesting example of an *underlying unity* between the Sacred and the Profane.

THE BRITISH

If there is one people or one nation that symbolizes the rejection of garlic (just as Provence or Spain or Italy symbolize the love of garlic), then it would be the English. Perhaps it was the cold climate that made it difficult to cultivate Allium Sativum (although a wild, bitter garlic — Allium Vineal —flourished like a weed in the English countryside, as if garlic were having its revenge on the Alliumphobic British), or perhaps the high civilization in England kept the garlic suspect. Insofar as the English climate influenced the quality of life and thought, one can speculate that the lack of passion for the pungent garlic was due to a general "coldness" in the British themselves. A cold, rational culture is unlikely to be partial to the Primal Lily.

In Victorian England and America, garlic was held to be *déclassé*, and the poet Shelley, in a letter to a lady friend from Italy, spoke thus of garlic:

> What do you think? Young women of rank eat — you will never guess what — garlick! (65)

A more hostile attitude was evident in the American colonial mind. John Evelyn, a 17th-century American and early spokesman for *Sallets* (salads),

90

spoke of garlic as:

>…dry towards excess and tho by both Spaniards and Italians and the more Southern People familiarly eaten with almost everything, and esteemed of such singular Vertue to help Concoction, and thought a Charm against all Infection and Poysen (by which it has obtained the name of the Country-man's Theriacle), we yet think it more proper for our Northern Rustics, especially living in uliginous and moist places, or such as use the Sea; whilst we absolutely forbid it entrance into our Salleting, by reason of its intolerable rankness, and which made it so detested of old that the eating of it was (as we read) part of the Punishment for such as had committed the horrid'st Crimes. (66)

THE RURAL BRITISH DISDAIN FOR GARLIC---Passing a field of Allium Vineal (a wild garlic)

This rhetorical repulsion of the humble garlic has been carried by the British into the 20th century. H.L.V. Fletcher has this to say about garlic's place in England in the early part of this century:

> I cannot remember anyone using it either as a flavoring or an herb. Then sometime after the First World War it became known as an herb that would cure almost anything. Whether it was the smell or whether it was that the panacea did not work I do not know, but it went out of fashion as quickly as it came in. As a flavoring it has never been as popular this side of the channel as it always seems to have been on the other. *For that I am heartily thankful for I like its taste no better than its smell.* (Italics mine). (67)

The English have paid a price for their alliaversion. It is claimed that during an outbreak of an infectious fever in the poor quarters of London in the early 19th century, the French priests who always used garlic in their daily diet visited the worst cases and never contracted the disease, while the English clergy — avid alliumphobes — caught the infection and fell victim to the disease (68). Of course many of the early English herbalists recommended the garlic as a medicine but there is lacking the passionate love of garlic as a food, and as a *way of life* that one finds in more southern European climates, and in Asian cultures.

THE ODORLESS GARLIC

The English and American puritanical disgust with garlic's smell and taste has led to the dream of an odorless garlic. A garlic lover like myself is hard-put to imagine such a mutation! Ever since the Romans theorized that if you planted the garlic when the moon was below the horizon and harvested it when the moon was nearest the earth, the garlic would not have a bad odor, men have been searching for ways of eliminating or hiding the smell of garlic. One American gentleman tried to develop a "kissable" garlic salad dressing. He was written up in American Magazine (February, 1955) in an article entitled "Kissable Garlic":

Sometimes a man will go to great lengths to get a kiss from the little woman, and Bill Deretchin of Brooklyn, N.Y., is that kind of man. Trouble was Bill liked garlic and Bessie, his wife, didn't! Not that she had any objection to the taste. Rather, it was the lingering aroma, especially after Bill had enjoyed a garlic-seasoned steak or salad for dinner. There were no kisses from Bessie for quite some time after such a meal, and that troubled Bill a lot. Fond as he was of the zippy seasoning, he seriously considered giving up the stuff.

Before taking such drastic action, though, Bill began a series of experiments in his food products plant where he cooked up and sold a variety of sauces. After 8 years of trial and error, he came up with the answer: a garlic sauce which, when sprinkled on food gives out with all the rich garlic flavor but leaves no after-taste or fragrance. It's all done with a secret formula, he says. He labeled the liquid "kissproof," and now bliss reigns supreme in the Deretchin household. His star customer for the new sauce? Bessie.

MODERN SCIENCE AND GARLIC ODOR

Modern science has been enlisted in this battle against the odor of garlic. Men of intelligence have always been curious about the perfidiousness of the garlic odor; how explain the phenomenon of rubbing garlic into your feet and breathing it out of your lungs later? A recent letter to the medical journal, *The Lancet*, (July 1973) expresses this same curiosity:

> *Garlic on Baby's Breath*
> Sir — Has the following observation been further studied? Garlic seems to be peculiarly capable of penetrating the placental barrier and has been noted on more than one occasion on the breath of the newborn infant delivered of a Pakistani mother.
> S.B. Snell

Science, that great alleviator of human woe, has determined that one millionth of an ounce of garlic oil is detectable in a single whiff of breath.

The traditional theory about the smelly breath of garlic-eaters was that very small particles of garlic got caught in the teeth of the garlic-eater, and that when he breathed, the air would flow over the garlic, picking up the alliaceous odor. From this theory have come countless mouthwash antidotes (parsley, cumin, caraway, etc.) which may help, but which really do not do the trick.

In working with patients whose oral cavity was, for one reason or another, inoperative, doctors have found that by feeding garlic directly into the stomach or alimentary tract, an odor of garlic would still be passed through the breath. The conclusion was that the essential oils and the accompanying chemical breakdown of these substances in the system would permeate through blood and tissue into the lungs where the essence would be passed out with each breath (69). Although the various antidotes for garlic odor will perhaps mask some of the odor, there is little one can do to completely eliminate the sulphuresque erruptions that accompany a proper garlic repast. It is true, however, that certain cooking and eating techniques will help in the control of the odor, and these will be described in the cookbook — Part Four, The Garlic Gala Gastronomique. Americans will just have to learn to accept the occupational hazards of one of humankind's favorite preoccupations — GARLIC.

GARLIC, ROMANTIC LOVE, AND STINK

Much of what may be called alliaversion is the product of psycho-social characteristics of the middle- and upper-class mentality. To what extent the dread of "stink" is linked to classical Freudian-type categories (anal retentive, obsessive-compulsive, etc.) is best left to the Freudians to determine. On the surface, it is obvious that styles of courtship involve deep, underlying attitudes about such things as body odor, and new research has been advanced indicating how we perceive subtle odors in our mating rituals that lead us towards or away from the potential loved one. It is also obvious that in American culture the smell of garlic, no matter how subtle, will tend to lead potential mates apart. The unspoken taboo against garlic in our culture is based not on the fear of offending a god, as was true of the Greeks, but on pragmatic grounds: Garlic will make breath and skin stink, and this will turn off a potential friend or lover. Indeed, in this culture — America, 20th century — "to smell" is *ipso facto* to smell *bad*. Alan Watts discusses these issues in his article, "Do You Smell?":

> ...The question seems impolite, and yet it is no more so than asking: do you see? Do you hear? Do you feel? Do you taste? We admire a person of taste, but what is wrong with a person of smell? The problem is superficially one of bad usage in English grammar. "To smell" should mean to sense through the nose, and "a smell" should mean no more than a nasal sensation. A person with offensive body-odor should be said "to stink", and an unpleasant nasal sensation should be called "a stink" or "a stench", never "a smell"...(70)

Watts concludes that this limitation in both our language and in our

95

perceptual range is the result of a repression, especially in materialist "WASP" culture, of the sense of smell. And when an entire sensory mode is repressed it becomes unconsciously powerful, opening up the possibility of irrational attitudes and actions against individuals, and indeed entire societies, who manifest the repressed qualities. Thus, the Koreans, Spaniards, Italians, and Jews are said to smell like garlic by non-garlic-eating ruling classes. With the ever-increasing sanitization and deodorization of our world, one can imagine the nose of man shriveling up from disuse — like the baby toe. G.K. Chesterton's poetry will be proved prophetic...

The noselessness of man.

A LOVE SCRIPT

Within our own WASPISH society, our ignorance of smell has perhaps been an underlying motivation for more than we might realize. It may be that our peculiar forms of government, social relations, mating behavior, etc., are built to some degree around this aversion to strong smells. The phenomenon of Romantic Love, expounded in novels, movies, television, and especially through the advertisement media, may be no more than a dream of purity and odorlessness. If we were to put the ideas behind Romantic Love into a script, it might go as follows: We approach our Love as if in a Dream, we unite or "know" one another, thus entering the Heaven of Union; nothing gets in our way. In fact, if all goes well, the Cosmos conspires to assist in the Union: Lawrence Welk (a profane Wagner), or Johnny Mathis ("Until the Twelfth of Never") create the mood of Sweet Eternity; the planets and the stars, if visible, form the canopy of the Love Nest; and our sweet odor-free breaths whisper the secrets of Pure Love. This techno-WASP vision of love sells millions of dollars in toothpaste, mouthwash, and breath mints every year to Americans, Englishmen, and more and more to Europeans and Asians.

Reality though is hard to beat. There is always something that gets in the way of the dream of Romantic Love. It may be a motorcycle suddenly breaking the poignant silence, or a commercial interrupting the TV or Radio symphony. Worst of all, occasionally we are thrust into the position of Adam and Eve who, seduced by the serpent of Reality, fall from the dream of Heavenly Paradise. And of course, GARLIC is such a serpent for there is nothing that destroys the bliss of Romance like the knowledge of *good* breath and garlicky breath! Right?

ALLIOCENTRISM

The connection between garlic and Satan has already been discussed. It has crossed my mind that perhaps the Serpent did not give Eve an apple at all, "apple" being a euphemism for Allium (onions and garlic). If this is so, then we have to imagine that Eve, the heroine of paradisiacal romance, is seduced by the garlic-bearing serpent, and in turn seduces Adam with said garlic, and in so doing violates the orders (odors) of the Father. Adam and Eve have come to know good smell and garlic smell — they are ashamed! They now know they both stink. Immediately, to cover up their naked odor, they reach not for a fig *leaf*, but for fig *juice* (or the juice of the leaf) so as to deodorize the naked smell of their breath and sweat (garlic is exuded from the pores, often hours or even days after consumption). As punishment for eating the fruit of the Tree of Knowledge, the Father thrusts hero and heroine out of the Sweet Garden, and into the Reality of the smelly Soil, where they must harvest garlic in a life of painful drudgery. So the Alliocentric view of human history becomes, given this transposition of imagery, a story of the first garlic-eaters aware of a sweeter past existence, yet immersed in the sad reality of the Earth — soil and toil and stink.

Thus the Christian vision of Original Sin as interpreted by Alliocentrists, is really telling us that Romantic Love doesn't work because Adam and Eve ate of the serpent's "Earth Apple" (Allium). To this day, all the promises of paradise, including Romantic Love American Style have failed to

Adam and Eve in the Garden of Garlic

destroy certain realities which must be confronted if man is to survive. If man will save himself and the Earth, he must bury himself once again in the painful drudgery of Reality. Garlic is Reality, and as such, it contains the seeds of both Good and Bad, sacred and profane. Those who deny Reality (smell, earth, toil) see garlic as Bad. Those who accept Reality rejoice in the primal qualities of Garlic, and in loving its pungency, transpose the seeds of Bad into Good, as did the Egyptian, the Jew, or the Italian peasant to whom the odor of garlic was as Perfume to the nose of a Prince as he smells his Lover coming. But heedless of this truth, the Argument Against Garlic continues its course, changing only in its particular focus and not in its inner intent.

THE FINAL SOLUTION — THE PILL*

The modern attack against garlic (and thus against "smell") just like the modern defense of garlic, is a scientific one. We have seen how science is enlisted in the battle against garlic's odor, and the *final solution* to garlic's earthy smell comes in the guise of humanity's most pernicious Nostrum — The Pill.

Now the pill is a mixed blessing. In terms of the use of garlic as a dietary supplement, large doses of garlic can now be taken without the accompanying odor, and without the necessity of eating dozens of cloves at one sitting. This in itself is not bad. Thanks to a German, Dr. J.A. Hofels, who first produced garlic in capsule form, garlic can now be taken in large doses for a variety of ailments by the squeamish and pruddish non-garlic-eaters. The

*I refer here particularly to the dehydrated and powdered garlic pill, and not to the garlic "perle", which contains the natural extracted oil of garlic. Although there is still controversy over the relative values of these two forms of concentrated garlic, my own attitude is to suspect the form most removed from the natural.

garlic pill has been designed to release small quantities of Allium Sativum along the intestinal tract such that quantities too small to detect on the breath are absorbed. This is a great boon for humanity and for garlic, but like all human advances, it is a double-edged sword. The tendency will be to get lazy about the wonders of fresh garlic. Like garlic powder, the pill will tend to antiquate Allium Sativum *qua* Allium Sativum, unless of course garlic lovers the world over maintain a vigilance against undue neglect of the real stuff. Whether or not scientists and gourmets (*false* gourmets) will press forward on the quest for an odorless garlic remains to be seen.

A MODERN ADAM AND EVE. Reprinted from the *Oakland Tribune* with permission.

CHAPTER SIX

IN DEFENCE
OF THE
STINKING ROSE

THE ARGUMENT against garlic is a pervasive one, and there is no sign that the anti-garlic forces in the world are about to capitulate. However, there are signs that the pro-garlic forces are growing in strength, and one sure sign of this is the popularity of Lovers of the Stinking Rose, garlic's fan club. Born in the pages of the first edition of *The Book of Garlic*, LSR grows daily. In the next few pages the reader will learn more about LSR, its publication *Garlic Times*, and by clipping out pg. 103 of this book you will have in your hands a questionnaire and application form to send to LSR. We look forward to meeting you.

LOVERS OF THE STINKING ROSE

The primary function of LSR is to promote and protect garlic. Through garlic festivals, the *Garlic Times* publication, and other functions, LSR tells the world that garlic tastes great, is good for you and should not be feared or loathed. Garlic lovers support LSR's efforts by joining the club, subscribing to the *Garlic Times*, giving gift memberships to friends, purchasing the mail-order items in *Garlic Times* and sending material—recipes, remedies, folklore, stories—for inclusion in the *Garlic Times* and future editions of *The Book of Garlic*.

ANTI-GARLIC CRUSADE CONTINUES

The most recent attacks on garlic have come from American mouth-wash manufacturers and their Madison Ave. hucksters, and from the Japanese who are set to market, so it is claimed, a new, odorless fresh garlic. The mouthwash people are claiming that garlic and onion breath are public odor number one. Although these clever fellows have literally created new kinds of bad breath—denture breath, morning breath, medicine breath, etc.—they still see fit to pick on garlic and onion breath. There is method in their madness, to be sure. After all, the enjoyment of good food is growing in America, so most Americans will end up with garlic or onion breath at some point or other. In other words, these marketeers are using America's growing love of garlic to sell mouthwash. And this is why Lovers of the Stinking Rose has called for a boycott of all mouthwashes that single out garlic and onion breath. LSR claims that garlic breath is *garlic breath*—not *bad* breath.

As for the new odorless garlic from Japan, very little is known yet. Claims have been made that a strain of garlic has been isolated that has the taste and odor of garlic going in, but not the taste and odor of garlic coming out. Smelling is believing.

It may be appropriate here to add that LSR is not alone in its attack on the mouthwash conspiracy. Journalists such as Charles McCabe of the San Francisco *Chronicle* have published telling exposés of the mouthwash industry. As we go to press, we have noted a new book that acknowledges America's neurotic fear of odor. Here is a short quote from Janet Hopson's new book, *Scent Signals* (Morrow): "Society is too willing to eradicate, ignore or deny human scents before we even know about them. That's what the whole deodorant thing is, really." Although Hopson doesn't recommend total avoidance of deodorants or mouthwashes, she is suggesting a greater freedom for naturalness. She backs up her position with scientific data that indicate that humans, like other animals, need their natural scents in order to be healthy and happy.

APPLICATION FORM FOR MEMBERSHIP IN LSR
1621 Fifth St.
Berkeley, CA 94710

Members of LSR receive *The Book of Garlic*, a five-issue subscription to *Garlic Times* and discounts on mail-order items. For those who have bought *The Book of Garlic* from a store, you may subscribe to *Garlic Times* at the member rate of $5 for five issues. (Non-members pay $6.50 for five issues). But you must send in this page to us to qualify for the discount subscription and discounts on mail-order items. So cut along dotted lines, fill out the questionnaire, and enclose your check made out to LSR. (Xeroxes of applications don't count). We will send you your first issue of *Garlic Times*.

If you are joining LSR, you can give gift memberships to friends for only $12. They'll receive the book, subscription, etc.

California residents please add 6% sales tax.

Name _____

Address _____

_____

Dear LSR,
Count me in!
I wish to be a member and enclose $14 _____.

I have the book already, so send me my member subscription to GT for $5.00 _____.

And send a gift subscription to the enclosed name at the member gift subscription price of $12 _____.

Cover of *Garlic Times* #1

Nah, I'm not going to join LSR until I see a *Garlic Times*. So, send me your current issue for $1.00 _____.

Just send me another copy of *The Book of Garlic* for the postpaid price of $8.95 _____.

I understand that prices on memberships and other items are subject to change without notice and I'll pay the small increases when notified. I'll also allow four weeks delivery time.

LOVERS OF THE STINKING ROSE QUESTIONNAIRE

We at Lovers wish to know more about you and your garlic habits. In our defense and promotion of Allium Sativum, we must not cease to open our ranks to new and enthusiastic Alliumphiles. Therefore, if interested in receiving future literature from LSR, please fill out this Questionnaire and return to us.

Bon Garlique!

Name _____ Occupation_____

Age _____ Address _____

Religion, Creed, Philosophy_____

National Origin and Heritage_____

ALLIUM CREDENTIALS

Most frequently used form of Allium Sativum: Powder _____ Salt_____ Minced _____
Granulated _____ Concentrated Oil _____ Pill _____ Clove _____
(You may indicate numerically the order of use)

How much used?_____ Which Meal?_____

How most commonly prepared? _____

_____

_____

Ever eat it raw? _____ Explain _____

_____

_____

Ever use Garlic as Medicine? Yes _____ No _____ Explain_____

_____

_____

Have you any good garlic recipes, jokes, stories, etc., for our archives? (Please indicate sources if possible. Use other paper if necessary.)_____

_____

_____

_____

_____

_____

Any questions or suggestions?_____

_____

_____

_____

_____

Cut along broken line

GARLIC IN THE NEWS

LSR Announces Boycott of Signal Mouthwash

It has come to the attention of LSR that Signal Mouthwash, a product from Lever Brothers, is being intensely promoted through television and magazine advertising. The gimmick behind the campaign is that Signal halts bad breath caused by the "strongest of all" mouth odors—garlic and onions. Not only is this claim questionable, but it suggests further that garlic and onion odor are socially undesirable, a view that LSR cannot let go unchallenged.

In this age of sophisticated culinary tastes, the lingering odor of garlic and onions on one's breath is a sign of cultivation. The ruin of any outstanding French, Chinese or Italian meal would be to kill the fragrant after-taste with a commercial mouthwash.

But on another level, the so-called clinical studies by Lever's own "specialists in oral hygiene" don't make sense. First, other clinical studies (objective studies *not* paid for by the product's manufacturer!) have shown that garlic odors come not from residual particles of garlic in the mouth, but from the lungs—the mouthwash is at best a *temporary* masking agent. Chewing clumps of parsley can also reduce the odor from garlic consumption.

More importantly, the Lever ad, by claiming that Signal combats garlic and onion odors in the mouth, suggests that garlic odor is emitted only from the mouth. The fact is that the odor of garlic is exuded in the normal process of perspiration—you could hold your breath indefinitely and *still* smell from garlic! And need we add that oral and dermal activity are not the only two outlets for garlic odor? Need we elaborate on the third?

LSR insists that Lever Brothers discontinue its disparaging remarks about garlic and onion odors being "offensive." But if they persist, we recommend that their ads should conform to scientific fact. We suggest that the ads recommend Signal baths and Signal enemas, for only then would the fumes of garlic be totally masked

—and then only briefly. Nature has put longer life into the odor of garlic and onions than into the masking powers of commercial deodorants and mouthwashes. (LSR does not recommend such activities. The only effective way to deal with garlic and onion odor is to socialize with other garlic and onion eaters—you'd be surprised at how dramatically and completely the odor is eliminated!)

Illustration by Lawrence Duke

A Clove A Day

All you garlic lovers, take heart.

For hundreds of years, the fragrant little herb has done yeoman's duty—seasoning foods. Recently organic gardeners have rediscovered it as an organic means of pest control. Herbal-medicine freaks have been proclaiming its virtues for years—to cure respiratory infections, to improve circulation and even as a simple antiseptic. Ginseng-and-garlic tea is allegedly one of the great cold-killers, miles ahead of Contac.

Now, modern medical science seems on the verge of embracing the stuff. According to a University of Minnesota study, taking garlic may be a way of cutting down, and even avoiding, heart disease. Student and teacher volunteers at the university's school of public health are being asked to ingest approximately 20 milligrams of garlic oil in pill form each day, the equivalent of two to three cloves of garlic.

Researchers say that rats fed a moderately high-cholesterol diet that also included two per cent garlic were able to maintain a cholesterol count close to normal. Other rats that received the same diet without garlic reportedly showed a 23 per cent increase in cholesterol readings.

Courtesy *Mother Jones*

garlic times

Sample pages from *Garlic Times*

GARLIC T-SHIRTS ANYONE?

Smell It Like It Is, Inc. is a Miami firm that manufactures T-shirts that smell—like bananas, oranges, rootbeer . . . and *possibly* garlic. The garlic shirt is not a current item in their line, but they are prepared to make them up should demand warrant it. They produce shirts in quantities of a thousand or more, but LSR is working on a plan to get 250 of the garlic-scented shirts with "Lovers of the Stinking Rose" printed on front —the roses on the shirt will smell like you-know-what. If you are interested, let LSR know, and perhaps the shirts will be available by our next issue—Spring, 1978.

Garlic Cousin Makes Guinness Record

In England, recently, a group set out to break various records in the *Guinness Book of World Records*. The pickled onion-eating record was topped by Keith Munns, who ate 19 large pickled onions in two minutes! Nice going Keith. Why not try, now, a few jars of miso-pickled garlic bulbs found in your local Oriental market. If you do, let us know! You will become LSR's garlic-eating champion, and an honorary member!

ANTI-GARLIC LAW LINGERS

There are many whacky food laws in cities and states across the USA. Many are no doubt left-overs from earlier days. Since garlic was scorned by our Puritanical fore-fathers, its not surprising that anti-garlic laws would have been passed. In fact, garlic was seen as a punishment in Colonial America. One surviving law is on the books in Gary, Indiana: It is illegal to take a streetcar or go to the theater within four hours of consuming garlic.

Leslie Cabarga

Italian Waiter In London Stinks

Reuters reported that a waiter, Umberto Berlen, 39, was fired from his job at an exclusive London club because he served claret over a diner's left, instead of right, shoulder. But Berlen claimed that he was fired from Les Ambassadeurs Club because he smelled like garlic, something Prince Charles, a member, might not approve of. Berlen states, "I had eaten some garlic, it is true, the night before, but it was to cure a bad cold I had." The club secretary commented, "I will not have anybody who lowers the standard of my club, which we have worked for years to put at the top." Berlen is taking his case to the courts, claiming unfair dismissal. LSR is trying to follow up this story and will report its findings in the next issue.

Many Americans Say 'No' To Garlic

The punitive value of garlic is re-enforced by the fact that garlic is, according to L. M. Boyd in his "Grab Bag" column in the S. F. *Chronicle,* the *numero uno* hated odor in America. His survey showed that the odor of lard was second and olive oil third. Two odors indispensable to good eating—garlic and olive oil—seem to have powerful enemies in America. The odors Americans like best: hot coffee, strawberries, and apples.

Letters Continued

Have you heard about the Carson Pass garlic crash? A huge two-trailer semi loaded with seed garlic from Nevada went over the side near the crest of Carson Pass, spilling and breaking sacks of garlic over several acres of granite. Word spread through the Mother Lode, and hundreds of veteran Italians flocked to the site, bags and boxes aplenty, combing the talis for every last bulb they could find.

- David Cavagnaro,
  Santa Rosa, CA

Allium sativum is a grass / Whose delight no Epicurean can surpass / And to learn of its roots / Be you commoners or snoots / Read L. J. Harris' Book—it's a gas! (But try to convince my wife!)

- Andrew Drury Elder,
  Sebastopol, CA

Here's a true garlic story: Jeannie ate garlic sandwiches for lunch which contained a whole bulb of garlic. Early the next morning she gave birth to a healthy baby. When the baby was 2 days old, Jeannie's doctor asked her: "Do you like garlic? Your baby still smells strongly of garlic!"

- Mrs. C. T. Endemann,
  Calistoga, CA

I feel that I have no choice but to join LSR after discovering that my girlfriend eats sandwiches of peanut butter and sliced raw garlic. Common sense would seem to dictate my eating garlic if only in self-defense.

- Paul Koehn,
  Albany, CA

LSR's Lloyd "John" Harris sits in official garb in front of garliciana.

GARLIC PRESS INVENTOR WANTS FEEDBACK

Greg Bedayn of Tacoma, Washington, has a better mousetrap—that is, garlic press, and before he goes into production, he'd like to hear from garlic lovers about their ideas for the perfect garlic press. Says Greg, "Can I get some feedback from your readers? My press is designed and ready for production, but I could still make crucial changes if anybody has a hot idea!"

If you have hot ideas about garlic presses, send them to LSR and we'll pass them along to Greg. If you have just plain hot ideas, keep 'em to yourself! (If you have hot ideas about Chef Aidells—pictured on the cover—he'd appreciate receiving them in envelopes marked "Personal".)

CHAPTER SEVEN

A GARLIC HERBAL

THE following garlic remedies are taken from a wide range of cultures. It is hard to know the exact origins of any given brew, as they are filtered down through many lands, and in the process are changed. Many of these "recipes" are obviously of English origin, but then the English herbal tradition has roots in Roman and Greek medicine.

The value of these remedies is not absolute. They may work for some and not for others — which is true of modern chemical drugs as well. The scientific basis for many herbal medicines has not been totally elucidated, although we have mentioned in the introduction that garlic contains active ingredients such as allicin and germanium, which will be shown in Part Two to be anti-bacterial, anti-viral, and even anti-carcinogenic agents. The traditional use of garlic makes use primarily of its "mechanical" function as expectorant, diuretic, diaphoretic, antihelminthic, stomachic, etc. A Glossary follows the remedies and will explain some of these herbalist terms. Again, I must add that these remedies are not being "prescribed" as an alternative to necessary medical treatment by your doctor.

GARLIC IN RUSSIAN FOLK MEDICINE

We know that garlic was native to a region in Siberia, and so it is not strange that garlic should have such a prominent position in the folk medicine of Russia, Siberia, Poland, and other surrounding lands. In fact, garlic was so highly praised by Siberians that until the middle of the 18th century, they still paid their taxes in garlic:15 bulbs for a man, 10 for a woman, and 5 for each child (71). The following Russian Couplet expresses in another way the value placed on garlic as a medicine (a ransom is a wild garlic):

Eat leeks in tide, and
ransoms in May
And all the year after
physicians may play.

This enthusiasm has not been diminished with the advent of modern medical science. The Russian (Soviet) peoples are still very much involved in their folk traditions, and the garlic has not been made "obsolete" by advanced chemo-therapeutics. Garlic has even made a reputation for itself in recent times as "Russian Penicillin" because of its general and successful use as an antibiotic.

Soviet scientists reported recently that they have in production an actual pharmaceutical antibiotic, "Allicin," which kills only specific bacteria, leaving natural *healthy* bacteria untouched, something our more "sophisticated" drugs do not always do. And indeed, the Soviet government encourages the use of folk remedies. Garlic is of course only one of many natural herbal cures still used by the Soviet people, and it is to the credit of the Soviet phenomenon that the valued and tested "old-fashioned" ways are allowed to flourish side by side with more modern methods of medical treatment. One is perhaps amused that in a day and age when the most advanced chemical and electrical technologies are being used to treat most disease, the Soviet government has been known to have emergency shipments of garlic flown in from Europe in times of flu epidemics! In one recent case 500 tons were imported! It may be absurd to suggest that garlic may be the cure for the "common cold" (although this idea is poetically attractive), but that millions of Russians inhale garlic vapors for colds and bronchial disorders cannot be dismissed as mere superstition. In fact, there have been studies that indicate garlic's value in the treatment of cold symptoms. My own experience justifies in my mind these claims for garlic, and since I am of Russian and Polish descent, I will present my personal testimony here. I have had much success in treating my own cold symptoms with garlic: As nose drops, as relief for sore throat, and for headache and fever. The "recipes" for these treatments can be found in the following section — Miscellaneous Garlic Remedies.

RUSSIAN REMEDIES

The following recipes are part of a very old tradition of folk medicine, and they are still used to this day by the slowly vanishing breed of tribal medical men (shamen, natural medicine practitioners, *znakhari*, folk healers, etc.).

FOR ARTERIOSCLEROSIS

This remedy is recommended to all aged people, to be taken every 12 months. A glass jar is filled ⅓ with finely chopped garlic and then filled to the top with good vodka and covered. This mixture is kept in a warm place for at least 2 weeks (preferably in sunshine during the day). After 2-week period, mixture is strained and the infusion is ready to use.

Dose: Begin with 2 drops in warm water before lunch. The dose is then increased by one drop each day up to 25 drops. Then, dose is *reduced* daily in the same way, one drop a day. This treatment can be repeated after a 2-week break.

NERVOUS SPASMS AND SEIZURES

Garlic Milk Potion: One clove of garlic, crushed, boiled in a glass of milk and taken hot.

HIGH BLOOD PRESSURE

One clove of garlic per day taken every morning. Clove should be swallowed whole. Garlic pills can also be used. A glass of water can follow the swallowed clove. This remedy will quickly lower blood pressure in almost all cases.

COUGH (and whooping cough in children)

1. Eleven sliced garlic and onion heads are boiled in one quart of unpasteurized milk until soft. Strain. Then add honey to taste.
Dose: One tablespoon each hour of the day. Mixture should be warm. This western Siberian cure is claimed to break even a bad cold in one day.

2. Siberian practitioners used to apply unpeeled garlic directly to the child's throat at night, held in place by a bandage.

3. Inhaling steam of garlic milk is also recommended.

OLD AGE TONIC (especially for arteriosclerosis)

Fill pint bottle ¾ full of finely shredded raw garlic and fill with alcohol (same as above).

SIBERIAN ENERGY FORMULA (for fatigue, loss of energy, senile debility)

4 small heads of garlic crushed.

4 medium onions run through a meat grinder twice, preserving juice.

½ lb. barley in quart of water until water is boiled away, then run through meat grinder.

½ lb. fresh oats treated same as above.

2 oz. dried valerian roots (valeriana officinalis) finely chopped.

All this combined with 2 lbs. of honey and cooked over a slow fire until the mass assumes the consistency of very thick cream. This preparation is then spread out on a plate, one inch thick, to cool. When this mass sets, it is cut into squares about one inch across, and kept in a cool place.

Dose: 3-6 squares a day before meals. It is a very valuable food supplement for persons 50 years and older.

SIBERIAN OLD-AGE REMEDY (for last stages of senility—general debility, angina pectoris, loss of energy, breath, etc.)

⅓ lb. garlic, ½ lb. onion, 1 lb. honey, 2 tbl. vinegar (preferably apple vinegar).

Garlic and onion run through meat grinder twice, and vinegar then added. Let stand in warm place 24 hours. Honey is heated over slow fire until it is near boiling point. Garlic, onion and vinegar are then combined with hot honey, mixed thoroughly, and left to "ripen" for seven days in a warm place. Then strain through sieve.

Dose: Once a day, four teaspoons taken in succession, not all at once. Continued indefinitely. This remedy has a cumulative effect.

UKRAINIAN ELIXIR

Used over 500 years in Kiev and Kharkov areas for old age combined with obesity.

1 lb. garlic finely ground combined with juice of 24 lemons and left standing in glass jar covered with cheese cloth for 24 hours. Shake before taking.

Dose: 1 teaspoon at night with ½ glass warm water. It takes about 10 days for improvement in body tonus to be noticeable. This can be used also by younger people suffering from fatigue or low blood pressure.

 # Miscellaneous Garlic Remedies

FOR COLDS, COUGHS AND RELATED RESPIRATORY DISORDERS

A GARLIC SYRUP FOR LUNG DISORDERS: A quart of boiled water poured over 1 lb. of fresh garlic cut into slices is left to stand in a closed vessel for 12 hours. Sugar or honey is then added to make a consistency of syrup. A little vinegar will improve this remedy and the addition of caraway or sweet fennel seed bruised and boiled will lessen the garlic odor.

A GARLIC SYRUP FOR SHORTNESS OF BREATH OR HOARSENESS: Peel and slice garlic cloves and put into a soup plate. Cover each slice with honey, and in an hour or so a syrup will have formed. Take it by the teaspoon several times a day.

A COLD REMEDY: Cut cloves and rub them into soles of feet before sleep and at intervals during the night.

A COLD REMEDY: A cut clove held on either side of the mouth between the cheek and teeth — cloves should be replaced every few hours. You can make small cuts in the clove with your teeth to release small amounts of the juice, but this will increase both the sensation of heat and of odor.

FOR BRONCHITIS: The Russians inhale garlic vapors for this and related lung problems. Steam the garlic cloves whole, or press the juice into steaming water.

FOR TIGHTNESS OF CHEST, BRONCHITIS, COUGHS, AND WHOOPING COUGH: Chop garlic cloves finely and place into a jar with equal parts of Vaseline. Stand on a warm surface (the top of an oven) until Vaseline has melted. Then stir and allow to cool. Do not strain. This mixture is to be massaged into chest and back as a liniment. Onion can be used but will not be as effective.

FOR WHOOPING COUGH: A poultice is placed on the bottom of the feet. Chop a peeled garlic finely, enough for a ¼-inch-thick cover for the bottom of the feet. Spread evenly on soft cloth and then place a thin piece of cloth over garlic. Grease bottom of feet with lard or Vaseline before applying poultice to prevent blistering from the heat of the garlic. Now place a poultice on feet with a suitable cloth for binding the poultice to feet overnight. Cover both foot and poultice with a sock to prevent it from being kicked off. Remove in the morning and make a fresh one. This is valuable for any hard cough.

FOR SINUS CONGESTION: Chop two cloves; add about 2 oz. of water and stir, letting garlic settle to the bottom. Use the clear liquid, dropping a few drops into each nostril. Sniff and hold head back. This will be very hot, but invaluable. Jeanne Rose, an herbalist, reports that she cured a long-standing sinus condition by this method. The amount of garlic to water can be adjusted. I have used this mixture as nose drops for stuffy nose. It must be repeated fairly often.

FOR ASTHMA (based on Dr. Bowles' Asthma Cure): Boiled cloves of garlic with vinegar and sugar are stored in an earthenware jar. A dose of the syrup plus one or two of the cloves can be administered daily.

ACHES AND PAINS

FOR EARACHE (or infections in the ear): Place a peeled but uncut clove in the ear. Let it sit in ear through the day. Cloves can be changed daily.

FOR TOOTHACHE: Mix salt, oil, pepper and garlic, and bind mixture as poultice on the pulse; leave overnight. Garlic cloves also can be held directly on tooth.

FOR STOMACH ACHE: Slice garlic into yogurt. Leave standing for several hours before eating. You can remove garlic before eating mixture if you do not like the taste or effects of raw garlic.

FOR HEADACHE: Garlic is applied to the temples in a poultice.

GOUT AND RHEUMATISM

The Russians drink vodka in which garlic has been standing. They claim this also dissolves kidney stones. Garlic mixed with lard is used as an ointment directly on affected areas. Moxa cones can be applied to points of soreness or to specific acupuncture points for neuralgia and rheumatism pain.

ARTERIAL TENSION AND HIGH BLOOD PRESSURE

Up to 30 drops of fresh garlic juice can be taken orally or intravenously. Garlic pills are also used.

FEVERS

DR. MINCHIN'S FEVER TEA: One dram (⅓ oz.) of fresh garlic juice in beef tea or other similar fluid taken every four to six hours for typhoid or other fevers.

CONVULSIONS

In infantile convulsions and other nervous and spasmodic affections, garlic is applied as a liniment.

FAINTING

Garlic juice is applied to the nose.

EPILEPSY

An infusion of crushed bulbs is given before and after meals.

PARASITES

Mustard or coconut oil in which garlic has been fried is applied for scabies and maggots.

RINGWORM

The cut end of a clove, or the juice is applied to affected areas.

ACNE

Cut cloves are rubbed into pimples several times a day. This will not prevent acne, but will cure it once it has developed.

HEMORRHOIDS

Peel a garlic clove, oil it with lard or Vaseline or vegetable oil, and insert as a suppository. Keep in overnight. For tenderness, soreness, and hemorrhaging of the anus.

HEAD AND SCALP PROBLEMS

DANDRUFF TREATMENT: This garlic rinse should be used prior to regular shampooing. Make a garlic rinse by mashing garlic (5 cloves) and adding 2 cups of hot water (you can add wine or vinegar). Macerate the garlic in the water and allow to sit or infuse for 2 hours. Strain off or decant the liquid and pour through wet hair, allowing liquid to drain into a bowl. Re-pour and massage into scalp. Two to three hours later, shampoo, adding herbs to mask odor — if you must. (72)

FOR BALDNESS: Wine of garlic is made by macerating 3-4 bulbs in a quart of proof spirit. This lotion is massaged into scalp before shampooing.

OPEN FLESH WOUNDS

Garlic applied to open wounds is an effective disinfectant and was used in World War I. It is claimed to have prevented gangrene and loss of limb and life.

INTESTINAL AILMENTS

DR. FERNIE'S TINCTURE (1887): The essential juice of garlic mixed with wine and taken 10-20 drops in water several times a day. Also can be taken in pill form.

NEURALGIA AND RHEUMATISM

We have mentioned the effectiveness of moxa and garlic for respiratory ailments. This is also effective in cases of neuralgia and rheumatism when applied over affected areas, or over the specific points designated on an acupuncture chart.

POISON IVY

A poultice of crushed garlic is placed on affected areas for about 30 minutes. Remove if too hot, or if skin begins to blister. Apply an oil to reddened parts.

ATHLETE'S FOOT

Wash affected areas in hot soapy water. Rinse well, dry and apply the oil two to three times a day.

INSOMNIA

Garlic is recommended as an alternative to sleeping pills for insomnia. Professor Watanabe (*Garlic Therapy*, 1974) explains that the allicin in garlic, which has an oil-soluble property, combines with lipoids (fatty compounds) in nerve cells, thus calming down the action of the cells. Watanabe noticed that the sedative power of garlic is increased when added to comfrey and *herba epimedii* in an alcoholic liquid (not enough alcohol to cause drowsiness by itself). The alcohol contributes to the speed with which the garlic is assimilated into the system.

GARLIC AS AN APHRODISIAC

As we have seen, garlic has a long history as a popular sex stimulant. Although the smell of garlic turns most people off, the power of garlic to turn people on has through history turned the celibate clergy off. Thus, we often find garlic as a forbidden food in the "by-laws" of various religions. In support of this claim of arousal, herbalists point to the warmth that develops throughout the body, and especially in the abdomen after garlic consumption. It is also claimed, although I have not seen any evidence for this, that garlic stimulates the central nerve of the penis, contributing to erection.

Like other aphrodisiacs (Spanish Fly), garlic is used in the East as a temporary and immediate arousal agent, but unlike these other short-lived stimulants, garlic is said to create a long-lasting effect; Japanese researchers point to garlic's power to stimulate and invigorate hormonal and gastric secretions. This results in a general revitalization of the entire organism. Sexual potency is increased as a by-product of general organic potency.

In China, the Ammites are said to credit garlic for their sexual vigor and health. In India, men rub a garlic and fat ointment on the penis and lower back to promote and maintain erection. (From *Sex, Drugs and Aphrodisiacs*, by Adam Gottlieb, 1978)

TASTY CONCOCTIONS FOR SENSITIVE CONSTITUTIONS

Pickled Garlic

A good way to eat garlic without cooking it is to pickle the cloves in vinegar, soy sauce, honey, or wine. These liquids can be mixed in various combinations. The garlic retains its active principles, yet it is not as harsh. The liquids in which the garlic has been preserved for weeks or even months, absorb the strong odor and the clove becomes soft and mild. Vinegar prevents the garlic from sprouting and thus preserves the garlic. The sprouting process changes the substances in garlic which increase the odor. Make sure that the jar in which the garlic is pickling is air-tight, since any air will oxidize the garlic. Store in a cool place. A whole clove, preserved in any of the above liquids can be taken with some of the liquid as a medical preparation or as a snack.

Candy-Coated Garlic for Kids

Take sliced cloves of garlic and sprinkle with sugar, allowing to dry in the open air. The garlic will be very agreeable to children who usually turn away from garlic. If you are repulsed by sugar and prefer honey as a sweetener, give the honey-pickled garlic to your children (whole cloves covered with honey and sealed in a jar for several weeks).

For Those With Sensitive Stomachs

Not everyone can handle raw garlic or even pickled garlic. Those with stomach problems should not over-do garlic, and it is advised that they cook the garlic before eating. The recipes in Part Four will satisfy the palate and the sensitive stomach. Although the heat of cooking destroys the enzyme in garlic responsible for garlic's medicinal compound, allicin, this only delays the effectiveness of the garlic. The allicin will be formed in your system, and the harsh odor of garlic will not be as evident.

GARLIC OIL

The extracted oil of garlic, which contains the active sulphides of garlic, is available in gelatin capsules from most health food stores. The capsules come in five or ten "minim" strengths. A minim is a "drop". A salesman for Makers of Kal, Inc., a distributor of garlic capsules or perles, told me that there are 275 mg. concentrated garlic oil in five minims, and 500 mg. in the ten-minim strength. This works out to about one fifty-sixth of an ounce of oil in the ten minims. This oil is, of course, very concentrated. A spokesman for Gentry International, the manufacturer of the pills and perles (in Glendale, California), told me that one part essential oil of garlic is the equivalent of 700 parts dehydrated garlic, and 3,000 parts fresh garlic. This is not to say that garlic perles contain pure "essential oil", for 10 minims of essential oil would be roughly equivalent to *3 pounds* of fresh garlic. The minim quantity includes the vegetable oil carrier and other additives, I believe. Frankly, no one in the industry—from producer to distributor to health food store—has been able to tell me how much raw garlic one would need to match the potency of 5- or 10-minim perles.

UPDATE: *There are products now that spell out the equivalence in fresh garlic. There are also new garlic supplements that use sophisticated extraction techniques. One company, Arizona Natural Products, in Scotsdale, claims that their method retains garlic's enzyme activity in their garlic purée and capsule products, while eliminating odor.*

JEANNE ROSE, GARLIC HERBALIST

This material is excerpted from Kitchen Cosmetics *by Jeanne Rose. Jeanne is LSR's herbal consultant and the author of several herbals. Her own line of cosmetics, and her books, can be obtained from New Age Creations, 219 Carl St., San Francisco, CA.*

I love garlic and I love to eat garlic. We use it daily in the house for its known medicinal qualities. It is most definitely a vermifuge, antiseptic, diaphoretic, diuretic, stimulant and expectorant. I have *not* used it externally as a cosmetic although it has great value when applied as a topical ointment to skin conditions such as acne or other types of pimples.

Our favorite way to use the garlic, nature's miracle medicine, is to eat it daily in tortillas. Fry tortillas in a little corn oil, drain them, fold them, add yogurt or mayonnaise, alfalfa sprouts, chopped garlic, sliced avocado, beans if you have them and whatever else might be of interest. I probably eat 3-5 raw garlic cloves a day.

If you have a cold, substitute garlic soup for the traditional chicken broth. If you wish to impress a renowned chef, make garlic chicken with a freshly butchered bird. Add salad and wine and you have a meal fit for a king. Divine!

Garlic is used internally to protect a body from disease and externally as an antiseptic to protect the skin from germs and disease.

Garlic Honey

INGREDIENTS: *Garlic cloves, Honey*

TO MAKE: Peel garlic cloves and put them in a jar. Add honey, a little at a time over a couple of days until the jar is full. Set in a sunlit window for 2 weeks to a month or until the garlic has turned somewhat opaque and all the garlic flavor has been transferred to the honey.

TO USE: This Garlic Honey is an excellent cough syrup. Just take a teaspoonful every couple of hours or whenever it seems necessary. You must remember though that the honey has a lot of concentrated garlic power in it and one teaspoonful can represent many cloves of garlic. If you are giving this syrup to a child, you should dilute each spoonful with a bit of water. Garlic Honey also soothes a sore throat. As an application for acne or herpes it has no equal because it is both healing, soothing and slightly anesthetic. I also like to baste chicken with Garlic Honey, it's delicious.

TIP: You have to add the honey very slowly to the jar full of garlic because it takes time for the thick honey to totally fill all the spaces between the garlic cloves. Honey liquefies as it absorbs the garlic juices and the garlic gets rather limp and almost tasteless in time.

JENNIFER MOORE'S HERBAL REMEDIES

Jennifer Moore is an herbalist living on Catalina Island in California. Here are some concoctions that she has used with her clients. For more information, write Jennifer at Box 1359, Catalina Island, Avalon, CA. 90704.

Liver Flush

This tonic drink helps cleanse the liver of accumulated waste. It is promoted by the Polarity Massage Institute. For a healthier liver and elimination system, this drink is taken in the morning, one-half hour before eating.

2 oranges and one lemon, juiced
2-3 cloves garlic, chopped or pressed
2 tbl. olive oil, cold-pressed preferred

You can use grapefruit with or instead of the oranges, but the lemon, garlic and olive oil are essential. Mix together in a glass and swallow. The taste really isn't bad and if you drink this daily, it improves your skin and hair texture.

For Insect Bites and Stings

Rub a cut clove of garlic over the bite. This is also useful for boils and pimples. You can even leave the clove over a boil with a hollow cut in the clove to fit over the raised bump in your skin. Leave this on for several hours like a poultice and the boil may come to a head or burst. This is a Mexican Indian treatment as taught to me by Javier Lomili.

For Vaginal Yeast Infections

Insert a clove of peeled but unbruised garlic into the vagina in the evening. Leave it in overnight and remove in the morning. It will be covered with a foamy bad smelling slime. Do this for 3 nights. If you wear your clove in the day, the heat of bodily activity gives your underwear a permanent garlic smell. This may be OK with you, but according to Rita of Luna Menstrual Sea Sponges, evening treatments will suffice. If this method doesn't work, write me and I'll tell you my herbal methods.

garlic

Heather King ©Faitoute

123

GLOSSARY

DECOCTION: This is a preparaton made by putting pieces of the dry plant in boiling water, and then straining the water. It is better not to boil the plant, as this may in the case of garlic reduce its medical potency by burning away certain sulphide compounds.

INFUSION: Extraction of active properties of a substance by steeping or soaking in water or other liquid.

MACERATE: No heat is used. The plant is left standing in cold water for a time before mixture is filtered.

TINCTURE: This is a macerate made with alcohol instead of water. The dry plant is left standing in the alcohol for several days, after which time the active principles will have dissolved into the solvent.

EXTRACT: Once a tincture or macerate is formed and the solution is then allowed to evaporate, then the concentrated fluid left behind is called an extract. The more fluid that evaporates, the drier the extract, and when completely dry the extract can be powdered.

POWDER: A powder can also be made from the original plant that has been dried either in the air or in an oven. The dry tissue is either crushed or ground, and later sieved or sifted. Garlic is also freeze-dried, and this avoids excessive heat.

SYRUP: If a quantity of sugar is added to a juice, infusion or decoction, a syrup is formed. This is done chiefly to hide a specific taste. For those who are sensitive to strong tastes such as ginseng or garlic, this is a useful way of getting the medicine down. Also honey or molasses can be used instead of sugar.

POULTICE: For external application; a paste made of the plant plus oils is laid against the skin between layers of soft fabric such as linen which are tied to that portion of the body being treated. A Plaster uses wax, resins and fats and is applied in the same way.

LINIMENT: A medicine applied to the skin or rubbed into the scalp. Thinner than an ointment.

PILL: Incorporating powders or extracts in a base such as starch, or gum. The mixture is made into a ball, held together by the filler ingredients, and can be coated. This is not the same as a tablet which is held together by being compressed in a machine—this is the common practice today in medicine.

CARMINITIVE: A substance that relieves flatulence, expelling gas from the intestines.

DIAPHORETIC: A substance for increasing perspiration. Also sudorific.

DIURETIC: A substance that helps the body to dispose of water by increasing the production of urine.

EXPECTORANT: Any agent which promotes the ejection of fluid from the lungs and trachea.

HOMEOPATHY: Opposed to Allopathy. Treating disease with small amounts of the substance that in a healthy person would cause symptoms like the disease. Techniques of immunization are not unrelated to the principle of homeopathy.

II

GARLIC THE SUPER HERB

*A Survey of Recent Clinical and
Experimental Studies Indicating
Garlic's Effectiveness as
A Medicinal Agent*

INTRODUCTION

The remembrance of . . . astounding folk discoveries should sober our thoughts when we criticize too freely the old pharmacopoeias. It is easy to make fun of medieval recipes; it is more difficult and may be wiser to investigate them. Instead of assuming that the medieval pharmacist was a benighted fool, we might wonder whether there was not sometimes a justification for his strange procedure.

Professor George Sarton (1)

I HAVE tried to show in Part I the controversial but substantial place garlic held in the diet and medicine of earlier civilizations. But to "justify" the use of garlic today to an American medical doctor might be very difficult. Not only would the idea of herbal cures be suspect, but the suggestion of garlic as a cure might well receive even greater scorn. Garlic and pizza, yes! But garlic and cancer? (laughter follows).

Nevertheless, the open-minded reader may find in the following pages reason enough for returning garlic to its former highly praised position. If in the course of my appraisal of garlic as medicine I reveal a profound distrust and disdain for the *professional* medical establishment, I hope the reader will be patient (no double entendre intended), and not judge garlic poorly by virtue of my perhaps over-zealous need to bad-mouth Western medicine.

We live in an age of *Proof*. We must justify our justifications. The justification for the use of garlic as a magical-medical agent has always been, simply, that it worked. For the ancients "proof" consisted in observation of a substance's effect on a sick person—trial and error. If the patient got better after garlic treatments, then a curative power was attributed to the herb and a traditional cure was in the making. No chemical analysis or theoretical explanation was necessary if the herb worked repeatedly. It is almost as if the early attempts by humans to heal themselves came out of the same instinctual centers that motivate other animals to use the natural environment for cure and comfort of their group.

Today, however, cynicism and its polite front sophistication are rampant in the land. *Tradition* no longer holds water in the Western scientific community where a "tyranny of the new," evident in excessive consumerism, is seen also in the administration of drugs—if a new super drug is available, an older "tried and true" drug may be skipped over. So, relying heavily on ever newer synthetic chemo-therapeutics, and often forgetting the plant origins of many modern drugs, the medical profession has all but ignored the current counter-culture trend back to the "roots" of medicine. Scientific studies indicating the value of many traditional plant remedies are also ignored.

THE NEW OLD-FASHIONED WAY

There are signs, however, that change may be coming, even within the medical establishment. Slowly, recognition of the values in the old-fashioned way is arising among medical doctors who are beginning to see that people are not as healthy as they should be, given all the so-called advantages of new medical treatments available in the West. A reawakening interest in traditional healing techniques is growing in the wake of the almost epidemic popularity of such practices as acupuncture, yoga, and other folk and/or Eastern medical/mystical practices. The common denominator in all these areas is *prevention,* and the preventive emphasis in medicine grows in inverse proportion to the failures of modern medicine in coping with what seems to be an increase in degenerative diseases, such as heart disease, which cannot be simply knocked out by germ-oriented (allopathic) super drugs. Dr.

Aubrey T. Westlake describes this problem in his book, *The Pattern of Health* (Shambala, 1973):

> Disease appears, almost frighteningly, to be hydra-headed. We get rid of one disease only for others to appear in its place, and the new ones are usually more intractable . . . Thus we have in the main eliminated the infectious fevers, only to be confronted with . . .systemic diseases, so that more than five and a half million people in this country (England) suffer from some sort of severe rheumatism or arthritis, 14% of the entire population. We lower the infantile mortality rate, but are faced instead with cardio-vascular disease. We materially reduce the incidence of tuberculosis, only to be confronted with an increase in cancer, particularly in its most distressing form, cancer of the lung (2).

ORTHODOX VS. UNORTHODOX

The kind of thinking that allows for a multiplicity of attitudes towards health is, of course, attacked by medical conservatives who wince at the mention of herbalism, or nature cure and homeopathy, which are modern developments from older natural medicine traditions. These practices are seen as naive, primitive throw-backs to pre-science; other labels might include faddism, quackery, and even criminal malpractice. One Naturopathic doctor I talked with about her use of garlic in her rather large practice told me of the on-going harassment she must endure from the medical profession. One time, a photographer was sent with a referral patient from an M.D. He was supposed to get a picture of the Naturopath illegally "turning" the pregnant patient's baby who was in the wrong position for delivery. The Naturopath, whose name I promised to withhold, refused obviously to see the patient with the photographer.

I cannot deny that a part of this fervor over natural cures is generated by less-than-honest opportunists. But even within the antiseptic domain of establishment medicine, one can find ample instances of criminal malpractice. One need only mention certain super drugs that were thrust upon the market as "laboratory tested" only to end up in the annals of medical history as potential and sometimes actual killers and cripplers (Thalidomide to name one).

Western medical assumptions about the nature of disease, and the means of curing it, cannot tolerate the holistic approach of "unorthodox medicine", to use a term from *The Case for Unorthodox Medicine*, by Brian Inglis (3), which says essentially that good health is a state of mind-body that can be encouraged from within by adjustments in diet, and by proper exercise and rest. Arguing against the preoccupation of Western medicine with germs, unorthodox "theory" points out that germs are always present in and on the body, and that disease occurs when the organism can no longer protect itself with its own defense mechanisms. Germs are secondary; a strong, balanced body is primary. In the West, this order is reversed, and people spend more energy keeping themselves clean than strong. This emphasis on prevention and "right living" would, of course, mean a de-emphasis on chemical medicines, the backbone of the AMA-FDA academic/pharmaceutical monopoly in the U.S.

Garlic, ignored along with other members of the herbalist's pharmacopœa, has been singled out for attack by virtue of the quantity of disorders and diseases it has historically been held to benefit. This list would sound like a catalogue of human complaints. Any single substance held valuable for the relief of so many "plagues" is, *ipso facto*, sheer poppy cock (my expression). I am referring here specifically to W. W. Bauer, M.D. who pooh-poohs garlic in the book, *Potions, Remedies and Old Wives' Tales*, (Doubleday, 1969). Dr. Bauer and his sophisticated cronies are obviously not aware of recent clinical studies indicating the value of "poppy cock" in cases of narrow-mindedness, bloated ego, hyper-rationality, and pseudo-pomposity (the control subjects, who could not tolerate doses of open-mindedness and free-thinking, all remained unchanged).

I am not prepared to prove garlic's value as a virtual panacea, but from the evidence I have found, there is reason to believe that garlic may have a multiplicity of beneficial functions both as a dietary nutrient and as a medical specific. If one considers nutrition a key, if not *the* key to sound health, then there is no reason why a simple food like garlic, shown to be so effective as an antimicrobial within the intestinal tract, cannot be useful in all the diseases and disorders associated with pathogenic intestinal bacteria.

If garlic is linked to the optimal performance of the digestive organs, as the following studies indicate, and if recent reports concerning garlic's anti-cancer and cholesterol-controlling action are even partially correct, then the medical conservatives will have to "eat their garlic." We may come to respect, if not entirely agree with, the following advice of a 17th-century writer:

> You are still sending to the apothecaries and still crying out to fetch Master Doctor to me; but our apothecary shop is our garden and our Doctor a good clove of Garlic (4).

It is *not* my advice that we renounce Modern Medicine. The advances of medical knowledge over the last several centuries boggle the mind of any sincere soul; but we tend to throw out the baby with the bath water when we take to heart the prejudice of modern scientists and doctors against so-called quackery, old wives' tales, primitive medicine, witchcraft, and all the other traditional techniques and cures of popular medicine. It is to the credit of some researchers that they have taken medical history seriously, and have applied modern techniques of analysis to the old brews and concoctions of herbal practitioners. Their hypothesis is simple: in exploring the folk medicine of the past, new cures will be found for the future. Witness the "re-discovery" of digitalis, the dried leaf of the Foxglove plant containing active ingredients which are used today as a heart stimulant. It is inconceivable that other plants do not contain healing ingredients waiting to be "re-discovered" by modern science.

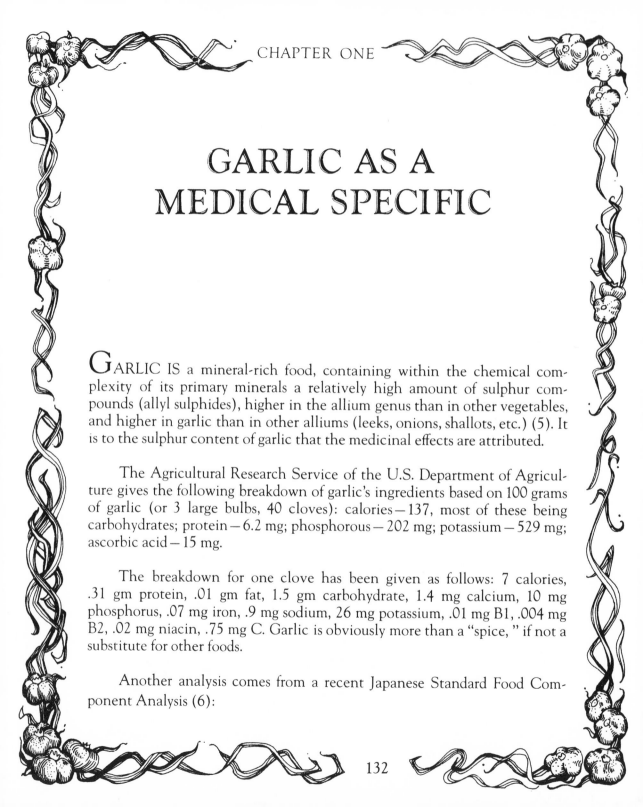

CHAPTER ONE

GARLIC AS A MEDICAL SPECIFIC

GARLIC IS a mineral-rich food, containing within the chemical complexity of its primary minerals a relatively high amount of sulphur compounds (allyl sulphides), higher in the allium genus than in other vegetables, and higher in garlic than in other alliums (leeks, onions, shallots, etc.) (5). It is to the sulphur content of garlic that the medicinal effects are attributed.

The Agricultural Research Service of the U.S. Department of Agriculture gives the following breakdown of garlic's ingredients based on 100 grams of garlic (or 3 large bulbs, 40 cloves): calories — 137, most of these being carbohydrates; protein — 6.2 mg; phosphorous — 202 mg; potassium — 529 mg; ascorbic acid — 15 mg.

The breakdown for one clove has been given as follows: 7 calories, .31 gm protein, .01 gm fat, 1.5 gm carbohydrate, 1.4 mg calcium, 10 mg phosphorus, .07 mg iron, .9 mg sodium, 26 mg potassium, .01 mg B1, .004 mg B2, .02 mg niacin, .75 mg C. Garlic is obviously more than a "spice," if not a substitute for other foods.

Another analysis comes from a recent Japanese Standard Food Component Analysis (6):

Based on 100 grams of garlic

nutrient absorption rate	25%
calories	84 Cal.
moisture content	77%
protein	2.4%
lipid	0.1%
galactolipid	19.3%
fiber	0.7%
ash content	0.5%

MINERAL MATTER:

calcium	18 mg
phosphorous	67 mg
iron	1.7 mg

VITAMIN CONTENT:

vit. A effective value	16 I.U.
carotin	50 I.U.
B_1	.22 mg
B_2	.08 mg
C	20. mg
Nicotine acid	.4 mg

Some early researchers based their claims for garlic's value on the bulb's vitamin and mineral content. Two doctors in New York, Edward Kotin and David Stein, made the following statement:

> An excellent medicament for employment in a diversity of conditions. We believe that the vitamin and mineral factors do much to cause this to be a drug of noteworthy usage.

These doctors made their claim in *The New York Physician* in September, 1937, based on studies with patients who suffered a variety of complaints.

The presence of vitamin C in garlic perhaps explains garlic's traditional use in various vitamin C deficiency diseases such as scurvy. One Elizabethan doctor prescribed for cases of scurvy a concoction of garlic, balsam of Peru, and other ingredients. One would have to eat quite a load of garlic, however, to keep up with Linus Pauling's regimen of 3,000 to 5,000 units of vitamin C a day. In this case, it behooves one to make use of the modern vitamin pill.

GARLIC'S HEALING INGREDIENTS

Alliin, Allicin, Allinase

Most researchers point to the high sulphur content in garlic as the medicinally active agent. Toward the end of the 19th century, after 6000 years of garlic use, German scientists succeeded in extracting from garlic a volatile oil containing allyl compounds (diallyl disulphide, diallyl monoside). Louis Pasteur, as far back as 1858, had fueled interest in garlic by his favorable reports on garlic's antiseptic powers. Further exploration in the 1940s by Dr. Arthur Stoll, a Swiss Nobel Prize-winner, uncovered in garlic a substance named alliin, which was later determined to be S-allyl-L-cysteine sulphoxide (7). Alliin was found to be the "parent" compound that must be broken down before any anti-microbial effect is possible, and before any of the characteristic odor of garlic is evident. This catalytic breakdown is accomplished with the enzyme allinase, which is also present in garlic. Alliin and allinase are separated by garlic's cellular membrane, and the garlic clove must be crushed before they come into contact. When they do, they produce allicin, known more technically as allylthiosulphinic acid allyl ester (Pensky and Weisenberg, 1957). Allicin evolves into both diallyl disulphide, which is the odiferous agent, and allyl thiosulphinate, the medicinal essence of garlic. Cavallito and Bailey in 1944 demonstrated that allicin was responsible for the bactericidal action of garlic. It was active in concentrations as diluted as 1:100,000 against a variety of micro-organisms (Tynecka and Gòs, 1973). Allicin is so highly thought of in the Soviet Union that they have it on the market as an antibiotic; they call it Russian Penicillin. Although allicin drugs are not as powerful as penicillin, it has been stressed by researchers that garlic is effective against certain germs that are difficult to destroy with conventional antibiotics, particularly the gram-negative organisms which are responsible for most hard-to-treat bacterial infections in the U.S.

Selenium and Germanium

Garlic is a complex substance and so it is not surprising that there are substances in garlic that are little known or not yet known. Germanium, for instance, is not a recognized substance in the West. But it is claimed that it is effective against cancer by stimulating circulation of oxygen throughout the human organs. Other disorders held to be benefited by germanium are cerebral tumors, rheumatism, asthma and many others (8).

Garlic is also an excellent source of biologically active selenium. Selenium is a recognized trace element in human nutrition, and is becoming a popular health food store product. Garlic's antiatherosclerotic effect may be due to its high selenium content. It is also said that selenium normalizes blood pressure and is a powerful anti-oxidant. This may explain claims for garlic's anti-aging powers.

Garlic's value for the heart is discussed in Dr. Richard Passwater's book, *Super Nutrition for Healthy Hearts* (Jove). It's a rather complicated issue and Dr. Passwater's book is very helpful.

THE HEALING MECHANISM

The exact mechanism whereby garlic kills bacteria and viruses is still rather unclear, especially to a layman like myself. Allicin and germanium have been mentioned as garlic's healing ingredients. The Russians have talked about "phytoncides" as garlic's curing agent. No two researchers agree on the exact nature of garlic's anti-microbial mechanism. In the forties there was much disagreement on very technical matters, even when all claimed garlic's value. The work of Volrath, Walton, and Lindegren (1940) ruled out diallyl disulphide (the odor-producing agent) as the anti-microbial substance in garlic. Their work presented allyl aldehyde (or acrolein) as the possible active agent. Another researcher, Semmler, supported the general notion that allyl or sulphur compounds are responsible for garlic's value, noting that sulphur derivatives play an essential role in good digestion.

In 1950 a German, Dr. J. Klosa, made the following claims about garlic's mechanism in the *Medical Monthly* (March, 1950). He said that garlic oil kills dangerous organisms without hurting beneficial ones. The sulphides and disulphides unite with virus matter, he claimed, in such a way that inactivates viral activity, preventing viruses from reforming. It has been added by others that garlic limits bacterial growth by helping to destroy the germs' oxygen metabolism.

In terms of garlic's larvacidal or pest-destroying ability when used as a spray in agriculture, K.C. George and S.V. Amonkar studied how garlic kills various plant-destroying pests. They determined that garlic interferes with the organism's ability to synthesize proteins, and they denied garlic's role in suppressing the respiratory metabolism of the pest larvæ (9).

The Bactericidal Mechanism

Very precise biochemical information is now available defining the

136

mechanism by which garlic inhibits pathogenic bacteria. It has been found that a certain grouping of molecules (-SO-S grouping) in the garlic oil compound is responsible for inhibition of enzymes in micro-organisms. I am not a biochemist, so I cannot elucidate this process any further except to say that in the chemical process whereby allicin combines with the bacteria, the organism's respiration stops. The bibliography at the back of this book lists the journals in which this process is given more technical expression, and I direct your attention to them if you are so inclined.

GARLIC AND VITAMIN B$_1$

A Japanese researcher, Fujiwara (*Pakistan Medical Times*, May 16, 1961), discovered that garlic increases the capacity of the body to assimilate vitamin B1. There occurs a quicker and easier penetration of the intestinal wall by vitamin B1 which is ordinarily not easily digestible and slow to penetrate. When combined with garlic into a substance he calls allithiamin (alli= garlic or allium and thiamin is vitamin B1), Fujiwara found that vitamin B1 becomes available quicker and in greater amounts. Further, blood concentration of thiamin increases ten-fold to a level impossible to achieve except through injections.

This power of garlic to increase the availability of B1 is very important in the treatment of certain disorders, such as chronic inflammation of the nerves, extreme nausea in pregnancy, and mental depression. This may also explain claims that garlic is a prophylactic against liver and gall bladder damage, since cocarboxylase (which acts beneficially on the liver cells) is produced by B1 (10).

Watanabe explains further this relationship between garlic and vitamin B1. Allicin oxidizes vitamin B1 when they are combined, but at the same time allicin is deoxidized by the hydrogen of vitamin B1. Allithiamine is the chemical compound formed by this process of oxidation and deoxidation. Watanabe claims that this allithiamine holds the B1 until it can be absorbed by the body; the B1 then returns to its original state. Alone, B1 loses much of its effectiveness. This development has caused a vitamin boom in Japan. A synthetic and less expensive allithiamine is now on the market. It is called allinamine, and is being used as a supplement for vitamin deficiency in the Japanese diet which consists largely of white rice.

Garlic's Route Through the Body

Many researchers have pointed to garlic's usefulness in digestive disorders. Not only does garlic kill pathogenic bacteria in the intestine, but it also stimulates digestive juices. Emile Weiss (1941) reported findings of an autopsy of an accident victim who had evidently eaten garlic prior to his accident. The examiner, Kretschmer, reported that the stomach and intestine were empty except for a few shreds of garlic. The gall bladder was filled with bile and entirely normal except that it had a strong garlic odor. Kretschmer concluded that garlic, after entering the oral cavity and flowing from the esophagus to the stomach, reaches the liver and gall bladder where it increases bile secretion. Kretschmer thought that at this point the garlic stimulates production of digestive ferments, and together with the increase in bile, affects growth of normal intestinal flora in opposition to pathogenic bacteria.

A META-SCIENTIFIC EXPLANATION?

Theories have been presented that there is something "in" garlic that works "below" the level of garlic's chemical effects on the human organism. The chapter on The Meta-scientific Explanation at the end of this survey of garlic's medical uses will investigate these ideas concerning the "spirit" side of garlic's powers. At some point, we may come to understand how the "matter" and the "spirit" of health work together.

CHAPTER TWO

THE CLINICAL EVIDENCE

SINCE World War I, extensive research has been carried out on garlic in many European and Asian countries. Part of this interest in garlic is a result of the successful use of garlic as an antiseptic in cases of gangrene and other serious infections. In the First War, garlic was applied to wounds to control suppuration (the formation and discharge of pus). In World War II, garlic was given credit for lowering the incidence of septic poisoning among wounded soldiers; not one case of gangrene or septic poisoning was reported among men receiving the garlic treatments.

The following information has been organized both according to areas of research (hypertension, cancer, the common cold, etc.), and within these areas, chronologically.

GASTRO-INTESTINAL DISORDERS AND HYPERTENSION

During W.W.I, Marcovici, an army doctor on the Eastern front in 1915, carried out many experiments with garlic. For 25 years thereafter he used garlic therapy successfully in many gastro-intestinal disorders, and reported his findings in the *Medical Record* (January, 1941). In his experiments during the war with cases of dysentery, he administered one bulb of garlic per day, prepared in various forms. Rapid improvement followed both for subjective and objective symptoms. Evacuations decreased and appetite returned.

When garlic pills came on the market, Marcovici began to use them instead of fresh garlic. In 1925, Sandoz Company introduced Allisatin, a pill that contained the active principal of garlic, allicin, plus vegetable charcoal —the absorptive quality of this additive allowed the allicin to be released slowly enroute through the intestines, thus limiting the odor of the garlic. Marcovici used allisatin successfully in dyspepsia, diarrhea, enterocolitis, fermentation, and as a treatment for symptoms of hypertension. His therapy consisted of 2-4 garlic tablets 3 times daily. Larger amounts were sometimes administered, but this increased the odor factor.

Later Marcovici was encouraged by clinical results with experiments undertaken at the Sero-therapeutic Institute of Vienna. These experiments were conducted with rabbits.

THE EXPERIMENT: Rabbits were fed dried garlic powder for several days. Dysentery toxins were then administered intravenously. Results: 2.5 grams daily of powdered garlic for three days prior to injections protected animals against a ten-fold dose of dysentery toxin. The garlic cured rabbits when it was given concomitantly with toxin (but not before injections). Many of these rabbits became ill, but none died. All of the control group given toxin but no garlic, died.

Marcovici also found garlic effective against hypertension. One of the symptoms of hypertension is high blood pressure. The exact causes of high blood pressure are complex, and many of those who studied garlic's power to reduce blood pressure could not agree on how it did the job. Marcovici said that the effects of garlic were not due to any specific vasodilatory effect of garlic, as claimed by Loeper and Debray, who in 1921 experimented successfully with a garlic tincture in cases of high blood pressure. Marcovici claimed that the lowering of blood pressure was the result of garlic's power to control and purify intestinal putrification. Marcovici worked with aged hypertensive patients who suffered high blood pressure, chronic constipation, chronic appendicitis and fecal stasis. As a result of these intestinal problems, the incompletely digested food undergoes pathological putrification, and toxins are absorbed and carried into the blood stream; this causes symptoms of headache, dizziness, fatigue, capillary spasms, etc. By controlling this putrification, garlic was, for Marcovici and others, a valuable treatment for all the symptoms associated with hypertension.

Marcovici's findings were confirmed by other researchers. In 1929, Ortner in Germany used garlic to lower blood pressure in 80 cases of hypertension. Other researchers in Germany found garlic effective against intestinal putrification.

In 1941, Weiss in Chicago reported a complete change in intestinal flora after garlic treatments (11). This flora is the bacteria living in the intestine, some of which helps in digestion, and some of which is harmful, causing putrification. Weiss noted that symptoms of headache and diarrhea vanished, while healthful bacteria increased in the intestine. Working with 22 subjects, all with intestinal disorders, garlic was administered over a two-week period, during which time urine and feces were collected and examined. A control group received no garlic. The 22 subjects taking garlic improved and all symptoms disappeared; but, more importantly, a complete change in the intestinal flora was noted. By the end of the two weeks of garlic treatment, Weiss observed that the beneficial bacteria increased, and the harmful bacteria decreased. The control group remained unchanged, both symptomatically and according to bacteriological counts.

In 1941, Damsau also worked with garlic to lower blood pressure (12). Experiments with cats having high blood pressure showed that intraperitoneal injections of garlic concentrate gave an immediate reduction in blood pressure. Control animals remained high. Damsau also made the link between garlic's ability to control putrification and the lowering of blood pressure.

Some researchers, such as G. Piotrowsky, have claimed however, that garlic actually dilates the blood vessels, thus reducing pressure. This would be very important in the treatment of fatty deposits in arteriosclerosis. In the journal, Praxis (July, 1948), Piotrowsky, working at the University of Geneva, claimed success in lowering blood pressure with garlic in experiments with 100 patients. His treatments began with large doses of garlic, decreasing over a two-week period. Symptoms of dizziness, angina-like pains, head and backache were gone in 3-5 days.

FUNGUS INFECTIONS

Medical opinion from India or Libya doesn't carry much weight in America, so in spite of the many studies on garlic from outside the U.S., doctors here don't give garlic much credit. One American researcher who does take garlic seriously is Dr. Michael Tansey of the University of Indiana, Department of Plant Sciences. Two studies by Dr. Tansey, one with Judith Appleton and the other with Frank Barone (both published in the respected *Mycologia*—Vol. LXVII, No. 4 and Vol. LXIX, No. 4, 1975 and 1977 respectively) suggest garlic's potential as a drug for fungus infections. These infections in humans are now treated with drugs that either have side effects or produce resistant strains. According to the 1975 study, "an aqueous extract of garlic bulbs inhibits growth of many species of zoopathogenic fungi at the concentrations used." In the 1977 study this conclusion was verified using allicin against *C. albicans*. "Allicin [a sulphur compound in garlic] may provide a model system for chemotherapy of *C. albicans* infections."

In a letter to the author, Dr. Tansey elaborated on his study of garlic:

> Our work on garlic is continuing along orthodox lines . . . it is the systematic and painstaking testing and retesting that goes into the development of any potential antimicrobial agent . . . garlic has sufficient potential as an antimicrobial agent to warrant cautious and conservative investigation . . . There is a long and honorable tradition of the transfer of folk plant medicines into modern medical practice.

ARTERIOSCLEROSIS

UPDATE: *A network evening news program carried the story recently of Dr. Hans Reuter of Cologne, West Germany. Dr. Reuter claimed that his clinical studies prove garlic's effectiveness for controlling cholesterol, blood pressure and fatty deposits in the arteries. Reuter recommended 1-3 cloves of raw garlic be added to the daily diets of anyone interested in their cardio-vascular health.*

Recent medical studies support the claim that garlic actually affects the factors responsible for arteriosclerosis or hardening of the arteries: Hyperlipæmia (excess blood cholesterol levels) and hyperglycæmia (high blood-sugar levels associated with diabetes). In a December 29, 1973 issue of the prestigious British medical journal, *The Lancet*, letters from two cardiologists, Drs. Bordi and Bansal, of the Department of Medicine, R.N.T. Medical College, Udaipur, India, stated that the addition of garlic to the diets of test subjects actually controlled the amount of cholesterol in the blood. These tests were conducted on five subjects with garlic juice, and on another five subjects using the oil extract of the juice. All subjects were in good health, and the garlic juice and oil extract produced similar results.

The Tests

The doctors added to the regular meals of their subjects 100 grams or ¼ pound of butter. Three hours later, the subjects averaged a blood cholesterol of 237.4 milligrams per cent, which was up from a fasting level before the meal of 221.4. When the juice or oil from 50 grams of garlic was added to an identical meal with the same amount of butter, the blood cholesterol level three hours later was only 212.7 milligrams per cent, which was *down* from a fasting level of 228.7 before the meal.

The addition of butter without garlic also brought the level of plasma-fibrinogen (the precursor of fibrin which is involved in the blood clotting mechanism) to 320.9 up from a fasting level of 249.8. When garlic was added the level was 256.4 which, again, was down from a fasting level of 281.3. These are both significant drops especially in view of the fact that the garlic brought the cholesterol and fibrinogen levels down below the normal levels before the addition of the fat. Bordi and Bansal concluded that:

It is obvious that garlic has a very significant protective action against

143

hyperlipæmia and blood-coagulation changes, which are normal after fat ingestion.

In discussing the other drugs on the market which control these blood factors—drugs which are either very expensive or transient in effect—these researchers added finally that:

> Clinically, garlic could avoid most of these drawbacks and could be recommended for long-term use without danger of toxicity. It would be particularly useful in preventing alimentary hyperlipæmia *in persons who do not have manifest signs of arteriosclerosis but are predisposed on account of diabetes, hypertension, family history of stroke and heart-disease.* (Italics mine) (*The Lancet*, Dec. 29,1973, pp.1491-2)

Well, that means *me*, and millions of other Americans. If there was ever a doubt in my mind about why I am taking a lot of garlic in my diet, this statement by Bordi and Bansal erases it.

NEW RESEARCH

The work of Bordi and Bansal is being confirmed, and it appears more and more likely that garlic really does control cholesterol. A recent paper published in *Atherosclerosis* (Vol. 29, 1978), by Drs. Jain and Konar makes the following points: that garlic lowers blood cholesterol and is, indeed, a protective agent. That the anti-atherogenic action resulted from an approximate daily dose of 1-6 mg of the active principle of garlic (the oil extract), or approximately 15-60 grams of fresh garlic. (There are about 28 grams in an ounce).

Other studies by Jain, in the *American Journal of Clinical Nutrition* (September, 1977) go even further, stating that garlic discriminates between low-density lipoprotein (LDL) cholesterol and high-density lipoprotein (HDL) cholesterol. It is LDL that increases heart disease risk, and this is the cholesterol that garlic appears to reduce.

LEPROSY

In ancient Greek and Hindu medicine, garlic was used in the treatment of leprosy. In fact, Lepers were called Pilgarlics because they were left to peel their own garlic. A study undertaken in India in 1962 has shown garlic to be an effective agent against many types of leprosy. Garlic was administered by syrup, pill and ointment. While several subjects improved dramatically in many of the indices of improvement (subjective well-being, regression of lesions, decline in bacteriological index, etc.), the control case, not receiving any treatment, deteriorated so rapidly, that he was immediately given a conventional treatment. The experimenters enthusiastically encouraged further testing (*Journal of Indian Medical Association*, November, 1962).

TUBERCULOSIS

At the beginning of this century a doctor, W.C. Minchin, practicing in Ireland wrote letters to a British publication, *The Lancet*, relating his success with garlic in treating the number-one killer at the time, tuberculosis. Working in a Dublin hospital, Minchin used garlic as an inhalant, in internal medications, compresses and ointments. His results were so good that other medical experts marveled at his treatment and in many cases did not even know that ordinary garlic was being used. The public responded to the *Lancet* articles with testimonials to their own success with garlic for a variety of ailments including the common cold.

Around the same time, in New York at the Metropolitan Hospital, Dr. M.W. Duffie also found garlic to be the best treatment among 56 other treatments for tuberculosis. His findings were published in the *North American Journal of Homeopathy* (May, 1914), under the title "Tuberculosis Treatment". Duffie wrote:

> Garlic is the best individual treatment found to get rid of germs and we

believe same to be a specific for the tubercle bacillus and for tubercular processes no matter what part of the body is affected . . . thus nature, by diet, rest, and exercise, baths, climate, and garlic, furnishes sufficient and specific treatment for the medical aspects of this disease.

There are many drugs now that deal very effectively with TB, so garlic may have completed its mission as a therapeutic agent for tuberculosis.

THE COMMON COLD

We have already mentioned Dr. J. Klosa's opinion that garlic oil (containing the sulphides and disulphides of allicin) combine with viral matter in such a way as to inhibit their activity, while leaving beneficial organisms alone (the nature of this anti-viral mechanism has not been fully demonstrated to my knowledge). His opinion was based on experiments with a preparation of garlic oil and water. He used the solution in doses of 10-25 drops over four hours taken orally and through the nasal tract. I quote from *Nature's Medicines*, Richard Lucas, 1966:

> In 13 cases of grippe: Fever and catarrhal symptoms were cut short in every case. No complaints of jaundice, muscle and joint pain, chronic lung inflammation, etc. The usual convalescent period was shortened.

> In 28 cases of sore throat: Burning and tickling disappeared in 24 hours. If caught in the first stages, further development of sore throat could be stopped completely by administering 30 drops or two normal doses.

> In 71 cases of clogged and runny nose: Taken in nose and mouth, garlic solution cleared the congestion in 13-20 minutes with no further complaints.

Another medical opinion concerning garlic's effectiveness in treating the common cold comes from Dr. Kristine Nolfi, M.D., in her book, My

146

Experiences with Living Food. She states:

> Garlic has also a curative effect on chronic diseases in the upper respiratory organs provided one keeps garlic in his mouth day and night (not while sleeping), removing the cloves every morning and evening after they have absorbed the poisons. This applies to chronic inflammation of the tonsils, salivary glands and neighboring lymph glands, empyema of the maxillary sinus, severe pharyngitis and laryngitis, bronchitis . . .

Dr. Nolfi offers the following cure for colds:

> If one puts a piece of garlic in his mouth at the onset of a cold, on both sides between cheek and teeth, the cold will disappear within a few hours or, at most, within a day.

CANCER

Plant remedies for cancer were recorded as early as 1500 B.C. in the Ebers Papyrus, and Hippocrates prescribed eating garlic for uterine tumors in his book *De Malierum Morbis.* The Bower Manuscript from India (450 A.D.) gave garlic as a cure for abdominal tumors. There is also evidence that where garlic eating is copious, cancer is uncommon—southern France, Bulgaria, Korea.

In the U.S., garlic cropped up as a possible cure for cancer during the illness of John Foster Dulles. He received numerous letters suggesting herbal cures, and several of these letters mentioned garlic. One letter was from a physician in Victoria, B.C., reputed to be treating malignancies successfully with a diet of garlic. Most of the letters came from areas where garlic production is high—Texas and California in the U.S., and Italy.

The first experiments carried out with pure Alliin (the parent substance of allicin) was in 1949, conducted by Hans Von Euler, a German. He tested the growth-inhibiting action of alliin on various tumors and observed that transplanted tumors of Jensen sarcoma in rats regressed, or even disappeared, after injection of 1-3 mg. alliin given intra-muscularly or directly into the tumor. Also, alliin inhibited growth of benzpyrene-induced sarcoma in rats (14).

In a 1957 issue of *Science*, Pensky and Weisenberg claimed that extracts of garlic contain powerful bactericidal and tumor-suppressing agents. Working with allicin, the researchers carried on studies with sarcoma tumors in mice. Treated and untreated tumor cells were injected in the mice, and no deaths were recorded from injections of malignant cells with allicin. Untreated tumor cells induced death in the mice. A third group was injected with untreated cells, and then garlic was injected. In these cases, tumor formation was delayed, and in many cases, prevented altogether. It was found that garlic must be re-administered often for continued effects.

Kimura and Yamamoto examined the work of Weisenberg and Pensky in 1963. They studied garlic's effect on MTK sarcoma III, an ascites tumor found in albino rats. The garlic extract produced marked damage to tumor cells. Damage increased with time after injection of garlic, and 3-6 hours after injection, the number of tumor cells with chromosomes with arrested development increased considerably. Ultimately, the cells died, although in these experiments, no complete regression of tumors was reported. Kimura and Yamamoto believe that experiments with allicin and other plant extracts "may lead to an effective therapeutic attack on the cancer problem" (15).

An antigen is a substance that produces an antibody when introduced into an organism. It is generally believed that tumors act "antigenically" and that immunization of the host animal prevents tumor growth on later introduction of the same virulent cells. Fujiwara and Natata discussed their findings in a 1967 issue of *Nature*. They worked with Ehrlich ascites tumor cells and treated them with an extract of fresh garlic. They found that:

> Mice injected with these (treated) tumor cells developed strong immunity to same type cells. Tumor cells treated with extract of boiled garlic and injected into mice did not bring about immunity. Mice in the control group all developed cancerous tumors.

In another experiment, 100,000 live tumor cells were injected into mice two weeks after a fresh garlic innoculation, and none of these mice developed tumors within a period of 100 days. It was concluded then, that pre-treatment of tumor cells with an extract of fresh garlic is effective, and that mice injected with these cells developed strong immunity to the same type of tumor cell (16).

It is yet to be demonstrated that garlic will become an effective preventative or cure for cancer in humans. The above experiments have, however, aroused interest in garlic within the cancer research establishment. Dr. Loren White, a noted cancer specialist in San Francisco told me that the National Cancer Institute is sending out teams to investigate herbal medicine in India and China. He mentioned that extracts of Periwinkle are being used for certain leukemias and that there is a growing interest in garlic and other herbs.

This is a very good sign that the prejudice against herbs is declining among researchers. This is not to say that officials within the AMA will not be very hard on simple, safe, and cheap herbal cures. The research end of medicine is always more advanced and more open than the administrative arm of medicine. It can take many years for a drug to go from the testing stage to the marketplace. Once a drug does make it, and if it should prove to be dangerous, it may take a long time to get it off the market—the particular pharmaceutical manufacturer fighting to keep his drug alive.

Dr. Irving Penn of the University of Colorado believes that certain anti-cancer drugs on the market may permit or even promote the growth of later, unrelated cancers despite controlling the original cancer. The second cancers may develop because these synthetic drugs are "immunosuppressive agents" and thus depress the body's defense mechanisms. Penn has data on many of these cancer-causing cancer cures (17).

This kind of situation suggests that safe *plant-derived* drugs deserve a closer look. As we come to understand the herbal techniques of the Chinese, Indians, Russians and others, perhaps Herbalism will be brought back out of its exile as Magic and returned to its rightful place as Medicine.

MEDICAL SUMMARY

The evidence for garlic's anti-bacterial, anti-carcinogenic and cholesterol-controlling activity is rather impressive, at least to this observer. I have encountered very few arguments against garlic, although this book may engender quite a bit of antagonism. That garlic is safe is uncontested. Of course, anything can be overdone. One believer in garlic does warn that excessive use of raw garlic can affect the liver adversely, but garlic perles allow a heavy but safe use of garlic's essential oil.

It is difficult to prove that anything is a "cure" because there are so many variables involved in the phenomenon of cure. Synthetic medicines which are put together from "scratch", as it were, are known quantities tested in laboratories. Unlike substances of natural origin, these man-made drugs are fairly uncomplicated, and their exact chemical structure is known. But even these "laboratory-tested" wonder drugs have future unknown effects, can even kill, and are often removed from the market when dangerous side-effects arise. (18)

We have seen the clinical evidence for garlic's powers as a medical drug. But studies with "x" numbers of subjects and control groups are not always as accurate as they seem. The same study can be repeated with different results. Laboratory studies are often more telling in that they have fewer variables. One can know more about what is happening under a microscope than within the complex system of a human being. The following studies dramatically show that garlic kills germs. If this point can be made conclusively, then I think garlic will be accepted in the West as it is in the East as a powerful therapeutic agent.

In many of the experiments with garlic, it has been shown that allicin can destroy gram-negative bacteria. In 1944, Calvalitto et al. used allicin against gram-negative and gram-positive micro-organisms. The studies showed allicin's effectiveness against staphylococci, streptococci, E. typhosa, Bacterium dysenteriae, Bacterium enteritidis, and Vibrio cholerae (19). One can recognize the related diseases in the technical names of these bacteria.

An experiment in 1954 showed conclusively that garlic is a powerful antibacterial. T. D. Yanovich, a Russian, introduced garlic juice directly into bacterial colonies. Within 3 minutes the bacteria ceased to function. In bacterial cultures, garlic juice caused bacteria to disperse to the edge of the culture, and within 10 minutes all activity ceased, and within only 2 minutes, immobile bacteria began to appear. Yanovich claimed that fresh juice was more effective than diluted or preserved samples (20).

In 1969, M.G. Johnson and R.H. Vaughn found garlic to be a powerful antibacterial against Salmonella typhimurium (food poisoning, diarrhea) and Escherichia coli (urine infection). (*Applied Microbiology*, June, 1969.)

In a very recent article entitled, "Inhibitory Action of Garlic on Growth and Respiration of Some Micro-organisms", Tynecka and Gòs summarize their findings thus:

> . . . garlic, in the form of the juice, is a very potent antimicrobial agent, both to bacteria and pathogenic yeasts. We can thus suppose that at least Staphylococcal and fungal skin and alimentary tract diseases can be effectively cured by juice of garlic (21).

Reports of garlic's medicinal value are appearing in medical journals at an accelerating rate—especially in journals from Japan, Germany, and Russia (and its satellites). Garlic cannot be avoided for too much longer by change-resistant Western medicine. It behooves those truly interested in "cures that do not kill" to examine the possibility of organic and natural cures for the inner plagues of humankind.

It may be that, like the old and lame folk in Serbia who every autumn go on a pilgrimage to the forest to eat the Ceremissa, a wild garlic, and return home invigorated, we in the West will come to take a daily pilgrimage to our kitchens to eat the cultivated Allium Sativum.

A FINAL NOTE—ON "HERBISM"

There is, of course, a middle ground that must be taken in matters of health. While I advocate the actual and possible value of garlic, I do not prescribe it as a cure for all of humanity's diseases. If someone is bleeding to death, it is not wise to advise taking an herb used to heal wounds. But likewise, if someone has a sore throat, it is not wise to prescribe a broad-spectrum antibiotic to knock out the germs in every case.

The AMA is wise to examine drugs before they are put on the market, but the prejudice against natural medicines is overwhelming and counter-productive. Control has led to a kind of racism against herbs, or "herbism". This prejudice has been aimed especially at garlic.

FRIEND OF HERBS: Dr. Paul Lee

Dr. Lee is the executive director of the Herb Trade Association in Santa Cruz, California, a non-profit, tax exempt corporation representing the national herb industry and directing the herb renaissance in America. The HTA engages the FDA in dialogue, gathers data on the safety of herbs, etc. Here are the words of Dr. Lee:

> No one can question the renewal of interest in herbs, tantamount to an herb renaissance. All you have to do is look at the growth pattern of any herb company in the country or take account of the very large corporations in the food industry now making plans to bring out herbal lines, from Lipton tea to Stuckey's. We can look forward to the most intense interest in the field of herbology, medical botany, pharmacognosy (medicines derived from plant sources), and a renewed interest in medical anthropology and the history of medicine, going back to earlier times when herbs were the main reference point for illness and disease.
>
> It has taken exactly a century and a half—from 1818 to 1978—for a certain trend, known in the textbooks as *Physicalism,* to eclipse the knowledge and use of organic products of natural origin, known in the textbooks as *Vitalism.* In 1828, a German chemist, Wolfgang Wöhler, artificially synthesized urea, a product of the kidneys, and opened the way for organic chemistry, the proliferation of synthetics, and the emergence of the large pharmaceutical companies.

That nearly exclusive trend has come to an end and the rediscovery of herbs is upon us. It is in line with a need for roots. Industrial society is responsible for uprooting us all from the environment. Industrial society is a world "above" the given world of nature and therefore lacking vital roots. We mean to find the root again."

HTA is now the Platonic Academy. Those interested in joining can write them at Box 409, Santa Cruz, CA 95601. Tell 'em LSR sent you.

Bumper sticker available from LSR .

CHAPTER THREE

AN ALTERNATIVE
INSECTICIDE

And wholesome berries thrive and ripen best
Neighbored by fruit of baser quality.

THE ABOVE line is from Shakespeare's *Henry V*. It is hard to say whether the Bard is being merely "philosophical" or whether he is referring also to early agricultural techniques. "Companion Planting" is a very old idea—the understanding that pests thrive best when plant species are segregated, a mass-agriculture technique. Recent studies have shown that pests are deterred when hit by a mixture of subtle chemical signals emitted by a variety of plant types. A plot of a particular species is more easily penetrated. Chemical fertilizers also have the effect of destroying a plant's inherent protective mechanism. More on this in The Meta-Scientific Explanation.

FOR THE BIRDS

Garlic was a known insecticide from the earliest days. Pliny, the man with 61 garlic remedies, had a recipe for keeping the birds away from the fields. He speaks of a kind of garlic called Alum, which grew wild in the fields (perhaps Allium Vineal). This Alum was boiled to prevent a second germination, then thrown to the birds so they would eat the seeds. This would numb them so that you could catch them by hand, and if you waited longer, the birds would fall into a deep sleep.

GARLIC AND DDT

Today, it is common for organic gardeners to border their crops with rows of garlic, and spray their plants with a garlic solution. The same characteristics which act as a bactericide in human beings serve to keep pests away from plants. In a 1970 issue of *Newsweek* (Volume 75) an article carried the story that, "Garlic extract kills mosquitoes, including those carrying yellow fever and encephalitis."

Now that the U.S. and other nations have banned or phased out DDT, the search is on for substitutes that do the job *safely*. Unfortunately, there has been a shift to "safe" chemicals which, according to Dr. G. Pank (*Journal of the American Medical Society*), "although much less persistent than DDT, are far more poisonous." These new organo-phosphorous compounds are not new at all, and in the five years before 1963, they killed 6,000 farm workers in Japan. (22)

Many recent studies indicate that perhaps garlic can be one of the effective, safe and cheap agents needed to keep the Green Revolution green. David Greenstock, Vice-Chairman of The Henry Doubleday Research Association in England, has found that garlic can do the job. His work with researchers in India has produced a garlic killer for the malaria mosquito which has become increasingly immune to DDT. The following figures show "kill" percentages of various pests using garlic emulsions and solvents:

87% of fireworm infestation
83% of cockchafer larvæ
91% of mole crickets
82% of grey field slug
95% of onion fly larvæ
98% of cabbage white and ermine moth caterpillars

In a laboratory experiment, the garlic solution killed 87% of pea weevils, and this discovery promises success against the related boll weevil in cotton, which many American growers claim needs DDT.

The fact that garlic does not kill many of the harmless bugs and beetles that co-exist with dangerous pests is another of garlic's assets. In fact, when Greenstock fed his emulsions to chicken, mice and rabbits, he established that the garlic sprays were harmless to livestock, wild life and birds, and in fact, the garlic brews improved the health of the experimental animals compared to the non-garlic-receiving control animals. An accidental outbreak of myxamatosis in rabbits showed the garlic-eating rabbits gained greater resistance (23).

HEALTHY GARLIC

Greenstock also indicated that the enzyme activity in garlic that creates the active agent allicin, is dependent on the proper balances of assimilable sulphur in the soil. This sulphur is produced in the soil by a number of micro-organisms, mainly certain tiny fungi that cannot grow without ample humus. Garlic grown in an unbalanced soil will fail to have the effect of the properly balanced garlic.

Other researchers are also working with garlic insecticides. Amonkar and Banerji report garlic's effectiveness against species of mosquitoes in the Culex and Aedes genera, which are among the most insecticide-resistant mosquito populations. They also claim that the diallyl disulphides and diallyl trisulphides in garlic are effective against potato tuber moth, red cotton bug, red palm weevil, and the perennial housefly.

THE LARVICIDAL MECHANISM

The debate over garlic's actual larvicidal mechanism mirrors the debate over garlic's bactericidal mechanism in humans. George and Amonkar have shown in their report, "Effect of Garlic Oil on Larvae", that the larvicidal properties of garlic are not due to a suppression of the respiratory metabolism of larvae, but rather to the inhibition of protein synthesis. They also point out that garlic acts fast and the effect on protein synthesis is irreversible (24).

GREENSTOCK'S FORMULA

The following insecticide has been used effectively against a variety of pests. It is noted by Mr. Greenstock that one should use the best garlic available—"organic" garlic will probably be the richest and most balanced of the commercial garlics.

> Take 3 oz. of chopped garlic and let soak in 2 tsp. (50cc) of mineral oil for 24 hours. Then slowly add a pint of water in which ¼ oz. of oil-based soap (Palmolive) has been dissolved, and stir well. Strain liquid through fine gauze and store in a china or glass container to prevent a reaction with metals. Use it in a dilution of 1 part to 20 of water to begin with, then 1 to 100 thereafter. Apply to plants as a spray.

This simple and non-toxic means of controlling pests may become a very important "home brew" in the years ahead, especially if it becomes necessary for City Dwellers to cultivate their own produce.

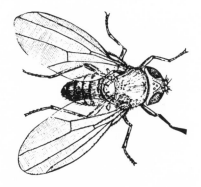

CHAPTER FOUR

JAPANESE GARLIC THERAPY

IT SEEMS that Japan is producing the most sophisticated systems of garlic therapy—this in addition to the plentiful laboratory studies by research teams at major universities in Japan.

Two recent books, both by men dedicated to the use of garlic for a variety of ailments, outline systematic therapeutic garlic regimens. Although both of these books were written originally in Japanese and appeal perhaps to a Japanese audience, they both contain a wealth of information on the preparation and use of garlic as an herbal therapeutic.

If these books do not attempt to prove garlic's medicinal powers, they certainly give the believer a solid vision of how garlic, given its value, can be used with maximum pleasure (minimum odor?) and multiple medical benefits. The Japanese—somewhere between Western medicine and their heritage of herbal medicine—recognize that the whole body must be treated, and not just symptoms of disease. In garlic, they have a medical specific, a general tonic for stimulation of the entire organism, and a dietary delight.

FLOW-LEBEN: ODORLESS GARLIC MEDICINE

While researching this book in 1973, I came across a book by a Japanese researcher, Yoshio Kato, who has developed a machine for the scientific application of garlic therapy at the Oyama Garlic Laboratory in Amagasake, Japan. Over 20,000 copies of his book, *Garlic, the Unknown Miracle Worker*, have been sold in Japan, and in the introduction to the

English version the author writes:

> This is not a fiction or other type of entertainment book, nor is it on the best-seller list.

Rather, the book is a reflection of what Kato calls "Creative Health". A testimonial by Kato was given in the Introduction.

Announcing the cure of 15,000 patients in his clinic, Kato goes on to explain why garlic cures (I have included data in "The Healing Mechanism"). Then, a very precise system for preparation of garlic medications is presented, as well as a survey of those diseases and disorders curable either by garlic taken internally or applied externally by his machine. Kato lists the following curable ailments: Stomach cancer and stomach ache, gastric ulcer, gastritis, liver disorders, heart disease, hyper- and hypotension, paralysis, TB, pneumonia, frostbite, neuralgia, backache, headache, parasites, constipation, and more. It is not Kato's desire to have his book serve merely as a do-it-yourself medical manual, but enough information is presented such that the reader can begin to introduce garlic into his diet as a supplement or preventative measure, and, in addition, can apply the various garlic preparations (designed to eliminate garlic's odor) for certain disorders in conjunction with medical treatment.

Kato's book leads inevitably to the introduction of his own special garlic therapy system which he calls *Flow-Leben* or "Flow of Life", and he presents it as a challenge to modern medicine.

> With garlic, the patient himself is doctor, pharmacologist, nurse and pharmaceutical manufacturer all in one. He himself alters his physical condition. (p. 173)

Kato believes that his garlic therapy system, which features an incredible garlic-spraying machine, can be installed to cover the needs of a population of 15,000 per machine system. This system is for sale through Oyama Industrial Co., Ltd. Applications for patents have been made in ten countries and have already been granted by five: Republic of China, Italy, France, Germany, and the United Kingdom.

The machine itself is described by Kato, and several pictures of the garlic-spraying device are provided. As Kato announced in his introduction, this book is not a fiction or entertainment—he must have been anticipating the inevitable response to his machine. Fiction? No. *Science* fiction?

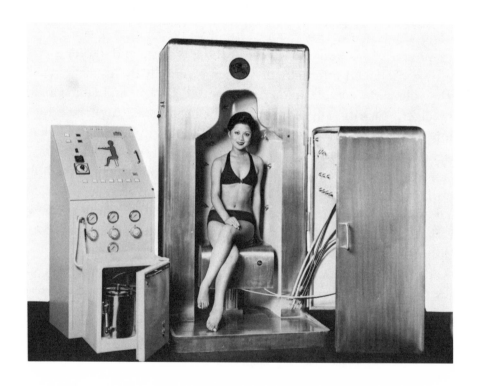

TODAY, AT THE OYAMA GARLIC LABORATORY IN JAPAN, this machine is spraying solutions of garlic and water on thousands of patients for a variety of ailments. Photo: Courtesy Oyama Garlic Laboratory, Amagasaki, Japan. U.S. Patent Document 3,868.950 Copyright©1975.

Garlic Therapy by Professor Tadashi Watanabe, D.Sc., is less "revolutionary" than Kato's book, but is perhaps more readable in its English translation. Like Kato's book, though, it presents a vast amount of information explaining garlic's mechanism and its use in herbal therapy and diet. Also, again like Kato's book, no *proof* of these claims is offered other than to mention that proof exists.

KYOLIC: ODORLESS GARLIC MEDICINE

The newest garlic development from Japan is Kyolic, a preparation with all the benefits of garlic but without the odor—or so the manufacturers claim. By an elaborate process, which involves curing garlic in huge vats for 20 months without the use of heat, organically grown garlic loses its odor through a natural fermentation process. It can be bought in a liquid or tablet form from health food stores. It is a popular supplement in Japan and has been tested by research clinics there and in Australia.

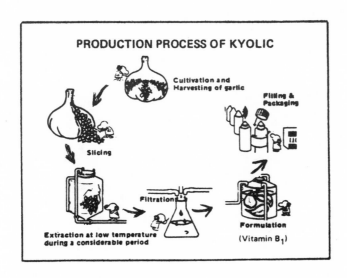

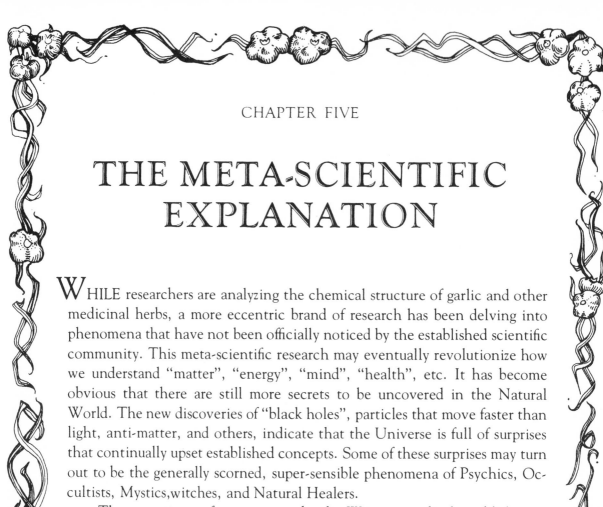

CHAPTER FIVE

THE META-SCIENTIFIC EXPLANATION

WHILE researchers are analyzing the chemical structure of garlic and other medicinal herbs, a more eccentric brand of research has been delving into phenomena that have not been officially noticed by the established scientific community. This meta-scientific research may eventually revolutionize how we understand "matter", "energy", "mind", "health", etc. It has become obvious that there are still more secrets to be uncovered in the Natural World. The new discoveries of "black holes", particles that move faster than light, anti-matter, and others, indicate that the Universe is full of surprises that continually upset established concepts. Some of these surprises may turn out to be the generally scorned, super-sensible phenomena of Psychics, Occultists, Mystics,witches, and Natural Healers.

The acceptance of acupuncture by the Western medical establishment is a first step in the direction of embracing the view that there are very subtle, and generally unrecognized, energy fields operating in Nature; and these energies or vibrations or radiations are essential for *Health*. Technology is being used to gather evidence for these phenomena, and machines are being engineered to record these previously undemonstrable energies.

The names for these "life forces" have changed with the particular tradition or discoverer. Acupuncture stimulates the energy flow known as *Chi*, and it is claimed in Oriental medicine that the stimulation of this *Chi* (*Ki* in Japanese) by such herbs as garlic and ginger can actually bring about sudden cures in the early stages of diseases caused by blockages and imbalances in this vital energy. *Chi* may be related to Wilhelm Reich's Orgone Energy. Kirilian photography records on film the auras emanating from all life. Garlic, as we will see, has been associated with Mitogenetic Radiations. Whatever we choose to call these life forces, it can be assumed that they are all either the same force with a different name, or different aspects of the same life force. Orthodox science recognizes none of these energy systems.

If we are to change the focus of modern medicine from its narrow concern with disease towards a wider concern for Health, then the medical profession will have to start re-examining the prejudices that prevent so-called unorthodox areas of medicine from emerging. The following is, again, from *The Pattern of Health* by Dr. Westlake:

> The really interesting thing about the new medicine which is emerging is that, while it will deal with increasing competence with the physical, to do so it will have to include the meta-physical. It is becoming evident that a true understanding of the physical is only possible in terms of metaphysics, and vice versa. This will constitute a major revolution in modern thought. (25)

SOME CRAZY HYPOTHESES

> Modern science should indeed arouse in all of us a humility before the immensity of the unexplored and a tolerance for crazy hypotheses.
>
> Martin Gardner (26)

There is some interesting evidence that plants have a form of intelligence that responds very sensitively to the quality of human emotion and human health. Care, attention, love, pleasant music and gentle words are said to help plants flourish, whereas neglect, excessive noise, and hostile intentions limit plant growth and health. If this is so, then why not reverse this relationship and examine to what extent human health depends on *positive plant vibrations,* in addition to the vital oxygen we get from the plant world. The growing interest in the following "crazy" hypotheses indicates that we are heading back to the old mystical/spiritual notion that all life is interconnected and mutually inter-dependent, whether high or low on the scale of complexity; the health of the high is dependent on that of the low, and vice versa.

GARLIC AND BAD VIBES

Some modern herbalists have suggested that there is something in garlic's electro-chemical makeup that combines with the electrical charge of "evil" or negative energies emitted by diseased tissue. The phenomenon of "bad vibes" is probably related to that of "evil spirits" of olden days. If these vibes or spirits or negative energies exist, as para-psychologists believe, then they exist on some heretofore unrecognized level of the physical/psychic plane we know as Reality. The positive, health-giving energies of garlic are said to counteract the negative, destructive energies of diseased beings, diseased tissue, and diseased particles.

This is all highly speculative, but these speculations lead to interesting hypotheses which may explain the popularity of garlic and other herbs as protective devices against ghosts, demons, vampires, bad vibes, and the like. Parapsychologists, and the psychics, clairvoyants, and healers they study, believe that if science does come to accept or at least fully examine paranormal phenomena and positive energies , then perhaps we will see someday a Science that does not rule out large chunks of the total reality that we are.

MITOGENETIC RADIATIONS

In the 1920's, Professor Gurwitsch (or Gurvich), a Russian electro-biologist, made claims that a peculiar kind of ultra-violet radiation was emitted by onions, garlic, and ginseng (the potent mandrake of Oriental cultures). These radiations had the property, according to Gurwitsch, of stimulating cell growth in cell division or mitosis. Gurwitsch called these radiations mitogenetic, and claimed that their presence served as a powerful rejuvenator and cure for many diseases (27).

Gurwitsch initially observed that cells in the tips of onion roots seemed to be dividing at a definite rhythm, and he believed that this dynamic was the result of unknown sources of physical energy coming perhaps from other cells.

He tested his theory by mounting one root-tip in a horizontal position within a glass tube, and pointed it towards a similar onion root also in a tube, part of which was shielded by quartz coated with gelatin, which had the property of blocking the ultraviolet rays. After several hours of this radiation, Gurwitsch examined the different sections of the bombarded root and found that the exposed portion showed 25% more cell division than the blocked portion (28).

Other researchers following Gurwitsch had similar results. Scientists in Paris, Moscow, and Berlin all concluded that mitogenetic radiations, or M-rays, did in fact exist. An American physiologist, Dr. G.W. Crile, noted that the human body gave off a similar radiation. He concluded that M-rays serve as a general physiological revitalizer by irradiating the human system. A Russian biologist, Professor Lakhovsky, found that M-rays stimulate the endocrine glands and increase hormone-producing activity, thus making M-rays valuable as a rejuvenator. Gurwitsch's experiments were rejected by English and American scientists and forgotten. For a more detailed study of M-rays and related energy systems, see *Orgone, Reich and Eros* by Edward Mann (Simon and Schuster).

THE SECRET LIFE OF PLANTS

Recently, a book entitled *The Secret Life of Plants*, by Tomkins and Bird, has brought to the public's attention the work of such men as Gurwitsch. Their very readable book presents the experimental data that, if valid, would prove the "radiant nature" of all life, and elucidate the specific inter-relationships of Human Beings and Plant Beings.

Tomkins and Bird describe the case of Cleve Backster, a lie detector specialist, who innocently hooked up his electrodes to the dracæna plant in his office and discovered to his amazement what has become known as the "Backster Effect": Changes in the environment of the plant—threats of violence to the plant, different types of people in the environment—all these variables were "absorbed" by the plant and registered through the poly-graph mechanism. Backster and others have become convinced that plants are alive in a way resembling human life, rather than the passive "stony" existence we have come to ascribe to plants. The result of these experiments gave rise to the talk-(or sing)-to-your-plants craze, and the horde of books now on the market which give directions to the would-be green thumb/green tongue.

These claims by Backster are of course contested—even by those who are generally open to "possibilities" in the relationships between living or-ganisms. Robert Rodale, the editor of *Organic Gardening and Farming,* dis-putes in a recent issue (May, 1974) Backster's claims based on a visit to Backster's laboratory. At this meeting, Backster was unable to show that yogurt (or rather, micro-organisms inhabiting the yogurt) responds to threats and human emotion. Rodale emphasizes that although many of the claims for "secret" plant life may not be valid, there are many secrets that are. For instance, the subtle chemical communications that take place within and between plant and animal species. The existence and functioning of such agents as pheromones, allomones, and kairomones—exuded by the organism—proves that a language exists in the plant realm below the level of human perception. This chemical language gives cues that are roughly equi-valent to "fear", "sexuality", etc.

Perhaps Backster is guilty of a naive anthropomorphism in that he attributes human motivation to instinctual and chemical responses. But, I am not prepared to rule out that plants can "perceive" negative vibrations from humans. Given the chemical signaling system that Rodale describes, I can conceive that humans exude a subtle chemical signal that tells other animals and plants about specific intentions. After all, to say that plants don't have human attributes is not to say that humans do not share with plants a common biochemical make-up. I have already mentioned the pre-conscious odor signals that humans use to signal sexual attraction or repulsion. Perhaps other signals indicate states of anger or sympathy which are in turn registered by plants.

The fact that Backster's experiments are not always repeatable—especially in front of "critics"—does not disprove his claims. It is common in these esoteric experiments for there to be a high rate of failure. Perhaps because these experiments deal with sensitive and subjective phenomena, and are thus responsive to the environment and the experimenters, they cannot be repeated as easily as more "materialistic" and controlable experiments. Psychics are notorious for "blowing it" under pressure or scrutiny, and yet the existence of psychic phenomena is being recognized by many establishment scientists.

Other findings tend to support the idea of Health as a balance of energies existing within and between organisms. The work of André Bovis in France shows that foods grown in chemically fertilized soil, or foods that have been over-cooked or eaten after their peak of freshness, do not radiate the same vital energies as organic, freshly-picked and properly cooked foods. He developed a device to measure the radiant energy of plants and animals and suggested that when a sick man, radiating below the level of good health, ate a food radiating at the peak of its vitality, these vital energies of the food would raise the level of the sick man's vibrations.

VITAL GARLIC

The work of men such as Gurwitsch, Backster and Bovis may help us to understand the "magical" phenomena that have puzzled scientific thinking for centuries. In terms of garlic, how is it that a simple herb has been held so effective throughout history as a curative and protective agent? How do herbs "cure" and revitalize on the physical level, on the spirit level, and on connecting levels in between? Is it enough to say, as many now admit, that garlic's sulphur compounds kill bacteria? What kind of power exists in garlic and other herbs that explains their rejuvenating effects? A scientific-materialistic explanation may not be enough.

Even if we answer the above questions, and even if we come to accept and use the health foods such as garlic, will the herbs be healthy themselves—healthy enough to help us? In his work with garlic as a pesticide, Greenstock came to understand the necessity of using *vital* garlic. Much of our vegetables are crippled from a nutritional point of view by their soil deficiencies and poisons, and thus lack the proper chemical balances for effective use. In the words of Dr. J.E.R. McDonaugh, it is obvious that . . .

> . . . the health of plants depends upon life in the soil, and (the health of) animals and man upon the quality of the vegetable and animal food upon which they live . . . the maintenance of this harmony between soil, plant, animal and man is the only means by which the protein is able to protect its host against invaders . . . (29)

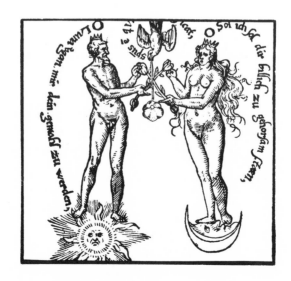

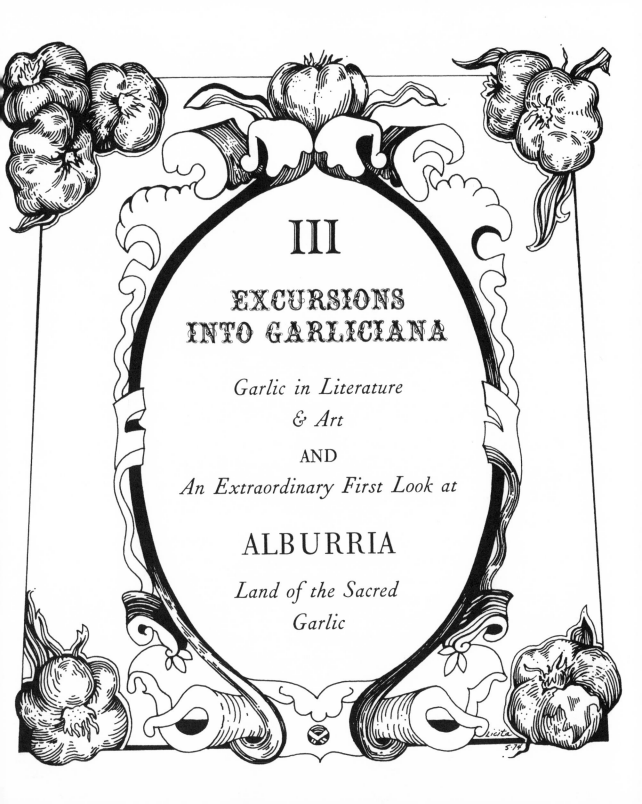

III

EXCURSIONS INTO GARLICIANA

Garlic in Literature
& Art

AND

An Extraordinary First Look at

ALBURRIA

Land of the Sacred
Garlic

INTRODUCTION

WHEREVER we fit on the scale between pro-garlic and con-garlic, we must ultimately admit that there is *something* in garlic, and that it indelibly marks garlic as the vegetable-herb of Mirth. Evidence? The immediate, and sometimes overwhelming, response of so many souls when confronted either at the dinner table or in conversation with the phenomenon of the pungent lily: Delight, chuckles, embarrassed giggles, painful hee-haws, outright bilious laughter, and indeed the entire range of Mirth spiced (or inflamed) by the perhaps unconscious restraints thrown up by the civilized super-ego as protest against basic animal pleasures of our lives (blushes, forced seriousness, etc.). Yet, in the final analysis, whether garlic is ultimately proven to be a panacea or a put-on, cure-all or con-all, it will not lose its characteristic funniness (unless, of course, science removes its characteristic stinkiness). Funny, I say, the way B movies are funny when the heroine of a Victorian love story accidentally reveals the white bony structure of her ankle, linking foot to calf-knee-thigh and fanny, to the hero who blushes with repressed erotic delight.

The mechanism involved here is typical: any dated taboo, whether against revealing ankles or eating garlic, will strike one as funny, and any demonstration of the antiquated taboo will bring some form of amused response. The historic ruling class taboo against garlic became the stuff of comedy from Aristophanes and Shakespeare, as we have seen, to Lawrence Durrell, whose short story, "If Garlic Be the Food of Love", is printed below. And yet the very strength of the mirthful response is in some sense a sign that the taboo, defunct as it may be, still carries, however subtly, a lingering trace of its former function, especially in the traditionally anti-garlic lands of

England and America. We do not laugh at things that lack Power, and the sacred-profane ambivalence surrounding garlic still generates a power sufficient to create Comedy.

In the following Excursions into Garliciana, the breath of this mirthful response to garlic will be revealed in the works of Rabelais, Ford Madox Ford, Lawrence Durrell, and Charles McCabe. Other poets, essayists, film makers, and artists are represented here who have produced work especially for *The Book of Garlic*. The special chapter on Alburria will present for the first time the Garlic Papers, correspondence between the highest officials of the Republic of Alburria, a Peoples' Garlic State.

SPECIAL APPENDIX — A Garlic Times Scrapbook

Since the original edition of *The Book of Garlic*, a lot of wonderful material has been received by Lovers of the Stinking Rose. In the appendix following the section on Alburria, some of this material is presented. Think of it as a scrapbook: odds and ends, letters, poems, etc., in no particular order. This section will grow through the years, for it is in this section that "future folklore" is in the making.

Postcard by Paul Wisswasser. Available from LSR.

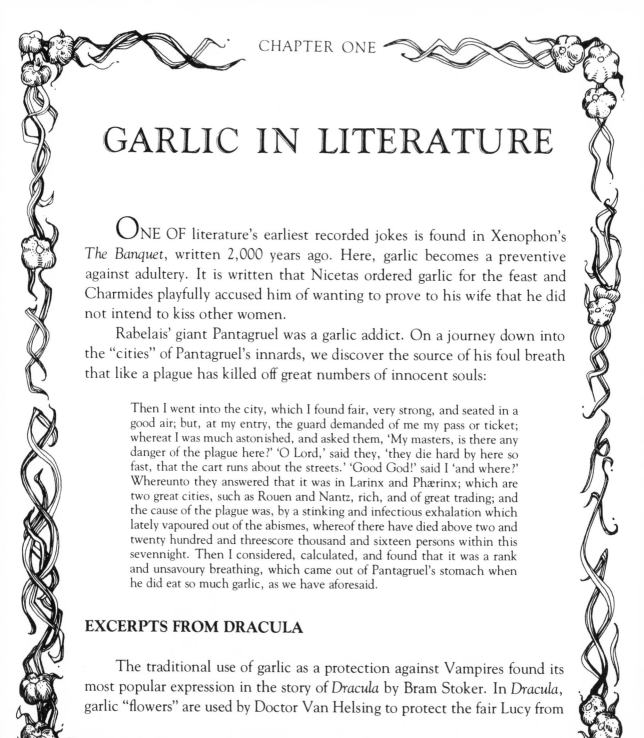

CHAPTER ONE

GARLIC IN LITERATURE

ONE OF literature's earliest recorded jokes is found in Xenophon's *The Banquet*, written 2,000 years ago. Here, garlic becomes a preventive against adultery. It is written that Nicetas ordered garlic for the feast and Charmides playfully accused him of wanting to prove to his wife that he did not intend to kiss other women.

Rabelais' giant Pantagruel was a garlic addict. On a journey down into the "cities" of Pantagruel's innards, we discover the source of his foul breath that like a plague has killed off great numbers of innocent souls:

> Then I went into the city, which I found fair, very strong, and seated in a good air; but, at my entry, the guard demanded of me my pass or ticket; whereat I was much astonished, and asked them, 'My masters, is there any danger of the plague here?' 'O Lord,' said they, 'they die hard by here so fast, that the cart runs about the streets.' 'Good God!' said I 'and where?' Whereunto they answered that it was in Larinx and Phærinx; which are two great cities, such as Rouen and Nantz, rich, and of great trading; and the cause of the plague was, by a stinking and infectious exhalation which lately vapoured out of the abismes, whereof there have died above two and twenty hundred and threescore thousand and sixteen persons within this sevennight. Then I considered, calculated, and found that it was a rank and unsavoury breathing, which came out of Pantagruel's stomach when he did eat so much garlic, as we have aforesaid.

EXCERPTS FROM DRACULA

The traditional use of garlic as a protection against Vampires found its most popular expression in the story of *Dracula* by Bram Stoker. In *Dracula*, garlic "flowers" are used by Doctor Van Helsing to protect the fair Lucy from attack. In the following excerpts, garlic is introduced into the story by Van Helsing, who is the only one who suspects vampires are the cause of Lucy's anemia and not a "disease".

Van Helsing receives garlic in the mail as reported in Dr. Seward's Diary entry of September 11:

This afternoon I went over to Hillingham. Found Van Helsing in excellent spirits, and Lucy much better. Shortly after I had arrived, a big parcel from abroad came for the Professor. He opened it with much impressment—assumed, of course—and showed a great bundle of white flowers.

"These are for you, Miss Lucy," he said.

"For me? Oh, Dr. Van Helsing!"

"Yes, my dear, but not for you to play with. These are medicines." Here Lucy made a wry face. "Nay, but they are not to take in a decoction or in nauseous form, so you need not snub that so charming nose, or I shall point out to my friend Arthur what woes he may have to endure in seeing so much beauty that he so loves so much distort. Aha, my pretty miss, that bring the so nice nose all straight again. This is medicinal, but you do not known how. I put him in your window, I make pretty wreath, and hang him round your neck, so that you sleep well. Oh yes! they, like the lotus flower, make your trouble forgotten. I smell so like the waters of Lethe, and of that fountain of youth that the Conquistadores sought for in the Floridas, and find him all too late."

Whilst he was speaking, Lucy had been examining the flowers and smelling them. Now she threw them down, saying, with half-laughter, and half-disgust:

"Oh, Professor, I believe you are only putting up a joke on me. Why, these flowers are only common garlic."

To my surprise, Van Helsing rose up and said with all his sternness, his iron jaw set and his bushy eyebrows meeting:

"No trifling with me! I never jest! There is grim purpose in what I do; and I warn you that you do not thwart me. Take care, for the sake of others if not for your own." Then seeing poor Lucy scared, as she might well be, he went on more gently: "Oh, little miss, my dear, do not fear me. I only do for your good; but there is much virtue to you in those so common flowers. See, I place them myself in your room. I make myself the wreath that you are to wear. But hush! no telling to others that make so inquisitive questions. We must obey, and silence is a part of obedience; and obedience is to bring you strong and well into loving arms that wait for you. Now sit still awhile. Come with me, friend John, and you shall help

LUCY FENDS OFF DRACULA with a braid of garlic. Actually, this is Margaret Whitton and Jeremy Brett in a 1979 production of "Dracula" at the Shubert Theater in Chicago. Photo by R. B. Leffingwell, courtesy *Chicago Sun-Times.*

me deck the room with my garlic, which is all the way from Haarlem, where my friend Vanderpool raise herb in his glass-houses all the year. I had to telegraph yesterday, or they would not have been here."

We went into the room, taking the flowers with us. The Professor's actions were certainly odd and not to be found in any pharmacopoeia that I ever heard of. First he fastened up the windows and latched them securely; next, taking a handful of the flowers, he rubbed them all over the sashes, as though to ensure that every whiff of air that might get in would be laden with the garlic smell. Then with the wisp he rubbed all over the jamb of the door, above, below, and at each side, and round the fireplace in the same way. It all seemed grotesque to me, and presently I said: "Well, Professor, I know you always have a reason for what you do, but this certainly puzzles me. It is well we have no sceptic here, or he would say that you were working some spell to keep out an evil spirit."

"Perhaps I am!" he answered quietly as he began to make the wreath which Lucy was to wear round her neck. The last words he said to her were:

"Take care you do not disturb it; and even if the room feel close, do not to-night open the window or the door."

"I promise," said Lucy, "and thank you both a thousand times for all your kindness to me! Oh, what have I done to be blessed with such friend?"

That night Lucy reports in her diary a new-found respect for the smelly flowers:

> . . .I never liked garlic before, but to-night it is delightful! There is peace in its smell; I feel sleep coming already. Good-night, everybody.

Unfortunately, the maid is ignorant of the purpose of the garlic and the necessity of keeping the bedroom windows closed. She removes the garlics as Lucy sleeps that night and opens the window. The following morning the maid tells Van Helsing of what she did:

> " . . .There was a lot of those horrible, strong-smelling flowers about everywhere, and she had actually a bunch of them round her neck. I feared that the heavy odour would be too much for the dear child in her weak state, so I took them all away and opened a bit of the window to let in a little fresh air. You will be pleased with her, I am sure."

Sure enough, Van Helsing discovers that Lucy has once again been sucked by a vampire, and he proceeds to give Lucy another transfusion. For the conclusion of this story of Vampires, Virgins, and Garlic, read the book.

FORD MADOX FORD from *PROVENCE*

...I came yesterday, also in Fitzroy Street, at a party, upon a young Lady who was the type of young lady I did not think one ever could meet. She was one of those ravishing and, like the syrens of the Mediterranean and Ulysses, fabulous beings who display new creations to the sound of harps, shawms and tea-cups. What made it all the more astounding was that she was introduced to me as being one of the best cooks in London — a real *cordon bleu*, and then some. She was as you might expect, divinely tall and appeared to appear through such mists as surrounded Venus saving a warrior. But I found that she really could talk, if awfully, and at last she told me something that I did not know — about garlic....

As do — as *must* — all good cooks, she used quantities of that bulb. It occurred to me at once that this was London and her work was social. Garlic is all very well on the bridge between Beaucaire and Tarascon or in the arena at Nimes amongst sixteen thousand civilised beings... But in an *atelier de couture* in the neighborhood of Hanover Square! ... The lady answered mysteriously: No: there is no objection if only you take enough and train your organs to the assimilation. The perfume of *allium officinale* attends only on those timorous creatures who have not the courage as it were to wallow in that vegetable. I used to know a London literary lady who had that amount of civilisation so that when she ate abroad she carried with her, in a hermetically sealed silver container, a single clove of the principal ingredient of *aioli*. With this she would rub her plate, her knife, her fork, and the bread beside her place at the table. This, she claimed, satisfied her yearnings. But it did not enchant her friends or her neighbours at table.

My instructress said that that served her right. She herself, at the outset

FERDINAND BINET is both the creator of this postcard, and an official of the town of Arleux, France. Arleux is the home of an annual garlic festival.

of her professional career, had had the cowardice to adopt exactly that stratagem that amongst those in London who have seen the light, is not uncommon. But, when she went to her studio the outcry amongst her comrades, attendants, employers, clients and the very conductor of the bus that took her to Oxford Circus, had been something dreadful to hear. Not St. Plothinus nor any martyr of Lyons had been so miscalled by those vulgarians.

So she had determined to resign her post and had gone home and cooked for herself a *poulet Béarnais*, the main garniture of which is a kilo — two lbs.—of garlic per chicken, you eating the stewed cloves as if they were *haricots blancs*. It had been a Friday before a Bank holiday so that the mannequins at that fashionable place would not be required for a whole week.

Gloomily, but with what rapture internally, she had for that space of time lived on hardly anything else but the usually eschewed bulb. Then she set out gloomily towards the place that she so beautified but that she must leave for ever. Whilst she had been buttoning her gloves she had kissed an old aunt whose protests had usually been as clamant as those of her studio-mates. The old lady had merely complimented her on her looks. At the studio there had been no outcry and there too she had been congratulated on the improvement, if possible, of her skin, her hair, her carriage …

She had solved the great problem; she had schooled her organs to assimilate, not protest against, the sacred herb ….

IF GARLIC BE THE FOOD OF LOVE
Lawrence Durrell

Every Wednesday now, in the winter, I lunch with Antrobus at his club, picking him up at the Foreign Office just before noon. I think he enjoys these meetings as much as I do for they enable him to reminisce about old times in the Foreign Service. For my part I am always glad to add an anecdote or two to my private *Antrobus File* — the groundwork upon which I one day hope to raise the monument of my own Diplomatic Memories . . .

Yesterday his memory carried him back to Vulgaria again where he had served under Polk-Mowbray — and over De Mandeville — as Head of Chancery. "Bitter days," he mused. "And perhaps one shouldn't talk about them. De Mandeville was in a queer state all that spring; perhaps it had something to do with the phases of the moon? I don't know. He was in a 'Hamlet, Revenge!' sort of mood. The trouble seemed to centre about the Embassy table — as Third Sec. he had a watching brief on the food. It started I remembered with a series of Constance Spry table-decorations which made that otherwise fairly festive board look like an illustration from the Jungle Books. One could hardly carry a fork to one's mouth without biting off a piece of fern by mistake. Slices of decorative pumpkin and marrow gave a Harvest Festival note to things. One peered at one's guests through a forest of potted plants. Finally Polk-Mowbray put his foot down. De Mandeville became huffed. The next thing was he ordered Drage to serve everything from the right — in deference to a left-handed Trade Mission chief who was staying with us. It may have been tactful but it led to endless complications with us right-handed trenchermen who found everything upside down, and had to scuffle to rearrange our table-patterns as we sat down. And then what with Drage coming in so fast from the wrong side one was practically always out, hit-wicket on the *soufflé*. I tried to reason with De Mandeville but he only pouted and bridled. It was clear that he was in an ugly mood, old boy. I feared the worst. I have a sort of intuition about these things.

"The next thing in this chain of progressive sabotage was curry. De Mandeville had a series of Madras curries served. They were of such a blistering intensity that the entire Dutch Embassy had the inside of its collective mouth burned away — peeled off like bark from a tree, old boy. The Minister called on Polk-Mowbray in *tenue* and wanted to know if a state of war existed between England and Holland. His wife was treated for soft palate. A *junior attaché* went about saying the Embassy food was full of quicklime and hinting darkly about damages. Naturally there were high words and massive contempts flying about which made Polk-Mowbray some-what nervy. De Mandeville was sharply taken to task, but without avail. He next served an onion soup and black bread without soup-spoons. You know how long a rich onion soup takes to cool. Our little lunch-party dragged on almost to dusk, and several guests were lightly scalded because they neglected to take thermometer readings before gulping. The whole thing was gradually working up towards a climax. I saw it all coming and mentally, so to speak, closed my eyes and breathed a prayer to the Goddess of Diplomacy. I could not, however, guess from which quarter this warped and twisted Third Sec. might deliver the knock-out blow.

"Then ... all this is in the strictest confidence, old man .... Then it came. Polk-Mowbray used to leave his office door wide open so I could see and hear all that went on therein. One morning I heard a familiar sort of row going on and I knew that the blow had fallen at last. Polk-Mowbray was hysterical. 'I adjure you by the bones of Cromer', he was yelling, 'to answer me without prevarication. *Have you been putting garlic in the food without telling anyone?* Did you, wittingly or unwittingly plug that *cassoulet*, impreg-nate that lustreless salad, order the peas to be lightly simmered in the stuff before serving? Answer me at once, or in Heaven's Name I'll ——'

"De Mandeville made a gobbling self-deprecating sort of sound and spread his manicured hands as he muttered something about garlic being eaten in all the best London houses. It toned up the nervous system. Some said it was the only specific for scabies. One would have to be very retrograde to imagine …. And so on in this style. Veins were throbbing all over poor Polk-Mowbray by this time. 'Do not try to justify yourself,' he thundered. 'Answer me with a simple yea or nea. And take that beastly sensual smile off your face. If you choose to dine on heads of raw garlic with your scabrous chauffeur it is your business. But the Embassy table is sacred, do you hear? *Sacred*. If you do not answer truthfully I shall make you the subject of a General Paper to the Foreign Secretary.' There was a short silence during which they glared at each other. Then De Mandeville threw back his chin and uttered the word 'yes' rather defiantly; he was wearing an obstinate Canine Defence League expression on his face. Polk-Mowbray levitated briefly and banged his desk with a triumphant, 'Aha! So you *did*.' It was clear that De Mandeville was in for one of those Searching Reproofs. His Chief now began to walk up and down his own carpet as he always did when he was moved. He Pointed The Finger Of Scorn at De Mandeville in no uncertain fashion. 'Wretch!' he cried in a shaking voice. 'Could you not see the harm that might come from such reckless and criminal cookery? Moreover you choose the *one* lunch party of the year which is of policy importance in order to do me the greatest damage. Think of the Naval Attaché! What has he ever done to merit that unspeakable lunch — at which he ate far too heartily? And my niece Angela — what of her? And the Head of the Foreign Ministry — what of him?'

"De Mandeville tried to make a few unavailing protests. 'Enough!' cried Polk-Mowbray hoarsely. 'Surely you know that to feed a Naval Attaché garlic is like stoking a coke furnace with dead rats? Did you see his face as he lurched out into the afternoon? You did not know, I suppose, that he was due to lecture to the Sea Wolves on Temperance and Self-Denial at sea? He created a very poor impression in a very short time. The wretch now fears court-martial. He says that now whenever his pinnace is sighted they raise a Yellow Fever flag and forbid him access to the ship. I do not doubt that the dirk-point will be facing him when he walks into the ward-room. All this is on your head and more. Don't interrupt me. That is not all. Do you realize that when I helped the Minister into his car he was making a noise like a bunsen burner? *You* would not care that he had to address the High Præsidium that afternoon on Foreign Affairs — moreover in a language so full of aspirates as to make the gravest demands on his audience! No, *you* would not care, with your pumpkins and pottery and left-handed table arrangements! On you go in your headlong career, weaving these devilish plots around my table. And apart from all this what about *me*. *You* cannot be expected to know that I was booked to read the Lesson at a Memorial Service in the British Baptist Chapel which is notoriously cramped and ill-ventilated. How did you think I felt when I saw the first two rows of the congregation swaying like ripened wheat in an east wind? How do you think I felt when it came to my turn to embrace the hapless widow? She was breathing as if she had slipped her fan-belt. Answer me! You see, you haven't a word to say. You are mumchance as you jolly well ought to be. Fie on you, Aubrey de Mandeville! *You* did not stop to think what effect Angela might have on Cosgrave after such a lunch. The engagement was pretty tremulous as it was — but you snookered the wretched girl well and truly. And what of the typists' pool? Girls keeling over one after another as they tried to take dictation from us. What of them?' For a moment words failed him. His face worked. Then he said in a low murderous tone, from between clenched teeth, 'I tell you that from now on there is to be no more garlic. Sage, yes. Thyme, yes. Rosemary, marjoram, dill, cummin, yes. Emphatically yes. But *garlic*, no!' And so the edict went forth and the sale of peppermints in the Naafi dropped off again."

Antrobus sighed sadly over these memories as he replenished our glasses. Then he said musingly: "I should say really that Garlic was the biggest Single Cross a Diplomat had to bear in the rough old times. It *had* to be banned, old man. Yet in a sense we were all Living A Lie, like the Americans under Prohibition; for we all secretly yearned after the stuff. (I say this in the strictest confidence. I would not wish to be quoted.) Yet it is strange that this noxious bulb should have such an allure for men. As for diplomats, it played havoc with Confidential Exchanges; and as for dancing with your

Ambassadress ... well. It was the quickest way to get posted. That is why I was so relieved when the Age Of Science dawned. I used to be *against* Science once, and for the Humanities — I freely admit it. But when at last chlorophyll came in I was instantly won over. What a boon and a blessing to dips! What an over-riding sense of relief! Many a breach was healed that day between man and man. Even Polk-Mowbray in the end allowed the salad-bowl to be lightly rubbed with a couple of heads before serving. And I don't know whether you noticed the rather respectable little *ragoût* we have just been eating? Not bad for the Club, is it? But fear nothing! In my pocket lies a phial full of those little grey tablets which make human intercourse a rational, easy, unbuttoned sort of thing again. No more shrinking from pursed lips in The Office. We can hold our heads high once more! Let's drink a final little toast to the Goddess of the F.O. shall we? I give you Chlorophyll!"

THE FEARLESS GARLIC EATER
Charles McCabe

GARLIC COUNTRY

Garlic, I have for a long time held, separates the men from the boys. And, if I may be so presumptuous, the chicks from the women.

I sleep on Telegraph Hill, but for the most part live in North Beach, which is garlic country as ever was. At the grocery where I shop the garlic is placed right next to the cash register, and sold to you when you go out, like cigarettes. This is presumably because both are addicting substances, and small enough to stick in your pocket when you're buying the filet of sole and the apple juice.

When I go to London I have to find my way to Soho where the bulbous-rooted plant is understood and respected. In N.Y. I hit Mulberry St. and the Italian restaurants near Police Headquarters on Center St. I don't like to be away from that pungent taste, that formidable smell.

It happened recently that I found myself away from garlic country. It was on one of those huge Italian liners that run from N.Y. to Naples. Italian liner? Yes, indeed. The shipping people pandered to one of the more obscure American prejudices, that against garlic. Not an item of food on the menu, including, as I thought the spaghetti sauce, had even a suspicion of the flavor of the most useful member of the lily family. This indeed garlic is, botanically. You could look it up.

After seven days of this Spartan regimen, it was indeed good to get back into true garlic country in Algeciras, at the Southern tip of Spain and in full view of the Prudential Insurance Company—i.e., Gibraltar. There you can almost spit across the Straits into Tangiers where garlic is really King, and browned fat ladies sell it strung together like Hawaiian leis. I once bought one of these garlic necklaces from a street peddler in Belgravia and tried to bring it into the good old U.S. The customs guy was so shocked by my temerity that he didn't even ask to open my bags.

There are people who like garlic even more than I. One was Mr. Guy Burgess, the late British diplomatist-spy who took off for Russia in the 1950's with Mr. Donald McLean. He used to eat it, not by the clove but by the bulb. He always had a couple of bulbs jingling about in his pockets. He was a pederast. Burgess also had an extraordinary number of friends who were neither garlic lovers nor pederasts. I often wonder how he fared in Russia, in the garlic department.

When I first came to Frisco, I used to lunch regularly at the old Buon Gusto on Columbus and Broadway with a friend named Tim. We discovered the beauties of *pasta con pesto* — spaghetti or ravioli with a ravishing green sauce made of lots of squashed garlic cloves, olive oil, and fresh basil leaves. Tim was married, I was not.

After 3 days straight of pesto, both of us were quite redolent. We were of the same species, though not of quite the same degree, as the old paisanos who sit on the benches at Washington Park, the smell of garlic oozing from their leathery integuments. Some of them hit you at five paces. These old boys really herald their presence.

The Pesto began to screw up Tim's marriage. After the second nite he would be expelled from the master bedroom. It was rapidly becoming a question of his pesto or his wife. I temporized for Tim, as I tend to do with my friends.

Lots of Parsley, consumed after garlic, tends to abate the ferocity in interpersonal encounters. This I told Tim, and it worked for a small while. He now lives in Washington, is still happily married, thanks·in no small part to having overcome his addiction to the dread smelly leek. I am still a garlic freak and quite unmarried, thank you. I wonder what I'm telling myself.

San Francisco Chronicle, July 11, 1973

ROMANCE AND GARLIC

Got into a rather arcane discussion the other night. When the pivotal point in the argument was reached it was necessary to descend to some form of definition, for there were a couple of Jesuit-trained products in the group. The gravamen of it all seemed to come to this: Have more couples been brought together by garlic than torn asunder?

It may seem to you that we gents didn't have much to do of an evening but that is where you underestimate the products, or the wreckage of a Catholic education. Our brothers and our priests and our nuns may have screwed us up in the sex department, but they gave us something in return. This is in many ways richer: an almost erotic pleasure of disputation, where we whet the long-disused machetes of the undistributed middle, the begged question, and dread solipsism.

An argument between college-educated Catholic laymen can be as formal as a Japanese Noh play, and as lacking in resolution as a Chekhov short story. Because you use the apparatus of Aristotelian logic, you have the illusion of thinking. It is merely musing you're doing. Daydreaming at night, within the comforting framework of "logic."

But back to garlic and romance. One logician was of the impression that garlic was so important, and its taste so delicate, that you should never use it when you are drinking alcohol. He wasn't necessarily thinking of the effluvium which results from the copious use of both at lunchtime; but that was not far from the minds of any of us.

No. This guy was and is a proper gourmet. He believed in garlic as flavoring, not as medicine, though he acknowledged that there is much to be said for it as medicine. Doctors in Mexico, who have gone to Cornell and Tulane and Columbia, still give cloves of garlic and a small shot of tequila to children who have been bitten by scorpions. I know. That's the treatment my own children got.

The proper gourmet, to get back to him, had the ideal way to revivify a failing romance or marriage, two conditions which often befall bar room logicians. The way is only to be recommended in extremis, as when the lady is having long, earnest talks with some Satanic graduate of Boalt Hall. The formula is simple: Go on the wagon, join the lady in a proper garlic debauch, and take a trip.

The proper gourmet did this very thing a year or two ago. He took his loved one, who happened by coincidence to be his wife, for six weeks to Ibiza, one of the Balearic islands off Spain. There are a lot of 18-karat freaks here who have a high tolerance for any habit, from cocaine to sobriety.

The p.g. and wife were drawn together like nut and bolt. The dry period made them so miserable, for the lady was partial to the creature too, that together they became company with a capital C. They needed each other, as misery needs company, which is one of the lesser known withdrawal symptoms of alcohol use. They sat in cantinas and drank gallons of lemonade, and talked about the kind of things they used to moot in college, like the Dodgers and The Cloud of Unknowing and whether Greer Garson liked girls.

The couple denied the temptation of boozers on the dry, the company of those who drank; and worse, those who filled the air with florid descriptions of the beauties of punching their way out of a hangover with Pernod or Amer Picon or whatever. The garlic, which they ate raw like olives, took care of that. It was, of course, bliss. Until they stopped, whereafter they lived unhappily ever after. They are still doing so.

The Lawry's spice people understand this. They have this ad about Meyer's girl friend, who found they were drifting apart. She tried Lawry's Garlic Spread. Voila! "Now my romance has a whole new air about it. Because of Lawry's Garlic Spread, Meyer and I are always alone. Together."

San Francisco Chronicle, August 1, 1973

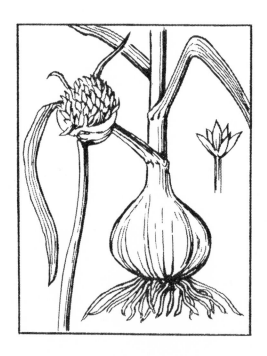

THE TRAVELS OF GARLIC

A Romantic Underview

by Sa Hog "The Bearer" Avedisian

MY INTEREST in garlic began when Lloyd J. Harris, one of the greatest raconteurs and tricycle thieves of all times, asked me to romanticize a history of garlic. Lloyd has great faith in my historical sense because he knows I have seen the movie *I Was a Teenage Caveman* three times.

Researching my mind very carefully, I discovered that garlic not only had a history, but that it has made its own history and is still to make more history. Let those who would scoff that garlic is its own miniscule microcosm scoff at their own risk. The future is fraught with *FANGERS* . . . . the Alburrians know this well.

Generally speaking, all herbs (garlic being an outstanding one) have yet to conclude their direct influence on our lives and fortunes. Roots have their own territorial imperatives, and too often and unbeknownst to us, these roots manage to use the passions of our loyalties to spread the tentacles of their interests. It would be wise to remember this as we begin to understand how garlic alone has generated enough energy to cross continents, create cosmic attitudes, and to write this book.

Without however knowing any of garlic's history, it would admittedly be difficult to believe that something as familiar as, say, the rise of gasoline prices would be directly related to as common an item as garlic. But it is. We can see this if we would follow the fortunes of a certain Semitic clan leader named Abraham, who, because of his great love and *mesmeration* of the omnipotent goodness of garlic (a plant he discovered inside of a burning bush), was driven from his home into the deserts of ancient Sumeria.

Garlic first left its scent on the footpaths of modern history 4500 years ago when the residing Fathers of the City of Ur, the hub of the Sumerian empire, chased Abraham from their town after he had convinced them that if they planted garlic next to their world-renowned tulip crop (which was the financial hub of the hub, celebrated in that ancient lute song—"a Hub-a Hub-a") they would have the world's only sweet-smelling garlic, thereby gaining for garlic the acceptance into the graces of the mighty, enriching the Sumerian empire even more. Unfortunately, instead of garlic smelling sweet, the tulips reeked of garlic and consequently the entire tulip industry perished, and with it the Sumerian glory.

The outraged Urians stoned Abraham from their city cursing after him the dreaded stigma "Jew", which in Urian means "May you never have a home, may you always have ten or twenty wandering tribes, may you be denied doctors and dentists, may you lack wit and wisdom, may devils guild your guile," and sadly, "may your fate be only as good as anyone else's."

—"Oh boy," Abraham shuddered under this strident curse.

—"What did he say?" asked one Urian to another. "I don't know. It sounded like 'Goy' [which in Urian means "The same to you in spades"]."

—"Damn Jew . . ."

In one whiff, therefore, garlic created the Jews and thus the Israeli-Arab wars, and to prove a point, *the rise in gasoline prices.*

Another ramification of the Tulip disaster was the development of what is known as European civilization. With the elimination of the Sumerians from the tulip economy, the "Shoes-of-Wood" people became the world's only tulip producers, a Dutch industry around which the nomads of Europe first settled into a persistent society.

Continuing our chronicle, let us follow garlic as it fled Ur riding atop Abraham's camel. The tribe stopped at a juncture called Harran, Turkey. A few among the clan decided to split, one group going south and the other north. "May God be good to you," Abraham said, "and remember if you should find a land of Milk and Honey, make sure it has some oil too." It was Abraham's decision to carry "Garlic-semitic" northward that eventually brought it to a bloody clash with "Garlic-aryan" in the fields of England.

The story of Garlic-aryan began at the top of Finland when Jan Viking tried to sell the town elders the idea that a garlic clove in the nose was better for a fever than crossing the appendix of a walrus over the forehead of a dead whale. "Blasphemy" cried the priest. "Socialized medicine" cried the doctors. Jan was ice-cubed out of town. He headed southward looking for more sympathetic lands.

How Garlic-semitic moving north and Garlic-aryan moving south met in westward England begins 12,000 miles to the east at the royal court of Genghis the Ginseng-eater Khan. It was during the time when Marco the Garlic-eater Polo and Ginseng Khan became involved in a heated argument over whether garlic was better on pizza than ginseng—the great, profound and jealous root of Asia. Sensing a threat to its sovereignty, ginseng triggered in Khan many memories of how well it had served the people and how it had saved his life during his tent days. "Genghis! Drink this ginseng tea or I'll break your neck," his mother admonished. He drank the tea and it saved his life.

Khan became so infuriated with Marco's insistence about garlic that he chased him clear back into Europe in a bloody attempt to enlighten the garlic eaters. The force of this chase, like a flying wedge, turned the northerly and southerly thrusts of Garlic-semitic and Garlic-aryan westwards towards England.

Because of the untimely death of Ginseng Khan, the first Ginseng-Garlic war ended before it was decisive. Again, the fallout from this war helped create modern Europe, and Khan's killing ways left Russia ripe for serfdom, which made it ripe for communism.

When Garlic-semitic felt a threat to its expansion into England (the last frontier of Europe) from the Garlic-aryan species, this created a sense of economic insecurity in William the Conqueror, the Franco-Saxon "Clover" king, who owned most of the garlic interests south of the Danube river. He invaded England to protect his interests. As garlics clashed, the death toll and anguish did not stop until it culminated in what is euphemistically called the "War of the Roses", or more accurately, the "War of the Stinking Roses." Because of the great personal misery suffered, Britishers to this day have an aversion to garlic, which explains why their cooking is without distinction, and why they suffer hemorrhoids and gout. Historically, this hatred of garlic politically unified the British to a degree which enabled them to create the world's greatest empire.

The Western anti-garlicum attitude has become a third and major force in the world's present political make-up. The other two powers at this time — Ginseng and Garlic — are again girding up for Ginseng-Garlic War II. The outcome of this war will be determined by who the anti-garlicum forces side with. I personally believe these anti-garlicum interests (elitist, puritanical, prejudiced) will ally themselves with the Ginseng forces (Asian, rigid communism, cosmic) against the Garlic forces (Russia, chaotic-communism, anti-elitist). Why? Because Ginseng is unodoriferous and because the bitterness of Ginseng makes it a natural for the slight bitterness the anti-garlicum elitist English love in their martinis.

There is only one way out of this approaching storm. Unless we learn to excuse our smells *and* our sterilities, unless we learn to live with spices *and* banalities, we will continue to be ruled by *Roots*. We must overcome the prejudices that roots cause among us (for their benefit). The bitter Ginseng, the pungent and fertile Garlic, and Blandness are meant to be our servants, not our Prime Political Movers.

192

Miscellaneous Bits and Pieces—

Modern plumbing developed as a response against the Stinking Rose War. The knights who fought the long hard war would sometimes have to stay in their armour for three or four days without change. Due to natural functionings, aided, perhaps, by the knights eating copious amounts of garlic to protect them from infections in case they were cut, their leggings would become receptacles for their egressions. If you can imagine how you would feel walking around in a tin-can filled with three or four days of such matter, the flush toilet would be a logical conclusion, and a blessing.

Another curious aspect of the Stinking Rose War, which reflects the power of garlic to make history even in a most incidental manner, involved one of the kings, Richard III, who lost his kingdom when his horse lost one of its shoes. While it was being shoed, the horse farted soon after having finished a breakfast of scrambled eggs and garlic. The blacksmith, who was shoeing the horse, passed out before securing the shoe. In the midst of battle, the shoe came loose causing the horse to throw-off his King, and this event culminated in that great line, "A Horse, a horse, my Kingdom for a horse."

In Napoleonic times, the battle of Waterloo was lost when as Napoleon embraced Josephine adieu, she, after also just finishing a breakfast of scrambled eggs and garlic, burped in his face. Napoleon turned his head sharply to the right, and while his head was so kinked, Wellington hit him from the left.

Garlic's influence on history has not only been associated with violence and bowel jokes. During mystical times it was believed that apes first started to leave the trees to retrieve dropped cloves of garlic. How the cloves got up into the tree was never figured out.

Garlic's highest political achievement is reflected in the ancient Mexican word "Democracy" which means "You have to let me breathe even if I eat garlic."

An example of garlic's reputation as an aphrodisiac is heard in the

Italian lament, "Oh so li me o", which means "May I rubba you with garlica oila before we rolla in the oreganoa."

The first time Adam made love to Eve was after she mistakenly passed a garlic bulb to him instead of that famous apple. Garlic's blood-warming tendencies soon made themselves apparent.

—"Hey, look at that," Adam said pointing to himself. "What is it?"

—"I don't know," Eve answered. "It's never been like that before."

—"Well, what is it?" Adam repeated.

By the time they found out Eve was pregnant. It was here then in the Garden of Eden that garlic first gained its reputation as an Aphrodisiac, and this first garlic repast led to the propagation of the entire Human race!

You see, I told you garlic had a profound effect on us. But as amazing as the history of garlic is, as amazing as its influence on our lives, even though it keeps us cool in the summer and warm in the winter, even though it is a People's Servant and even though it may save us from famine, pestilence and vampires, garlic is still best remembered for what it can do for a roast or a salad or bread or pizza . . . which tells the senses "Ahaaa . . . ."

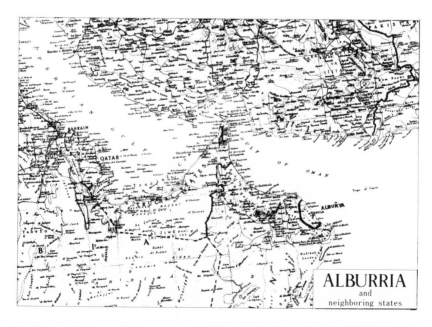

ALBURRIA
and
neighboring states

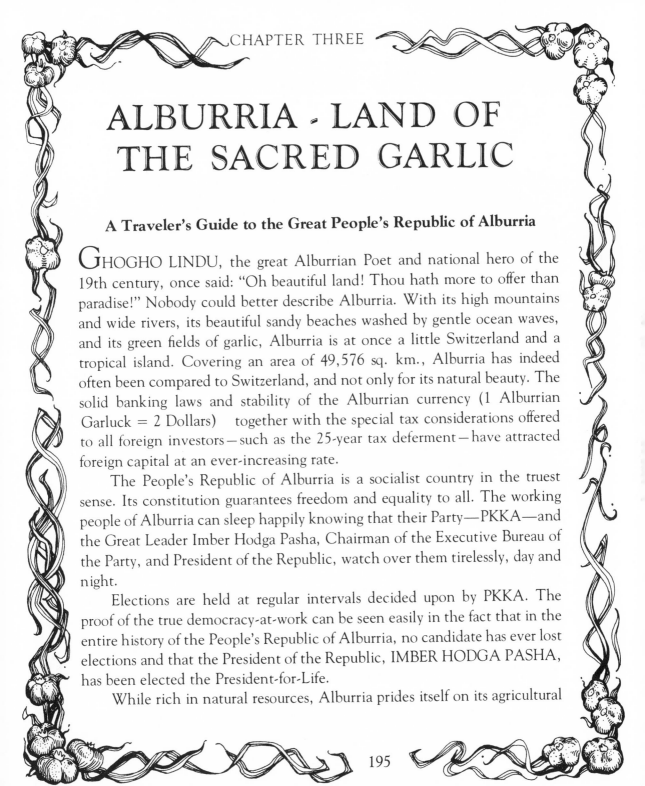

CHAPTER THREE

ALBURRIA · LAND OF THE SACRED GARLIC

A Traveler's Guide to the Great People's Republic of Alburria

GHOGHO LINDU, the great Alburrian Poet and national hero of the 19th century, once said: "Oh beautiful land! Thou hath more to offer than paradise!" Nobody could better describe Alburria. With its high mountains and wide rivers, its beautiful sandy beaches washed by gentle ocean waves, and its green fields of garlic, Alburria is at once a little Switzerland and a tropical island. Covering an area of 49,576 sq. km., Alburria has indeed often been compared to Switzerland, and not only for its natural beauty. The solid banking laws and stability of the Alburrian currency (1 Alburrian Garluck = 2 Dollars) together with the special tax considerations offered to all foreign investors — such as the 25-year tax deferment — have attracted foreign capital at an ever-increasing rate.

The People's Republic of Alburria is a socialist country in the truest sense. Its constitution guarantees freedom and equality to all. The working people of Alburria can sleep happily knowing that their Party—PKKA—and the Great Leader Imber Hodga Pasha, Chairman of the Executive Bureau of the Party, and President of the Republic, watch over them tirelessly, day and night.

Elections are held at regular intervals decided upon by PKKA. The proof of the true democracy-at-work can be seen easily in the fact that in the entire history of the People's Republic of Alburria, no candidate has ever lost elections and that the President of the Republic, IMBER HODGA PASHA, has been elected the President-for-Life.

While rich in natural resources, Alburria prides itself on its agricultural achievements. Within a short period of time since the Great People's Revolution, the country has become the major grower and exporter of garlic. In the past year alone, garlic production increased by 48.4% as compared with the pre-Revolution days of the stagnant regime of Pashuk II. Alburrian garlic can now be found in most countries of the world.

In Vervilla (population: 237,439), the quaint old capital city of Alburria, there are many things to see and places to visit. The Monument to the Unknown Hero; The Imber Hodga Pasha Museum of the Great Revolution; The Garlic Museum; the historic sites of revolutionary battles etc., are among them. At your request, the Alburrian People's Tourist Bureau (APTB) will arrange visits to garlic-processing plants, to the fields (at harvest time), or to workers' clubs on Saturday evenings where free "knob" (Alburrian drink) and souvenirs are usually distributed among visitors. (Ladies usually receive two-ounce complimentary bottles of the Alburrian-made perfume, The Spirit of Revolution, prepared from the rare blossoms of the pink garlic not found in any other place in the world.)

The Alburrian language, which traces its origins from the Indo-European group of languages, is spoken by 493,000 people of our country. The Turko-Yaffetic influence along with the Greek and Latin roots can be found in the Alburrian language. (For further information on this subject please be referred to the study by Professor Hel-Hodgi Hofi, "Historic Roots of the Alburrian Language", published by the Alburrian Institute of Linguistics in Vervilla.)

Alburria has come into the limelight of international tourism. Excellent swimming and hiking, healthy food and low prices make it an attractive vacation place for tourists from many countries. The Alburrian International Airways (ABIA), sometimes affectionately referred to as the "Flying Donkey Airways", has weekly flights originating in various parts of Europe and Africa. Its international network of routes is being expanded continually.

Come to Alburria—you will love it! We will greet you on our door-steps with the traditional "knob" and a warm SHINDET (peace)!

(This text printed in Alburria by the Alburrian People's Tourist Bureau, Revolusis Blvd. 17, Vervilla A-75, telef. 31-44.)

THE GARLIC PAPERS—Correspondence from Alburria

The following correspondence revolves around certain recent communications between Quonst Nik-kik, Commissar of Garlic Promotion; H.H. Krip, Immigration Services; Professor Nanos Valaoritis, poet and artist; Iris Clert, museum director; Alli Um von Sati-vum, a local garlic guru. Other names are mentioned in these letters, including George Hitchcock, poet and publisher living in Santa Cruz.

In this age of international intrigue and *personal* diplomacy, a glimpse at the motives and ideas that operate behind the facade of public understanding proves fascinating and instructive to students of history.

The Ambassador
of the People's Republic of Alburria

requests the pleasure of the company of

Prof. and Mrs. Nanos Valaoritis
to a garlic dinner on Thursday,
October 4 at 8:30 p.m.

R.S.V.P.

Alburrian Embassy
Athens

N-K:amr   31st August, 1973

Prof. Nanos Valaoritis,
3828 Landholn Avenue,
Oakland,
California 94605.

HIGHLY CONFIDENTIAL AND TOP SECRET

DESTROY BEFORE READING

Dear Comrade Professor,

     Thank you for your letter (undated for reasons of security)
and for your "Hired Hyroglyphics" and Hitchcock's "Another Shore",
all of which have been studied and have had a series of semi-public
readings here at the Embassy.

     At first, I was puzzled by Hitchcock's book. There was no
doubt whatever in my mind that he was an agent of the hated
Pashuks and that his book was an open offence to our beloved
country. I have since corresponded with our Commissar for Skryt
Bezpec, Hel-Hamir Krip, who has told me of Comrade Hitchcock's
true beliefs and has enlightened me about his invaluable work
towards furthering the cause of the International Garlic Revolution.

     However, dear Comrade Professor, we must always bear in mind
that, although the great Garlic Revolution has swept into the dust-
bin of history the running dogs of international imperialism and
their puppets, the Pashuks, we must be vigilant to their dirty
tricks. The Alburrian people, its beloved Party and its watchful
Leader will crush the enemies of the people wherever they may
happen to be. Therefore, I am sending you by carrier pigeon some
powerful garlic pills which you may drop into the drinks of those
whom you know to be endangering our cause. They will be put out
of action for several days. It was by using these same pills that
I myself was able to prevent the formation of a Pashuk Government
in Exile here in Athens.

     Both from reading your book, for which I congratulate you,
and that of Comrade Hitchcock, I have come to the conclusion that
both of you should apply for Alburrian citizenship. I have already
written to Hel-Hamir Krip and I am sure that if you write to him

cont. ....

yourselves, he will consider your applications favourably. However,
as direct communication between the U.S.A. and Alburria are out of
the question, I would suggest that you write to him via our Embassy
on the neutral soil of Japan. Please address him thus :

> Hel-Hamir Krip,
> Skryt Bezpec,
> Cefu III,
> c/o The Embassy of the Republic of Alburria,
> C.P.O. Box 870,
> <u>Tokyo, Japan.</u>

I think too, that it would be nice to send your books to our
learned Ambassador in Japan, whose name is Imver Ghogho Shirak
and whom you can reach at the same address. By the way, please
send me your book of subversive verses, as the Pashuk agents know
nothing about literature and would overlook their importance and
true significance.

Long live Alburria!

Long live our Great Leader Imber Hôdga Pasha!

Long live the Great Garlic Revolution!

I end this with the now famous lines of our Great Leader :

> "Kinshît Albuřidun zos
> Kinshitâs liderast
> Imner masüg!"*

(Imber Hôdga Pasha
1-4-70)

SHINDET!

Quönst Nik-Kik
Commissar for Garlic Promotion

* Excellent translations of his poems are now available in
Berkeley. The best English translation is by Sir Monitor
Lizard and the only one in Greek is by the Alburrian Class-
icist Dr. Alah Burr Nézos

N-K:amr   10th September, 1973

Prof. Nanos Valaoritis,
3828 Landholn Avenue,
Oakland,
California 94605.

Dear Comrade Professor,

    Herewith enclosed please find a copy of a letter
which our friend Iris Clert has just sent me from Paris
by diplomatic pouch. As you see, she too wishes to
become an Alburrian citizen. She also wishes to organize
a big Alburrian Happening at her art centre. You too, must
contribute to it, so write to her directly.

    I also enclose an invitation to the party which our
Embassy is giving on the occasion of the 5th Anniversary
of the Glorious Garlic Revolution. I hope that you and
your wife will be able to take the Alburrian Flying Donkey
Airways and be with us that evening.

    I look forward to hearing from you at your earliest
convenience.

        SHINDET!

Quŏnst Nik-Kik

        Quŏnst Nik-Kik
   Commissar for Garlic Promotion

encl.

PANJANDRUM PRESS

99 SANCHEZ STREET, SAN FRANCISCO, CALIFORNIA 94114
TELEPHONE: 861-5336

His   Excellency Quónst Nik-kik   1 Novermber, 1973
Embassy of the Republic of Alburria
Stadiou 10. Athens 133

My dear Commissar,

    The Doctrine of Simultaneity of Phenomena and the kind sup-
port of our dear Professor Valaoritis, Yogi Commissar of Telepathy
have conspired to bring your Government and my Intentions to this
common point in time and space. Truly, there is a Deity, and
one comes to Him, n'est pas, through a Garlic Diet-y!

    To think that just a short time ago I pressumed to be the
only Garlicomaniac extant....the ego of it! And such a lonely
position it was, carrying the burden of my Passion for that devine
bulb-toute seule- my shoulders heaving with the Agon, my breath
speaking/reaking to the world of my Woe. And now, a Homeland appears on the horizon of consciousness, a Holy Land where Lovers
of Allium can live and fantasize in Peace! The Glorious Garlic
Revolution is Balm and Nectar to my sagging spirits and I shall
dream and work for nothing less than that day when I set sail
for that "other shore" known as Alburria. May I live to inhale
the breath of the great Pasha whose Garlicodosis is legendary!

    But for now, I find myself engrossed in the Work of my life;
that is, the preparation and publication of the De-definitive text
on garlic. It was with the intention of enlisting Prof. Valaoritis' help in this project that I came to know of Alburria and
your great work in Garlic Promotion. My book (working title of
The Peoples' Book of Garlic) will outline the history of garlic
through all time as condiment, medical herb, folk symbol and
mandala, aphrodisiac, insecticide, and Panacea for a world limp
with pain. Collages, charts, maps, short stories, cartoons, anecdotes, recipes, graphs, documents and correspondence: all this
will form the Appendix to the History. I am busy now acquiring
permission to reproduce relevent data found in my researches.

    The Yogi Commissar of Telepathy has kindly shown me corres-
pondence from Alburria and I respectfully request permission to
reprint this seminal material in my book. I am told also that
a prospectus is available on Alburria, and I would be eternally
greatful if you could send it and any other information and/or
correspondence you deem fitting for public consumption-short of
classified material, of course.

    With your assistance, I can in my own small way bring the
Magic and Glory of Garlic to the stagnant consciousness of a
Mankind tottering on the brink of boredom and odorlessness, ignorant all-the-while of the Sacred Bulb that offers such succor
in this hour of crisis.

    I anxiously await your reply.

                      I am your servant
                      Alli Um Von Sati-vum P.U.

EMBASSY OF THE
REPUBLIC OF ALBURRIA
STADIOU 10. ATHENS 133

N: cet   November 13,1973

His Excellency,
Imver Gogo Shirak,
Embassy of the Republic of Alburria,
C.P.O. Box 870,
Tokyo, Japan.

Dear Comrade Shirak:

It is a long time since we corresponded, but I have been
in constant touch over the telephone with our future diplomatic
representative in Paris, Mme. Iris Clert.

She wants to stage an Alburrian feast in Paris on December 28.
This date is very good for me, but what about you?

Meanwhile, I have had a lengthy correspondence about our
Great Country with my cousin, Professor Nanos Valaoritis, who
is Professor of Poetry at California State University at Berkeley.
He has now put me on to the poet and writer, L.J. Harris, who is
so enraptured with our country and so enthralled with garlic as
a metaphysical concept, that he is publishing a book on it and
has taken the Alburrian name of Alli Um Von Sati-vum!

I enclose a copy of his letter to me. He asks permission
to quote my Alburrian correspondence with my cousin. From my
point of view the publication of my letters is quite in order,
as they do not contain classified information. However, do you
think that Kriz Bespek will have any objections? I shall not
answer him before hearing from you. I think, though, that it
would be quicker if you wrote to him directly, especially as
he asks me for a pamphlet on Alburria and I only have two left.
They are very popular!

Please let me hear from you soon.
Long live our glorious leader Imber Hodga Pasha!
Long Live Alburria!

SHINDET!

Quonst Nik-Kik
Commissar for Garlic Promotion

202

EMBASSY OF THE

REPUBLIC OF ALBURRIA

C.P.O. Box 870, Tokyo

Office of Immigration, Passport Section

December 21, 1973

Alli Um Von Sati-vum P.U.
1043 Cragmont Avenue
Berkley, California 94708
U.S.A.

Ref.: C-VI-SK-BZ-806

Dear Sir:

This office received information that you are desirous of becoming
a citizen of the People's Republic of Alburria.

In accordance with the provisions of the Immigration Order 399 (b),
Par. 17, Item 4f every applicant must submit a properly executed
application form, accompanied by two photographs. Upon receipt
of the above, the documents are passed over to Skryt Bezpik, Section
III, for security, idiological suitability, alliumphobia and other checks.
If the applicant is found eligible he is notified by this office, at which
time his Alburrian passport and other pertinent documents are forwarded
to him.

To expedite processing it is customary that the applicant make a voluntary
donation to the Cultural Fund of the Union of Socialist Garlic Growers.
Experience shows that a donation in the amount of $50. - (or equivalent)
assures a speedy processing of the donnors application.

GLORY TO THE ALBURRIAN PEOPLE AND ITS GREAT LEADER IMBER
HODGA PASHA !

SHINDET !

H. H. Krip
In Charge

Encl:
HHK/hh

P.S.   It is a pleasure to know of your efforts in compiling the long-overdue and
much-sought-after encyclopaedia of garlic-knowledge - THE PEOPLE'S
BOOK OF GARLIC. We shall await with suspense its publication and
hope that it will afford a great alliuminating experience to all its readers.

PANJANDRUM PRESS

99 Sanchez Street, San Francisco, California 94114
Telephone: 861-5336

January 20, 1974

Mr. H.H. Krip
Alburrian Embassy
Office of Immigration
Passport Division
C.P.O. Box 870, Tokyo

Dear Sir;

I am very proud to have received a passport application for
citizenship in the Alburrian Peoples' Republic (dated Dec. 21),
and I herewith enclose the completed application along with a
voluntary donation of $50 ("or equivalent") to insure a speedy
processing of these papers.

My donation is in the form of a $20 cashiers check and a receipt
for $30 worth of garlic books ($5 per book) payable to you on
publication of said Peoples' Book of Garlic. I hope this donation suffices to insure swift processing and security related
investigations.

Owing to accelerated publication date, it is my hope that a
passport can be issued before March 1, so that the book and
its author may arrive on the market with all proper accredidation

And may I ask once again for an Alburrian Prospectus. Prof. Valaoritis , Yogi Commissar for Telepathy has intimated the existence
of such a prospectus, and although I am quite familiar with the
Spirit and Odor of Alburria, I would be delighted to have more
data concerning the everyday aspects of this great land(geography,
economics, transportation, etc.). Lovers of the Stinking Rose
the world over await a more detailed account of their spiritual
homeland, and I hope that the Peoples' Book of Garlic can fulfill
this function!

Glory to the Alburrian People and its Great Leader Imber Hodga Pasha!

Yours very truly,

Alli Um Von Sati-vum

Alli Um Von Sati-vum P.U.
Director, An Aesthetic Prod.
A Division of Panjandrum Press

AUVS/ljh

PAŞPORT

ALBUŘYA KINŞIT REPUBLIK

PASSPORT ALBURRIAN PEOPLE'S REPUBLIC

Nr. 009151

This series of reproductions is taken from the passport issued to Alli Um Von Sati-vum, the code name for a powerful promoter of the *Stinking Rose*. Very few of these passports have been issued to non-Alburrians, and it is rumored that the latest passport has been issued to a famous Russian cellist now living in the U.S. (His name has been withheld for security reasons.)

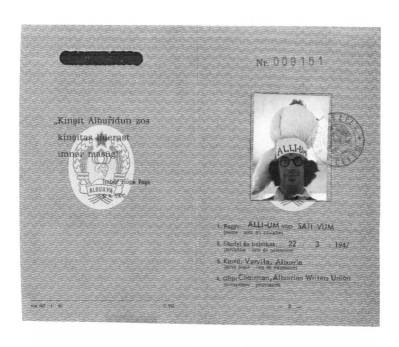

Nr. 009151

„Kinşit Alburidun zos
kinşitas liderast
imner mastig!"

Imber Höga Paşa
x 4 1970

ALBURYA

1. Bagyr: **ALLI-UM** von **SATI-VUM**
   (name - nom du titulaire)

2. Gladyl ka babirkas: 22 / 3 / 1947
   (birthdate - date de naissance)

3. Kinvil: Vervila, Alburria
   (birth place - lieu de naissance)

4. Ghir: Chairman, Alburrian Writers Union
   (occupation - profession)

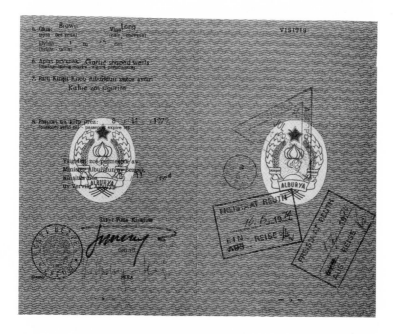

5. Okis: Brown   Vias: Long
   (eyes - les yeux)   (hair - cheveux)
   Dylds: 1   to   .8m
   (height - taille)

6. Abret prystiak: Garlic shaped warts
   (special distinguishing marks - signes particuliers)

7. Paru Kinşu Knoy Alburidun zagos şvdur:
   Kalur zos şigurta

8. Pasport uz kiti prez: 8 / 11 / 197.
   (passport valid till - passeport expire le)

Yaigidas zoe-permetor av
Minister Alburidun ni Bezage.
Kinşites zue
uv Yerviu, Alburria

ALBURYA

Sayr Polu Kinştar

VISITIŞ

ALBURYA

FREISTAT REUTH
EIN REISE
AUS

On Alburrian Linguistic Affinities

by Charles Perry, D. Alb.

The Alburrian people, as is well known, are a mixed race which traveled widely and suffered many political vicissitudes before finding their present happy situation. The Alburrians spent many centuries as one of the "submerged nationalities" of various Turkish and Slavic empires and at least some time in close contact with a Latin people, presumably the Rumanians. It was garlic that held them together more than their language.

All this has rendered analysis of their speech a thorny problem. Von Kretzmer considered them to be proto-Armenians, then changed his view to "ancient Anatolian" without specifying Cimmerian, Lydian or any one Anatolian people. Du Candolle flatly declared them to be a hitherto unknown "Eastern Albanian" tribe. Slavoj went so far as to call their tongue a "made-up language" *(pastishny jazyk)* which they did not actually speak except to scandalize linguists.

In my view, based on analysis of core vocabulary and "deep structure" grammar, Alburrian is a North-East Iranian tongue of nomad origin, most closely related to Ossetic, the language of the sedentary Scyths of the northern Caucasus. This basic Scyth-stratum is obscured by considerable Turkic, Slavic and Latin overlays.

The Latin vocabulary mostly comprises modern cultural elements. *Apert*, "clear, obvious"; *kresp*, "a kind of crepe flavored with butter, cilantro and garlic"; *skryt*, "signature"; *munyt*, "paper currency." The vocabulary of modern politics (*sigurita, polis,*

CHARLES PERRY, *garlic visionary, surveying the garlic-laden hills of Alburria.*

207

minister, permeşodi) is particularly influenced by French and Italian, usually assimilated in pseudo-Rumanian form.

The Turkish and Slavic elements were more prominent in the old language than in Modern Alburrian. Many Slavic lexical elements remain, such as *pryznak*, "sign"; Turkish words not related to food have survived less well. Examples are *bagyr*, "name" (Turkic *bagadir*, "hero," hence "fame, nickname"), *ĝaturm*, "garlic-stuffed pastry" (Turkish *qatlama*, "puff paste"). Turkish has, however, profoundly influenced morphology (the dative case ending *-ĝa*, the much-used causative suffix *-dir*).

But the basic vocabulary is North-East Iranian or Scythian. The very name of the Alburrian people, for instance, *Buȓi*, "garlic," is from the same root as Ossetic *bodaen* (Digor dialect), influenced by Iran dialect *nury*. The prefix *al-*, in my view, is related to Ossetic *aelaem*, "fruits or sweets, strung on a thread and hung from trees or around the necks of horsemen at funeral banquets." (Cf. Alburrian *zogal*, "to parade around with garlic strung around one's neck"; *zgalint*, "military decoration in the form of a stylized braid of garlic.") Thus, *albuȓidun* plainly means "garlic-braid people."

Significantly, the most famous line of the national poet Imber Hoĝa Paşa is all Scythian: "Kinşit Albuȓidun zos kinşitas liderast imner masüg."

Kinşit and *kinşitas* both go back to the root of Ossetic *chyndzaembal*, "young people." *Liderast* is related to Ossetic *laedaersyn*, "to flow down," and *masüg*, "creative," to *mysaeggag*, "invention." *Imner* is the untranslatable key word of Alburrian politico-culinary thought, usually rendered in En-

glish as "principle, strength, support." The second element, /ner/, may go back to the same root as Ossetic (Iran dialect) *nury*, "garlic." *Zos*, of course, is simply *sae*, "their". The poem may be translated, "The vigor of People's Alburria (or, the Alburrian People) flows from the creative principle," i.e., the "spiritual equivalent of garlic" so prominent in Alburrian philosophy.

All these elements are living linguistic factors. *Bezpek*, "legitimate," is compounded of Slavic *bez*, "without," and Latin *pek*, "fault." *Fiolluk*, "roasted or barbecued garlic," is the Ossetic *fizon (aeg)*, "shishkebab," with the Turkish suffix /-lik/. New compounds coined almost daily attest to the vitality of the Alburrian linguistic melange.

Note on orthography: The Latin alphabet was adopted after the Revolution. The vowels *a, e, i, o* and *u* are pronounced as in Italian. *Y* is an obscure vowel that varies between *i* as in *pin* and *u* as in *pun*; *ü* with the umlaut is like *u* in French. *Ş* with a cedilla is like English *sh and is usually transcribed as sh in State Department documents.* *C* is like English *ch.*

A circumflex accent is used over long vowels. Over the letter *g* the accent indicates a back-guttural representing Turkish *g* or *gh*. Over *r* it signals the most distinctive sound of the Alburrian language, the "nasalized *r*" which usually represents a Scythian intervocalic /-nd-/ or /-dn-/ and strikes a non-Alburrian as now an *r* preceded by a nasalized vowel, now a trilled *r* followed by an *n*. This "nasalized *r*" is conventionally transcribed in English as a double *r*, as in Alburria for *Albuȓya*.

MASTERWORKS FROM ALBURRIA

The following paintings are being shown to the world for the first time, thanks to the kindness of representatives from The Garlic Museum, and from the Imber Hodga Pasha Museum of the Great Revolution. In these works, the spirit of the Garlic Revolution can be felt in a heroic orderliness. The superficial similarity of some of these works to better known works of Western Art does not suggest that Alburrian art is in any way *derivative*. No, indeed. The common thematics of European and Alburrian art shows only a common groundedness in Humanity. That the Alburrians "see" garlic in everything (even in the great works of Western art), merely indicates a hyper-rational vision into one of man's most fundamental realities—Garlic.

The Great Imber Hogda Pasha

This is the central picture in the Pasha Museum in Vervila. The Alburrian Revolution is contained, symbolically, in this portrait. The Pasha is a gentleman—in his straw hat—but a soldier wrapped in a bandillero. Above Pasha is a gun, but in his hand is a dove. All contradictions are resolved through Pasha, the beloved Father.

David and Goliath

Alburrians interpret the David and Goliath myth in typical Alliocentric fashion. The Alburrian garlic is large, very hearty, and "hard as a rock". Goliath represents here the hated Pashuk conspiracy to destroy the Garlic Revolution. David is said by Alburrians to resemble the Great Imber Hodga Pasha in his youth, when he led the people of Alburria to victory over the Pashuks. The fact that a garlic is in David's sling shows the readiness of Alburria (Pasha) to destroy any "Goliaths" that may underestimate Alburria's power. Holding the garlic high, David seems to be offering the world a gift *and* a warning.

DAVID AND GOLIATH

THE GREAT IMBER HODGA PASHA

LA VIEILLE MAISON

Robert Charles is a celebrated restaurateur and the proprietor of La Vieille Maison, the Truckee, CA garlic haven. A native of France, Charles has had several smash hit restaurants in the San Francisco Bay Area. Now in Truckee, near Lake Tahoe, Robert and his wife Amora serve garlicky gourmet cuisine to skiers, gamblers, summer vacationers and garlic lovers from all over the world. Members of LSR receive a discount at La Vieille Maison.

Reservations: La Vieille Maison, Highway 267, P. O. Box 1298, Truckee, CA 95734. (916) 587-2421

Robert in action. He charms and mystifies his customers even before the food arrives at the table.

BELOW (from left to right): Wally and Carol, two of Truckee's most passionate garlic lovers; Robert Charles; George Lebugle, Robert's brother and a fine restaurateur in his own right. The group flew in Wally's plane to the Gilroy Garlic Festival.

A GARLIC MOVIE?

Michael Goodwin on Les Blank

I was a garlic virgin in Austin, Texas, just back from the lower Rio Grande valley, where I had been struggling to gather material for a *Village Voice* story about Les Blank, while Les struggled to shoot his Tex-Mex film, *Chulas Fronteras*. I had reviewed Les' films for several publications, but I had never hung out with him—especially when he was shooting—and he acted very uncomfortable with me. One morning he seemed particularly annoyed. "I had a dream about you last night," he said. "I dreamed that I made a big dinner for a lot of people, but you didn't come until too late. When you did show up I said, 'There was a good dinner tonight. Too bad you came late. And how come you never write about my cooking?' And you said, 'Generally I think your cooking is very poor.'"

After several weeks of tension, I decided to try and reestablish friendly relations. "Any chance of your cooking up a garlic feast?" I asked Blank, the day before I was to leave Austin for good. I meant it as a peace offering; I knew he was a big garlic fan. His eyes lit up.

When I walked into his girlfriend's house that evening I was terrified to see Blank chopping an entire head of garlic into a chicken sauce piquante! When that was simmering on a back burner he chopped up *another* big head and put that into a spinach casserole (subsequently baked under cornmeal).

"Isn't that too much garlic?" I asked.

"Too much garlic?" he asked, scandalized. "There's no such thing as too much garlic!" I abandoned hope.

The food cooked, we drank red wine, and presently the most wonderful aroma I had ever smelled began to fill the room. We hardly needed wine; we were getting drunk on the air-borne perfume of cooking garlic!

I asked him about his garlic film. "I have a feeling about garlic," he said, "like my feeling about Cajuns. I want the garlic film to make people feel as good as eating garlic makes me feel."

When the smell reached an ambrosial peak, Blank loaded our plates and we sat down to eat. I couldn't believe I was eating so much garlic and that it tasted so good. I had expected a harsh, nasty taste (like *raw* garlic)—but instead the food had a deep, rich bottom, a kind of extended bass, a little like truffles. The closest I could come to describe the taste was some culinary equivalent of the stomach-honk of a bass clarinet.

As the chicken went down, and bottle followed bottle, all the tensions of the Valley trip eased up. The high wasn't just wine—it was something else, a garlic high. "It does have residual effects," smiled Blank, "a feeling of well-being."

"Garlic and wine are one of God's great combos," I said without thinking very hard about it.

"Insanity is to art as garlic is to food," replied Blank.

I polished off a wing, feeling terrific. A warm glow was spreading through me. I felt a rush of love for everyone in the room, especially Blank, who had cooked this wondrous feed. "I think I just figured out your films," I announced. "You remember *Beat the Devil*, where everyone is trying to define time, and Peter Lorre says, 'Time is a thief.'? You make films about time, don't you? Time as a thief."

Blank's eyes grew sad. "It would be nice if time would disappear and leave us alone," he said.

Henry Miller holds a copy of *The Book of Garlic* sent to him by Lovers of the Stinking Rose. The photo is courtesy of Masako Tago.

In a letter to the author, Mr. Miller wrote:

> I have always considered garlic one of the four cornerstones of good health; the other three being honey, olive oil and yoghurt. I like it in small pieces in salads . . . I had a friend in Belgium who used to eat a whole clove of garlic with each meal.

To say that Henry Miller's life and work has been *garlicky* would not be inaccurate. In fact, Norman Mailer linked Miller with garlic in his book on Miller, *Genius and Lust* (pg. 371): ". . . Miller was a philosopher who cooked only with garlic, chopping boards full of garlic." That is, Miller's philosophy stinks. Whether true or not, the use of the image "garlic," rather than peppers, prunes or potatoes, is demonstration of garlic's literary/symbolic importance.

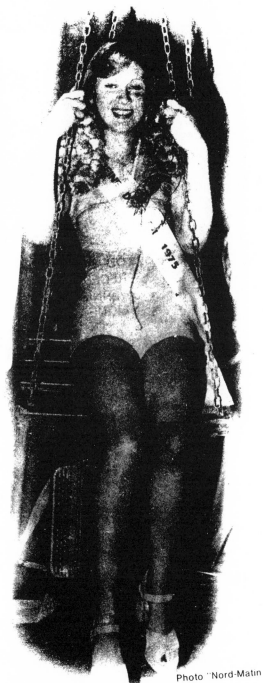

GARLIC HARVEST FESTIVALS *are com-mon in France, but only in Arleux, a small town north of Paris, do they elect a Miss Garlic beauty queen. Pictured above is the Miss Garlic beauty of 1975.*

Photo ''Nord-Matin

PARAMOUNT PICTURES CORPORATION

April 1, 1974

Mr. Lloyd J. Harris
1043 Cragmont Ave.
Berkeley, Cal. 94708

Dear Mr. Harris:

I am sorry I will have to disappoint you, but
I really know nothing about garlic except for
the fact that it is a fabulous remedy against
the vampires. Also the fact that the bloody
thing is awfully expensive, a factor we had
ignored until we started hanging wreaths and
garlands of it around the set.

Best regards,

Roman Polanski

RP/t

You may use this letter in your book with my blessing. Best of luck —
2.22.75

216

Dear Reader of *The Book of Garlic:*

MR. LLOYD J. Harris has asked me to deliver a message to his readers about what we call in Japan "pfiru" or garlic. He believes in garlic very much and that is good. He means well. He has been good to garlic and garlic has been good to him. I am touring the U.S., talking about garlic and all its wonders. I am watching the interest in garlic grow, as you say, like "hot cakes". I respect Western enthusiasm. Many an Easterner could be hit in the head with a ten-pound garlic and it would not awaken him. I am honest to goodness upset with Eastern lethargy. I hope *The Book of Garlic* reaches Japan, to wake up many lazy people.

My friends, garlic is the mysterious Mandala of Life. This not a joke, fellow man. You Westerners smell like porkchops and that is why you eat commercial variations on chlorophyll. Natural chlorophyll is good for you, but porkchops make your livers hard and your bile blue. We must have soft livers and yellow bile, or else we lose our jobs and maybe our lives, no? Mr. Harris is a good friend, and he follows faithfully the path of garlic. He has asked me to tell you about garlic, so "what-the-heaven," right? I am not sacred. Garlic is sacred. I am no Maharishi or Maharaj-ji. I am living-man living. Garlic is living *living*. We must all learn what this means, rather than be lived by living—hopeless, unhealthy, aimless

I have as you say, a gentleman's agreement with garlic. The Jew says I-Thou. That is good. We say Gar-lic; this is the same thing. Have you ever heard a garlic sing? The song of garlic is people eating it, no? Garlic is the Golden Rule. Do unto garlic what you would have garlic do unto you, a Christian might say. That is good, but do not expect garlic to do it as you do it. Garlic is a Bodhi Sattva, but you are a "No-bodhi". That is OK. I-Thou. We are content to be eaters of garlic and not the garlic. A Christian is not Christ and a garlic-eater is not Garlic.

Garlic comes from the ground but it is connected with the light that animates all things. I am in love with garlic and garlic is my guru. Garlic is a crystal ball: Look into it and you will see yourself reflected in everything else; Listen to garlic and you will hear the voices of history, the peoples' history, the history of people being people, eating garlic; Conceptualize garlic and see how the structure of the garlic imitates the structure of the universe, of the solar system, circles within circles, orbits around orbits; Smell garlic and you smell the earth; taste garlic and taste the heavens.

We are all by nature a tragedy and by habit a comedy. Garlic understands all this. Garlic is a means of focusing darkness and light into one structure that filters both into chemically and spiritually active forms of being healthy. In life, pick and choose what you will, but with garlic, what you pick will be what you choose.

Mr. Harris has been touched by the Spirit of Garlic. I can see it in his eyes and smell it on his skin and breath. But he knows he is not garlic. Therefore he will apologize to you for appearing to be a garlic. He is an actor, yes? That is good. He puts on disguise of garlic to better understand garlic and himself, but he always takes off his clothes at night. He need not apologize but he is a gentleman, no? He wishes you to like him and his book and that is OK too, because he is concerned about garlic very much and does not want to shed a false light on garlic. Mr. Harris has been possessed by garlic in a rather unusual way for a Westerner; he is not approaching the garlic from any conventional point of view. He is trying to let garlic in all its verification present itself, but being that he is not a garlic, Mr. Harris fails from time by time. He is like a preacher; it is easy for a preacher to forget he is not the God. But Garlic is grateful for *The Book of Garlic*, and Mr. Harris deserves credit for his encyclopedic efforts.

I apologize for my speech; I am, as you say, rusty on my English. May I finish with a word from my great teacher Master Chum Yosike: "In every man there is a Guru, but in every garlic there is only more Garlic." Good luck to you, and Garlic be with you.

Rev. Yorike Boshi*
Orinda, California—April, 1974

*Reverend Boshi is the guiding light of Lovers of the Stinking Rose, an organization created to support and study garlic as a food, medicine, and socio-political phenomenon. See the chapter, *The Argument Against Garlic* in Part One for more information on L.S.R.

GARLIC GOES FLAMENCO!

Garlic and Spanish Flamenco go together like Rum and Rumba. Where Spanish Gypsies live in the south of Spain, their food and music share an earthy passion that is symbolized by garlic. There is more than coincidence in the fact that so many stars of indigenous Flamenco are also butchers by profession. One such star is Anzonini del Puerto, the legendary singer/dancer. His recent stay in Berkeley, CA was a rare privilege for Lovers of the Stinking Rose; his music and his cooking were indeed garlicky!

Anzonini was shocked when he first learned of LSR. For him, garlic is a way of life that one does not think twice about in Spain. He was honored to learn of our passion for garlic, and dedicated several songs to LSR. Here are the lyrics to one verse, translated by Anzonini's guitarist, Kenny Parker. Unfortunately, the rhymes and word plays do not come through in translation:

Si quiere tener contento
 à tu marido en el trabajo
dirle à tu mujer que te eche
 en la comida 5 cabeza de ajo.

If you want husbands
 content with their work
tell their women to put
 5 heads of garlic in their meals.

This and other garlic verses were premiered at the home of LRS food editor, Bruce Aidells. Les Blank was on hand to add Anzonini to his garlic film, "Garlic is as Good as Ten Mothers."

See the *Garlic Times* Recipe Supplement, Page 270, for one of Anzonini's garlicky recipes.

Joke

A marriage broker arranges a meeting between a boy and a girl. The boy is shy, and asks the broker what he should say. The broker replies, "Ask her about her family. If that doesn't break the ice, talk about food. If she still does not respond, try philosophy."

The young man confronts the girl, who is also shy.
"Do you have a brother?" he asks.
"No," she replies.
Silence.
"Do you like garlic?" he asks.
"No."
Silence.
"If you had a brother, would he like garlic?"

—George Rhoads
Dundee, N.Y.

Ruthie Gordon's Garlic Song

There are spices and vegetables that you
    can grow
Some are under the ground, some grow tall.
Though they all have their qualities,
This you should know
That the garlic is best of them all.

You can use it in poultry, in fish and red
    meat
Or to spice up a vegetable stew.
In fact it improves everything that you eat
And it serves as a medicine, too.

Since Biblical times in all parts of the earth
It has cured countless sufferings and ills.
If we understood what the garlic is worth
We would throw out our poisonous pills.

The Egyptians, Phoenicians, the Vikings
    and Greeks,
Babylonians, Danes and Chinese,
On their voyages took enough garlic for
    weeks
And their enemies died on the breeze.

In Bulgaria's mountains and Russia's white
    plains
People live to a hundred years old.
For it's juice of the garlic that runs in their
    veins,
Oh, it's worth twice its weight in pure gold.

With selenium, germanium, allicin, too,
It can fight many types of disease.
So if you've got arthritis, T.B. or the flu,
Just say, "Peel me a garlic clove, please."

Plant some cloves in your garden to keep
    away worms
And the other bad things that kill plants.
If you're one of those people concerned
    about germs
You could drop one or two in your pants.

There are spices and vegetables that you
    can grow
Of all colors and shapes large and small.
After going through this I am sure you must
    know
That the garlic is best of them all.

IV

A GARLIC GALA GASTRONOMIQUE

The Pleasures of Garlic
In Soups and Sauces

WITH

Meat, Fish, Fowl

AND

By Itself

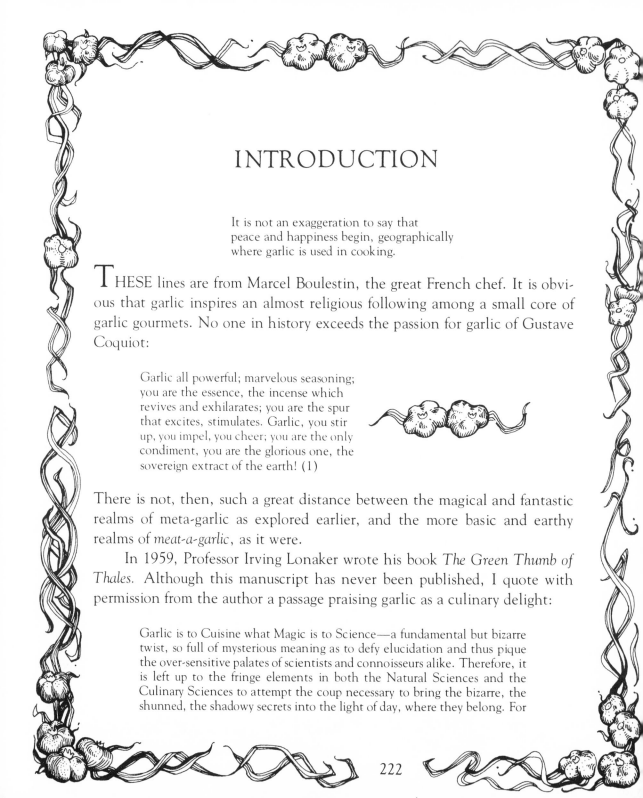

INTRODUCTION

> It is not an exaggeration to say that
> peace and happiness begin, geographically
> where garlic is used in cooking.

THESE lines are from Marcel Boulestin, the great French chef. It is obvious that garlic inspires an almost religious following among a small core of garlic gourmets. No one in history exceeds the passion for garlic of Gustave Coquiot:

> Garlic all powerful; marvelous seasoning; you are the essence, the incense which revives and exhilarates; you are the spur that excites, stimulates. Garlic, you stir up, you impel, you cheer; you are the only condiment, you are the glorious one, the sovereign extract of the earth! (1)

There is not, then, such a great distance between the magical and fantastic realms of meta-garlic as explored earlier, and the more basic and earthy realms of *meat-a-garlic*, as it were.

In 1959, Professor Irving Lonaker wrote his book *The Green Thumb of Thales*. Although this manuscript has never been published, I quote with permission from the author a passage praising garlic as a culinary delight:

> Garlic is to Cuisine what Magic is to Science—a fundamental but bizarre twist, so full of mysterious meaning as to defy elucidation and thus pique the over-sensitive palates of scientists and connoisseurs alike. Therefore, it is left up to the fringe elements in both the Natural Sciences and the Culinary Sciences to attempt the coup necessary to bring the bizarre, the shunned, the shadowy secrets into the light of day, where they belong. For

what would life be without magic or garlic, or the Magic *of* Garlic in this case . . .(2)

As we turn now to matters of cuisine, we will hold in the back of our minds that garlic is, as I have tried to show, more than a food, and that there is really no "correct" way of using garlic; nor are there absolute amounts of garlic to be used in the kitchen. Garlic is a personal experience. The following recipes and techniques come out of a tradition of garlic cuisine that may not necessarily represent your interest in garlic. I hope however, that you will try them and I will welcome any comments or suggestions you may have

GARLIC CUISINE IN HISTORY

Historically, garlic holds a special place in the cuisine of France, Italy, Spain, Greece, the Orient and Middle East, and the Slavic and Balkan countries. Michael Fields tells us that in the south of France (Provence), garlic is more often than not the *indispensable* ingredient (3). Italy is perhaps overrated as a garlic-eating country, and Spain is underrated. As we have seen, England, and until recently the U.S., have turned up their noses at the powerful garlic.

As early as 600 B.C. garlic was an important ingredient in Chinese cooking. The earliest surviving Chinese text is the *Shih Ching* or *The Book of Songs*. This collection of ballads, collected around 600 B.C., describes the life of the warrior-farmers of the northwestern highlands of Shensi. A spring expiation rite, held after the fields had been plowed, called for the sacrifice of a lamb which had been seasoned with garlic before being cooked over an open fire.

High we load the stands,
The stands of wood and earthenware.
As soon as the smell rises

God on high is very pleased:
'What smell is this, so strong and good?' (4)

The smell "so strong and good" is Garlic, of course.

In the 10th century, the Persians were avid garlic-eaters. From the verse of Ibn al-Mu'tazz, we hear a description of a tray of hors d'oeuvres at a banquet given by a 10th-century caliph:

> Here capers grace a sauce vermilion
> Whose fragrant odors to the soul are blown,
> Here pungent garlic meets the eager sight
> And whets with Savor sharp the appetite . . . (5)

Coming into the modern era, garlic has found traditional use in many recipes—especially in sauces, the perfect medium for garlic. One of the first sauce makers, the Roman, Apicius, was famous for his sauces flavored with wine, caraway, green coriander, pepper, raisin juice, and garlic. Provence has elevated the garlic sauce to the level of an art: aïoli, pistou, rouille. Variations on these can be found in the cooking of Spain, Italy, and Greece.

The Pungent Crescent

On a trip to Europe in 1978, the author made his way down the "pungent crescent," that Mediterranean arc that connects Spain, France, Italy and Greece. This was indeed the land of garlic, but surprisingly, not as garlicky as one might expect. Afterall, in the lands of the pungent crescent, no more attention is paid to garlic than a Floridian or Californian might pay to an orange. Where garlic has been used for centuries, it is almost taken for granted. Of course there are annual garlic festivals, but not the garlic mania so evident in America. It was exciting to see braids of garlic hung not only in food shops, but in travel agencies, doorways to homes, wherever. Garlic was most visible in Greece, as well as most evident in the food (many restaurants in Greece had tzatziki and skordalia, both garlic-rich appetizers—see pages 238 and 271). Garlic seemed least evident in Italy, American assumptions notwithstanding. One famous restaurateur in Venice told the author that Italians don't really like garlic because "they smell bad enough without it." Of course there are areas of Italy where garlic is bountiful (Piedmont and the Mediterranean seashore).

GARLIC TECHNIQUE

There are many techniques in using garlic, and each method of adding garlic to other ingredients will determine how much or how little, how strong or how mild the garlic flavor will be. *Quantity is not the key factor.* You can add forty whole cloves of garlic to a chicken or turkey stuffing, and the flavor of the meat and of the garlics will be less "garlicky" than if the juice of five or ten garlics was pressed into the same stuffing. In other words, what you *do* to garlic is what you *get* from garlic. If you leave the clove whole and cook it slowly, it will have a mild and nutty flavor with a consistency more resembling a baked potato. This is because, as I have said, the heat has destroyed the enzyme in garlic that creates the odoriferous compound diallyl disulphide. If you press or pound garlic in a mortar, you will bring out the stronger, more pungent flavor. The sulphur compounds in garlic create the characteristic garlic taste when the cell membranes are broken, releasing the sulphides that oxidize on contact with oxygen. The more violently one breaks down these tissues in the garlic clove, the more violent this chemical reaction, and the more "violent" the garlic taste.

So garlic can be mashed, pounded, pressed, diced, sliced, minced, powdered, granulated, or left whole. The powdered and granulated garlic available in markets is not to be used by anyone truly interested in the flavor of garlic, or in the food value of garlic (including the medicinal properties). In the processes used to reduce garlic to a powder or granule, the essential oils in garlic are often heated, and much of the value of garlic is thus lost. Some processes freeze-dry the garlic before powdering and thus heat is not used; but from the standpoint of flavor, the commercial forms of garlic,

225

including some rather dreadful sauces available in specialty markets, are not what garlic should be.

From the Garlic Press

Originally designed for pharmacological purposes, the garlic press has the advantage of yielding the oils and "meat" of garlic while retaining the pulp. It is this pulp that can be responsible for the mild form of indigestion some people feel after a garlicky repast. I have also found that if you press the unpeeled clove (as it comes off the bulb), the heavier outer skins will prevent the lighter pulp from clogging the small holes of the press. To clean the press, which can be tedious, you need only pull out the skin and rinse with hot water. This avoids the labor of poking at the holes.

To Separate the Head

One method is to hold the garlic bulb with one hand at an angle and hit the top with your other hand or a rolling pin. This however seems a bit dangerous. If a head is fairly dry, you can usually get a thumbnail behind a clove, and pry it out. The others will follow more easily. My method is to use an old potato press I found at the flea market; it looks like a giant garlic press, and the whole bulb can be placed inside. This device renders the bulb very easily into its constituent parts if you make sure before pressing that the vertical axis of the bulb is in a vertical position—that is, the root-end down and the stem-end up. Otherwise, you can smash the bulb down on a wooden surface.

To Peel a Clove

You can place the flat side of a heavy knife over a clove and bring your fist down hard on the blade. This will separate the skin from the naked clove, but at the same time break up the clove itself. This is fine if you are going to pound, press, or mince the clove. To get the skin off without injuring the clove, you can carefully strip off the skin beginning at the rough root-end. The thumbnail can get the skin loose and then it's a matter of stripping the garlic. You can also drop the cloves in a pan of boiling water and leave for 5-10 seconds. This softens and loosens the skins but it also cooks out some of the garlic's potency.

One need not always take the outer skins off the clove. If you add the unskinned cloves to a hot pan, the clove will cook rapidly without burning. Once soft, the darkened outer skins can be easily removed. Many recipes call for the discarding of the clove after it has completed its aromatic job. In stews and soups then, one need not peel the clove if it's going to be discarded anyway; often, after prolonged cooking, the skin will fall off the clove. I personally feel that to throw out the garlic meat is a high crime and mis-demeanor, worthy of instantaneous impeachment from the office of Chef.

VARIETIES OF GARLIC (from Jack Kakis' pamphlet)

Garlic (Allium Sativum) has a great number of varieties and strains. Some researchers claim over three hundred of them grown all over the world.

Most of the varieties are identified by local names in each country. The most common varieties grown commercially usually have some relation with the following groups:

LATE GARLIC is the most valued commercially for its long keeping qualities, the firm bulbs and the strong flavor. Late garlic can be distin-guished from all the other varieties by the narrow, upright, dark green leaves, the white sheathing surrounding the cloves. The color of the cloves varies from light pink to deep red. Late garlic matures in approximately eight months from the time of planting. It can be grown only within a relatively small range in latitude and climate because the plant is very specific in daylight requirements for bulbing.

EARLY GARLIC has the largest plant of most types. The leaves are broader than the late garlic and light green to pale green in color. Early garlic matures approximately one month sooner than late garlic. It produces bulbs very large in size, rather flat in shape and covered by an off-white sheathing, sometimes with purple veins. Cloves are large, asymmetrically arranged within the bulb and covered with a protective skin which is usually yellowish or yellowish pink in color. Early garlic is relatively easy to grow, and produces the highest average yields of all commercial varieties. Early garlic can be grown on a wider environmental range than late garlic.

CREOLE is a variety of garlic very common in Mexico and South America. The leaves resemble, somewhat, the late garlic but the plant is generally taller and lighter in color. During bulbing, it produces a seed stem which constitutes part of the bulb after harvest. The bulbs are composed of a large assortment of small cloves, at random, arranged within the bulb. Many of the cloves are "doubles," (two storage leaves in one sheathing). The skin covering the cloves is usually dark pink. Creole garlic is grown mostly for the seasonal advantages. It can be grown and produce bulbs in any latitude or climate.

CHILENO TYPE is an improved strain of creole with larger cloves and better-shaped bulbs.

CHILEAN, as the name indicates, is grown in South America. Strains of this type are grown in Japan, Formose, India and Spain. This garlic can be classified as early type because it matures only one to two weeks later than the creole. The plant resembles creole only because it is larger in size. The bulbs are white, flat, resembling a tangerine in shape and clove arrangement. Cloves are more or less even in size with a sharp edge toward the center symmetrically located around the seed stem. The color of the cloves is dark pink to wine. Chilean types, although fast maturing, are very specific in environmental requirements for bulbing.

EGYPTIAN garlic is very tall (over two feet average) and is a fast-maturing type. It produces large, white bulbs containing numerous small elongated cloves protected by white sheathing.

Related Alliums

Garlic's related Alliums are well known: onion, leek, chive, scallion, shallot. But there are some other alliums that resemble garlic very closely but are little known: Elephant Garlic and Rocambole.

ELEPHANT GARLIC (Giant Garlic): Although this allium (A. Ampeloprasm) is more closely related to leek, its flavor and shape resemble garlic. The bulbs and cloves are huge, several times the size of garlic cloves. The flavor is mild and cannot really substitute for the real thing. But, these cloves when sliced into salads, or baked as a vegetable are very tasty in their own right. They can be grown simply, much as you would regular garlic.

ROCAMBOLE (Sand Leek, Spanish Garlic): Rocambole (A Scorodoprasm) is very much like garlic in appearance. It is somewhat smaller and milder in flavor. Its flowers are light purple, not white like garlic's. The flower stalk is topped by a small white bulb which produces purple bulbils which can be planted. For dried flower enthusiasts, rocambole's stalks corkscrew into curlicues and spirals as they mature. When left to develop fully, the flower heads form a little globe of flowers, and after these, the tiny bulbils or bulblets. These can be peeled or left whole and used in soups and stews.

Where to Get Them

For growing garlic, you can use the cloves from your produce sections; use only the largest, most perfect cloves as seed. It is not as easy to get Elephant Garlic and Rocambole cloves. Here are some addresses:

FOR ELEPHANT GARLIC:
> Nichols Nursery, 1190 No. Pacific Hwy., Albany, OR 97321
> Fox Hill Farm, 343 Michigan Ave., Parma, MI 49269
> Yankee Peddler, Route 4, Box 76 Hwy. 36 N, Brenham, TX 77833.
> Metro Myster Farms, Route 1, Box 285, Northhampton, PA 18067.

FOR ROCAMBOLE:
> Le Jardin du Gourmet, West Danville, VT 05873.
> Casa Yerba, Star Rt. 2, Box 21, Days Creek, OR 97429.

GROWING YOUR OWN

In mild winter areas, plant the bulbs from October to December for early summer harvest, and where winters are severe, plant in early spring. Check with a local nursery to determine whether your soil needs nourishment. Garlic needs a loose, rich soil and sand must be added if there is too much clay.

The Procedure: You can use commercial garlic as your seed (clove), or you can send to a seed distributor such as Nichols (address listed under "Varieties of Garlic"). Begin by inserting cloves, point end up, ½ inch below the soil surface. Keep the cloves 4-6 inches apart to ensure large bulbs. Water deeply about once a week along with other vegetables, making sure drainage is good.

The bulb may take up to 9 months or a year before reaching its maximum size, and you will know the garlic is ready when the green leaf tips begin to fall and turn brown. The younger the garlic, the milder the flavor.

Indoor Garlic

You can plant cloves in a pot and grow them indoors in a sunny window box. Insert the cloves in a pot of rich soil, making sure there is an inch between the clove and the pot rim. Sit the pot in a hole in a partly shaded spot in your garden until it sprouts. If the soil looks dry after the first several days, sink the pot in a bowl of sun-warmed water that reaches up to the pot rim. The water will soak up from the bottom. Return to the garden after an hour or so. The garlic shoot will take about 2 weeks to show and at this point bring the pot into the house.

Green Garlic

The spear-like leaves sprouting from the growing bulb are very mild and very good in salads, soups, eggs, or whatever. By cutting the leaf tips from the plant you are directing the bulb energy into producing more leaf. This results in a milder and smaller bulb, if you are so inclined.

Elephant Garlic

This giant garlic is grown in the same way as ordinary garlic. It must be planted further apart (about 10 inches) so that the huge bulbs do not compete. It will tolerate damper climates with minimal sunlight and warmth. Plant in fall or early spring, and as late as May.

Rocambole

Plant in spring or fall if the winters are very mild. Keep cloves 5-6 inches apart, and 1-2 inches below the surface of the soil. Like garlic, rocambole needs sun and good drainage.

All of the above bulbs are ready to harvest when leaves dry out and turn brown. Garlic can take up to a year before fully maturing.

 GARLIC

CHEZ·PANISSE·GARLIC·FESTIVAL
JULY·12·16·1977
1517 SHATTUCK BERKELEY
548·5525

ABOVE: From the poster by David Lance Goines. RIGHT: Menu design and printing by Wesley Tanner. Both artists have worked closely with Alice Waters of Chez Panisse to create a festive but classy image for the Garlic Festival.

Garlic Frenzy!!!

Thursday Lunch $7.00. Choice of:
Aioli with Fish and Vegetables
Garlic Soup *and* Garlic Salad
Real Pasta Pesto *and* Garlic Tomato Salad

Thursday Dinner $20.00. With Cajun Music
Garlic Soufflé
"Lovers of the Stinking Rose" Salad
Garlic Beef Birds on Brochette
Fresh Fruits & Chocolate-covered Garlic Cloves

Friday Lunch $7.00. Choice of:
Whole-baked Garlic *and* Garlic Salad
Garlic Crepinettes with Garlic Potatoes
Hunan Garlic Chicken Salad

Friday Dinner $20.00. With Mandolin Music
Deep-fried Garlic Cheese
Pistou
Spit-roasted Garlic-stuffed Squab

Saturday Brunch $10.00. Comprised of:
Tomato Cocktail · Garlic Brioche
Grilled Garlic Sausages · Garlic Eggs
Orange Compote with candied Lemon
rind and Garlic

Saturday Dinner $20.00. Bastille Day
With French Folk Music
Grand Aioli
Charcoal-grilled Fish with Catalan Garlic Sauce
Chicken stuffed with Garlic and baked in a crust
Fresh Fruits & Chocolate-covered Garlic Cloves

July 12, 13 & 14, 1979

4th Annual Garlic Festival
Chez Panisse: Berkeley

THE RECIPES

The following recipes are divided into two sections. The first is a revised and expanded section from the original edition. New recipes have been added and a few old ones taken out. The second section is a *Garlic Times* Recipe Supplement. These recipes were first published in the third issue of *Garlic Times*.

Altogether, the recipes represent a wide expression of garlic cooking. Corrections, suggestions and new recipes will be gratefully received by Lovers of the Stinking Rose. If your recipe is published in *Garlic Times*, you'll receive a free subscription (five issues). LSR will also be sponsoring garlic recipe contests, and information will be forthcoming in *Garlic Times*. See the copyright page for the LSR address.

GARLICKED GARLIC

There are a number of recipes that treat garlic as it should be treated—as a *vegetable* and not merely a spice, herb, seasoning or flavoring. One eats onions baked, boiled, sautéed, broiled. Why not, then, garlic? The volatility of the garlic is, as I've said, mellowed with prolonged and moderate cooking, rendering the clove mild and even sweet. The following few recipes will surprise you if you have never experienced the pleasures of *ail seule* (garlic alone).

Roasted Garlic

10-12 large cloves	1 tbl. olive oil
2 tbl. butter	Salt to taste
1 tbl. peanut oil	Pinch of white pepper

Heat the butter, peanut oil and olive oil together in a casserole over medium heat. Put in peeled cloves, side by side, and make sure they are well coated with the fat. Bake in a 350° oven for about 20 minutes, basting from time to time. Add salt and pepper. One can also wrap the individual cloves in tin foil with a dab of butter and bake them. Serve as appetizer with toast or as vegetable side dish.

Poached Garlic with Butter

Place peeled or unpeeled garlics in gently boiling water. Let them simmer until soft, testing one with a fork. When soft, strain off the water and put butter (about a tablespoon for five cloves) and garlics into a warm pan. You can serve the cloves with the melted butter or you can sauté them until they are lightly browned. Add salt and pepper to taste. Spread the softened garlics on toast or French bread or serve as a side dish with meat, fish or fowl. I put the cloves in boiling water before adding eggs for poaching. By the time the eggs are done, the garlics are soft and can be spread on toast under the eggs. A great morning lift!

Charcoal-Roasted Whole Garlic

This is a Middle Eastern specialty. Whole bulbs of garlic are placed directly in the coals of a hot but not flaming fire. When the cloves are lightly browned and tender, it's ready. You can baste the heads with oil, salt and pepper or marinate the heads beforehand. Allow the bulbs to cool, then break off cloves. The meat can be easily pushed out of the darkened and hardened skins. Serve with any meat entrée.

Halved Heads of Garlic in Sauce

This is a delicious side dish with chicken. The whole heads of garlic must be large and very firm. Otherwise, when cutting them in half, they may fall apart. For smaller heads of garlic, just cut about ¼ inch off the root end; this will give you a surface to sauté, and will keep the bulbs intact.

4 heads garlic	1 cup white wine
1 tbl. olive oil	Pinch herbs (esp. thyme)
2 tbl. butter	Salt and pepper to taste
1 cup chicken stock	

Cut the four heads of garlic in half, as you would a grapefruit. The cut cloves will be held in their skins much as grapefruit segments are held together. Heat the oil and butter in a saucepan and sauté the bulbs cut side down over moderate heat until garlic meat begins to brown. Now add the chicken stock, wine and herbs. Cover the pan with a tight lid and braise over low heat until liquid is reduced and thickened and the garlic cloves are soft when poked with a knife. If sauce is reduced before cloves are tender, you can add more stock and wine.

To serve, place halved heads cut side up on a plate, and spoon some of the stock over each. This sauce can also be used over the chicken pieces. Eat the garlic like an artichoke, using your teeth and lips to pull the purée out of the skins. Serves 4.

Garlic Purée

2 dozen garlic cloves, or more
1 tbl. olive oil, or more
Pinch salt and pepper
Pinch herbs of choice (opt.)

Place whole, unpeeled cloves in a pot of boiling water for about 20 minutes or until clove meat is very soft when a knife is inserted. Drain and cool. When cool, remove skins and place cloves in a food processor or blender. Purée, adding salt, pepper, herbs and olive oil. Fill a glass jar, refrigerate.

Use this purée to thicken and flavor sauces, soups, stews, dressings and dips. Spread on croutons and serve with soups and salads. It can also be a sandwich spread for leftover meats.

Korean Pickled Garlic

1 quart unpeeled garlic cloves
1 cup vinegar
4 cups soy sauce
⅔ cup sugar

Place garlic in a jar, add the vinegar and enough water to cover the garlic. The cloves must be fully covered and not floating on the top. Close the jar and let stand for one week, then drain.

Boil the soy sauce and sugar for 10 minutes, then set aside to cool. When cool, pour over the garlic and seal the jar. The garlic will be ready to eat in three weeks, and it will keep indefinitely. To serve, bite or cut the tips from the cloves, and suck out the meat. If skins are tender, you can eat the whole thing. The younger the garlic, the more tender the skins.

GARLIC SAUCES

The classic garlic sauce is the French aïoli, which is a garlic mayonnaise made with olive oil, egg yolks, lemon juice or vinegar and, in some recipes, bread crumbs. In Spain this same sauce is called *ali-oli*. Aïoli may have come from the Greeks who have a very similar sauce called Skordalia, made with bread crumbs, garlic, lemon juice, oil, mashed potatoes or almonds and walnuts.

These sauces can be eaten with almost any meat, vegetable or soup. A meal based around aïoli can feature boiled potatoes, hot or cold cooked green beans, artichokes, cauliflower, broccoli; cold cooked shrimp and lobster; hot or cold poached halibut or other white fish; hard-boiled eggs; raw fennel, cherry tomatoes, mushrooms, turnips, zucchini and green peppers.

Another uncooked garlic sauce is called pistou in Provence and pesto in Genoa. This is a paste of garlic, basil, cheese, and olive oil. The only difference is that the French pistou does not have crushed pignolia nuts or walnuts which are added to pesto. The pistou is usually stirred into a vegetable-bean soup, whereas in Italy pesto is almost always used as a sauce for pasta.

Aïoli

4 large cloves	2 tbl. lemon juice
3 raw egg yolks	1-2 tbl. water or additional
½-1 tsp. salt, or to taste	lemon juice
2 cups olive oil	

Optional: pepper to taste, Dijon mustard, or vinegar as a substitute for lemon juice.

Although this sauce can be made in a blender for speed, it is better if it is made in the traditional manner with a mortar and pestle.

Peel the garlic and pound in a mortar until smooth. Add egg yolks and seasoning. Continue pounding until the paste is smooth. Then, beat in lemon juice or vinegar with a whisk. Start adding oil a drop at a time while continuing to pound. If you use a blender, whirl the garlic, lemon juice and egg yolks for about a minute until smooth and then add oil drops while blender is still on high. Using the blender may over-liquefy the aïoli, but it can be helpful if time is short (a hurried late-night urge for aïoli).

If the sauce gets too thick, add water, lemon juice or vinegar to correct the consistency. Never add more oil than can be immediately absorbed—no pools of oil. The main thing is to get the right consistency for this mayonnaise. There are many different recipes, some calling for more or less egg yolk, oil, lemon juice or vinegar. You can find your favorite aïoli by trying different ways.

This recipe makes about 3 cups. Serve with fish, meat and vegetables. Aïoli makes party dips taste as terrible and artificial as they really are. The sauce will keep about four days in the refrigerator.

Skordalia with Almonds

3 cups aïoli
¼ cup fresh white bread crumbs
   (French or Italian bread)
¼ cup blanched almonds, ground

Fresh lemon juice
3 tbl. finely chopped parsley
Salt to taste
Pinch cayenne pepper

Stir the bread crumbs, almonds and parsley into the aïoli in a glass bowl. Season with salt and cayenne to taste. Add as much lemon juice as tastes good to you.

Makes about 1¼ cups. Serve with a platter of cold vegetables, black Mediterranean olives, and black or white radishes. This sauce will keep a few days in the refrigerator.

Skordalia with Potatoes

1 pound baking potatoes
2 tbls. finely chopped
   garlic
1 tsp. salt

Fresh ground black pepper
2 egg yolks
½ - ¾ cups olive oil
2 tbl. fresh, strained lemon juice

Peel and cut potatoes into 2-inch pieces (about 2 cups). Drop potatoes into 3 quarts of rapidly boiling salted water and boil uncovered until they can be pierced easily with the tip of a knife. Drain and return to pan over a moderate fire until potatoes are dry. Mash them to a smooth purée and keep warm.

Pound garlic and salt to a smooth paste with a mortar or use a heavy bowl and wooden implement. Then beat the paste into the warm potatoes and, still beating, add the egg yolks one at a time.

Beating constantly, slowly pour in the oil, adding as much as you need to make a smooth dense mixture. Stir in the lemon juice and black pepper. Taste for seasoning and add more lemon juice if desired.

Makes about 1 cup. Serve like aïoli or Skordalia (with almonds), with fried vegetables (such as eggplant), or with poached or fried fish.

Rouille

Rouille is a hot garlic sauce that is served with French fish soups such as bouillabaisse or bourride. Michael Fields in *All Manner of Food* explains that the red pepper in rouille is known as *piment enragé* or "enraged pepper", so use with caution.

½ cup fresh bread crumbs (packed firm)	2 tsp. dried hot red pepper flakes
¼ cup cold water	½ tsp. salt
10 cloves garlic, finely chopped chopped	6 tbl. olive oil

Soak the bread crumbs in water for several minutes and then squeeze dry. Pound the garlic, pepper flakes and salt to a fine paste. Add the bread crumbs and pound slowly; when they are well incorporated, stir and pound in the olive oil, a tablespoon at a time. Use as much oil as is needed to make a smooth paste. This paste should almost hold its own shape in a spoon.

Serve with fish soups.

Lamb Sauce

This sauce is used with roast lamb and it incorporates the juices left in the lamb's roasting pan. I have not included a recipe for the roast lamb; I suggest you use your favorite recipe and simply add this sauce to it.

1 large head of garlic	⅛ tsp. rosemary or thyme
1 quart cold water	1½ tbl. raw white rice
¾ cup milk	1 cup lamb or beef stock or canned
Salt and pepper to taste	beef broth

Separate bulb and bring cloves to boil for 30 seconds. Drain and peel. Set again in cold water, bring to boil and drain.

In a sauce pan bring the milk, salt, herbs, and rice to a simmer. Add garlic and simmer very slowly for 45 minutes, adding more milk by spoonfuls if rice is about to scorch.

Pour in the stock and simmer 1 minute. Then force through sieve, or purée in electric blender. Correct seasoning to taste.

After roasting the lamb, deglaze the pan with 2 or 3 tablespoons of stock or water, scraping up coagulated juices. Strain into the hot garlic sauce and serve in a gravy boat.

Garlic and Sesame Sauce

4-6 medium garlic cloves, peeled and finely chopped	¾ to 1 cup cold water
1 cup tahina paste (ground, hulled sesame seeds)	½ cup fresh lemon juice
	1 tsp. salt

In a deep bowl, mash the garlic to a paste with a pestle or the back of a large spoon. Stir in the tahina. Then, with a whisk or spoon, beat in ½ cup of the cold water, the lemon juice and salt. Still beating, add up to ½ cup more of water, a tablespoon at a time, until the sauce has the consistency of thick mayonnaise and holds its shape almost solidly in a spoon. Taste for seasoning.

You can also use a blender with the tahina, water and lemon juice placed in first, and the garlic and salt added last. This recipe yields about 1½ cups and it is served over baked fish or cooked vegetables. You can also serve it as a dip with peta (Arab style) bread.

PASTA

Garlic sauces go nowhere better than on top of *fresh* pasta. With pasta, the sauce becomes totally incorporated into the dish—the pasta serving almost as a binding for the creamy garlic paste.

Fancy Pesto Genovese

1 cup fresh basil leaves, washed and dry
4 spinach leaves
6 sprigs parsley
3 sprigs marjoram
½ cup pine nuts

4 cloves garlic, crushed
¾ cup parmesan cheese or ⅓ cup parmesan and ⅓ cup romano or pecorino
½ cup olive oil
¼ tsp. salt

Blend these ingredients in an electric blender, adding the oil a little bit at a time. Serve over hot fresh pasta.

Pasta with Garlic, Butter and Cheese

A very simple and very delicious sauce for pasta is made with butter and garlic. Melt butter in a sauce pan and add 4 to 6 cloves of garlic that have been mashed until transparent. Simmer softly for 2 or 3 minutes without letting butter brown. Pour over hot pasta and grate fresh parmesan cheese on top. At restaurants you can ask for this sauce instead of the standard tomato sauces.

SOUPS

Garlic soup is a pleasant surprise for those who love onion soup and for those who cannot conceive of a soup made of large quantities of garlic. The gently boiling soup stock is a fine medium for garlic, rendering the cloves soft and mild.

Soupe à l'Ail

½ cup peeled garlic cloves
2 tbl. butter
4 tbl. olive oil
4 cups chicken stock, fresh or canned
3 egg yolks

1 tbl. finely chopped fresh parsley
½ tsp. salt
⅛ tsp. cayenne
A few gratings of whole nutmeg
6 slices of French bread (½″ thick)

Peel garlic cloves without cutting the surface. You can blanch them first in boiling water for a minute. Cool and peel. Over low heat, melt the 2 tablespoons of butter with 1 tablespoon of olive oil in a 2-quart sauce pan. Drop in the garlic and cook for about 15 minutes, turning the garlics often so they do not brown. Pour in chicken stock, raise heat, and bring to a boil. Then, half cover the pan and lower the heat to simmer the soup for about 20 minutes.

In a small bowl, beat the egg yolks with a whisk or rotary beater for about 2 or 3 minutes or until they thicken. Add remaining 3 tablespoons of olive oil, ½ teaspoon at a time, beating until the mixture becomes a thick mayonnaise.

Now, slowly stir into the mayonnaise 2 or 3 tablespoons of the soup, and return this mixture in a slow stream to the rest of the soup, stirring continuously. Heat almost to the boil, then pour the entire contents of the sauce pan, garlic and all, into a sieve set over a heated tureen. With the back of a wooden spoon rub and mash the garlic through the sieve into the soup and briskly stir in the salt, cayenne, and nutmeg. Continue to stir until the garlic purée and the soup are totally blended. Pour into soup plates over rounds of bread or toast and sprinkle with parsley.

I like to save some of the softened garlics to add whole to the soup. They add visual and tactile interest to the soup, and they taste like . . . garlic (although a very mild variety).

Bourride

This fish soup is made with aïoli and is a staple dish in Provence. The variations are innumerable.

3 pounds white fish (halibut, haddock or cod)	2 stalks parsley
	Salt to taste
Fish bones if available	4 or 5 cups water
3 medium onions	White pepper to taste
1 bay leaf	Aïoli, about 1 cup
1 tsp. thyme	3 cups heavy cream
5-6 pepper corns	15-20 slices French bread oven-dried

First, cut the fish into large bite-sized pieces and set aside. Then combine the fish bones, onions (chopped fine), bay leaf, thyme, pepper corns, parsley, and about 1 tablespoon of salt in a large, heavy casserole with a cover. Add 4 or 5 cups boiling water. Bring this to a boil, reduce heat and simmer for 25 to 30 minutes. Strain.

Now, rinse out the casserole and add the fish and the strained broth. Add more boiling water if broth does not cover fish. Bring to a boil, reduce heat to simmer and cook 10 to 12 minutes. Lift the fish into a heated soup tureen, cover, and keep warm in a low oven.

Measure out about 3 or 4 cups of the broth. If there is more you can reduce the fluid over high heat. Now mix in the aïoli with the broth, stirring constantly. Place over moderate heat and bring almost to a boil. Taste for seasoning, adding salt, pepper and a little lemon juice if desired.

Pour mixture over the fish in the tureen and sprinkle with parsley. Serve over the bread in a soup plate.

Puerto Rican Garlic and Egg Soup

3 tbl. olive oil	6 slices toast
6 cloves garlic	6 eggs
6 cups chicken broth	

Fry the garlic in oil and when golden brown remove from the oil. Add the broth to the oil and bring to boil, reduce to simmer. Poach eggs in the broth and oil and serve with broth over toast.

La Vieille Maison Soup

4-6 cloves garlic, minced	1 raw egg per serving
6 large onions, finely chopped	6 oz. grated Swiss cheese
4 oz. butter	6 oz. whipping cream
1 tsp. flour	Salt and pepper to taste
1 quart chicken stock	Pinch thyme
1 pint dry white wine	

This soup was first served in honor of Lovers of the Stinking Rose at Robert and Amora Charles' Truckee, CA garlic restaurant.

Fry onions and garlic in butter over low heat until they begin to brown. Add flour and fry until well coated. Add spices and wine, bring to a boil and continue cooking 30 minutes. Add the stock and bring to a boil. Continue cooking in a 350° oven for an hour in an oven-proof casserole.

244

Use a small oven-proof casserole for each serving. Beat an egg into each serving of soup and sprinkle grated cheese on top. Bake for 10 minutes in a 350° oven. When ready to serve, add 1 oz. cream to each serving. Serves 4-6.

FOWL

Forty-clove Chicken—Hermetically Sealed

There are many chicken dishes that call for 40 or more cloves of garlic. The garlic can be stuffed into the whole bird with other ingredients. Don't let the amount of garlic scare you; the garlic, after prolonged cooking has a mild, nutty flavor, and thus these chicken recipes are known as "pistaches" in France.

½ cup olive oil	1 two-pound chicken or capon
4 stalks celery	40 cloves garlic
1 tbl. tarragon	¼ cup cognac
Salt	¾ cup flour
Fresh ground pepper	Water
Nutmeg, freshly grated	Fried toast

Preheat oven to 375°. Pour olive oil into large casserole. To oil add celery which has been cut into thin strips, parsley, and tarragon. Sprinkle salt and pepper and nutmeg over chicken which has been cut into quarters. Add chicken to oil and vegetable mixture, turning to coat the pieces thoroughly. Add garlic, cognac, and ½ teaspoon salt.

Add to flour enough water to make stiff paste. Cover the casserole with the lid and make a hermetic seal by spreading flour and water paste on edges of lid and casserole. Completely cover top with aluminum foil. Bake the casserole for 1½ hours at 375°. Do not remove the top until ready to serve at the table. Serve with fried toast on which the garlic sauce can be spread. Serves 4.

CHARLES PERRY'S
Franco-Syrian Chicken

1 2½-3 pound frying chicken
4-5 cloves garlic
2 large lemons
1 cup dry white wine
2 tbl. oil or clarified butter

¼ cup pignoli (pine nuts)
1 tsp. salt
¼ tsp. pepper
½ tsp. minced parsley

Cut the chicken into frying pieces (wings, legs, thighs, deboned breast cut in quarters). Remove the fat and the skin. Squeeze 3 large garlic cloves onto the chicken pieces and rub them with the garlic all over. Let stand 10 minutes.

Squeeze one lemon onto the chicken pieces and marinate the chicken in garlic and lemon for another 20 minutes, stirring once or twice.

Scrape the garlic purée off the chicken and pat dry with a towel. Fry the pieces in the oil over a hot fire until the meat browns. Add the cup of wine and the marinade and simmer covered over low heat for 25 minutes.

Meantime, brown the pine nuts. Either put them in a 350° oven for about 20 minutes until they are evenly beige, or fry them in a little oil or butter over a very low heat, stirring constantly until light brown.

When the chicken is done, remove the pieces and sprinkle with parsley. Keep warm. Add the juice of the second lemon and one or two more squeezed garlic cloves and reduce the pan juices over highest heat for 5 minutes. Season with the salt and pepper and add the pine nuts. Serve the chicken with this gravy. Serve with French bread and cherry tomatoes.

As a variation, you can thicken the sauce with ground-up pine nuts. Serves 4.

Kelly's Asian Chicken

This recipe by Kelly Greene won top prize at the First Gilroy Garlic Festival.

1 frying chicken (3-3½ lbs.)
2-3 tbl. peanut oil
1 head garlic, peeled and
    coarsely chopped
¼ cup soy sauce

1 or 2 small dried hot
    red chili peppers (opt.)
½ cup white vinegar
3 tbl. honey
1 pound Chinese noodles

Cut the chicken into serving pieces and brown in the peanut oil in a wok or large, heavy skillet. Add the garlic and the peppers as the chicken becomes nearly brown. Then add the remaining ingredients except for the noodles. Keep cooking the chicken over high heat until it is done, about 10 minutes. There should be a few spoonfuls of sauce left to glaze the chicken and moisten the noodles.

While the chicken is cooking, plunge the noodles into boiling water until they are tender, about 3 minutes if they are fresh, 8 to 10 minutes if they are dried. Drain them well. Serve the chicken over the noodles. Serves 6-8.

FISH

Bacalao

1 whole dry codfish
3 tbl. olive oil
1 large onion, chopped
1 can pimentos

2½ lb. can Italian plum tomatoes
    (3½ cups)
3 tsp. minced Italian herbs
10 cloves garlic, chopped

Get a whole cod fish from an Italian grocer and soak in water in the refrigerator for 24 hours. Change water 5 or 6 times. Heat oil in dutch oven, add garlic and onion, and cook slowly until transparent. Add tomatoes and herbs and simmer while preparing the fish. Remove skin, fins, and backbone. Cut into serving-sized pieces. Add fish to the sauce and simmer covered for 1½ hours. Potatoes may be added for the last ½ hour of cooking. Serves 8.

Garlic Shrimp (Gambas al Ajilla)

2 pounds small shrimp	2 tbl. parsley, chopped
7 garlic cloves	½ cup olive oil

Clean shrimp and mix with 5 crushed cloves of garlic and parsley; set aside to marinate for 5-6 hours. Heat olive oil and add other cloves and shrimp mixture. Stir and cook from 3-7 minutes until shrimp are pink. Check for salt and pepper.

MEAT

Anne's Veal Shanks with Garlic

Third prize at the First Gilroy Garlic Festival went to Anne Epstein of North Hollywood, California for her veal dish.

3 hind leg veal shanks, cut into 3 or 4 1-inch pieces each	2-3 cups brown veal stock, chicken broth or beef broth, enough to cover the meat
½ cup vegetable oil	Salt, pepper
3 large onions, thickly sliced	4 heads garlic, separated and peeled
1 or 2 large carrots, thickly sliced	Chopped parsely for garnish
Bouquet garni (see note)	French bread, sliced and toasted
1 cup dry white wine	

Brown the veal shanks in the hot oil in a large braising pot. Remove the meat from the pot. Add the onions, carrots and bouquet garni (note: this is a bundle of celery, thyme and parsley that is removed from the dish before serving). Sauté the vegetables until they are browned and softened. Drain as much of the oil as possible. Heat the oven to 325°.

Spread the vegetables into a layer at the bottom of the pan. Arrange the veal shanks on top. Add the wine and let it boil away, but take care not to burn the meat or vegetables. Add the broth, bring it to a boil and add the garlic cloves. It is all right to smash the garlic cloves lightly to make them easier to peel. Cover the pot, place it in the oven and let it bake for 1½ hours or until the veal is fork-tender.

Drain the liquid and measure it. There should be 2 cups. If there is more, reduce the liquid over high heat. The vegetables may be puréed and added to the sauce to thicken it. Place the meat on a pretty platter and garnish it with chopped parsley. Serve the garlic cloves separately in a small bowl with a knife for spreading them on the toasted French bread slices.

Because of the lengthy cooking time, the garlic loses much of its pungency and becomes sweet, rich and buttery. Serve it with a robust red wine. Serves 6.

Garlic-Crusted Lamb

A five- or six-pound leg of lamb	1 tsp. salt
2 slices bacon, chopped	1 tsp. paprika
2 tbl. butter, softened	Fresh ground pepper
3 to 10 sprigs parsley, chopped	1 tbl. vinegar
6 cloves garlic, finely chopped	

Score the surface of the lamb, cutting ⅛ to ¼ inch deep in diagonal lines about an inch apart. Mix together all ingredients into a smooth paste. At least an hour before roasting the lamb, rub the paste into the scored slits and over the entire leg. Place on a rack in a roasting pan and roast in a preheated 325° oven for 12 to 15 minutes per pound or until meat thermometer reads 125° to 130° for pink.

Pork Kabobs

This is a simple variation of Shish Kebob. Marinate for several hours chunks of pork (from the shoulder) in soy sauce, vinegar, beer, chopped garlic, a tablespoon of brown sugar, oil, salt and pepper (determine amounts according to your taste). Add other spices—perhaps ginger or thyme. Then place meat and vegetables on a skewer and roast over charcoal. You can use mushrooms, green peppers, onions or whatever you like. I place unpeeled garlic cloves next to each chunk of meat. While the kebobs are roasting you should brush on the marinade to prevent the meat and vegetables from drying out.

Symiotic Keftedes

Keftedes are Turkish meatballs. The following recipe comes from Daniel Spoerri's book, *The Mythological Travels,* in which he describes his day-to-day existence on the small island of Symi in the Aegean Sea, an existence which revolved primarily around the local cuisine. Describing the use of garlic in this area, Spoerri notes:

> City dwellers would turn up their noses at us, because little by little our Gallic way of life is giving way to the Garlic way of life (p. 162).

Spoerri says of Greek cooking:

> Garlic is widely used in all Greek cooking, and they say that if you swallow a clove of garlic before eating a very garlicky dish you avoid bad breath . . . and there are those who firmly believe this. Try it at your next opportunity. Kosta Theos, our Landlord, the Son of God, claims that a few garlic cloves pricked with a needle and eaten raw is the best cure for "the runs". Proof of the very frequent use of garlic is that some Greeks call a mortar a skordostoupi or garlic-crusher.

1 pound ground beef
3 medium-sized onions, chopped
A sprig of mint
4 or 5 tomatoes, or medium can
    of purée

1 head of garlic, crushed
Salt and pepper
2 tbl. flour
2 eggs

Mix and knead all ingredients (adding the flour and eggs gradually) for 10 minutes. When this mixture is stiff, make small balls the size of a walnut and fry them in oil.

Garlic Sausages

This recipe is one of my favorites and it has been given to me by the nice ladies at a Berkeley "charcuterie" or French delicatessen. Their shop, *Pig-by-the-Tail,* offers the finest home-made French delicacies I have ever tasted (or seen).

The pork sausage is a fine medium for garlic. The ground meat and garlic is held together by a hog casing and gently simmered or boiled. Thus the meat and garlic paste become totally amalgamated into one tasty essence. If you have never made sausages from scratch, I recommend it as a truly "primal" experience.

2 pounds pork butt
½ pound pork fat
⅓ pound ham and ham fat
8-10 medium garlic cloves, peeled
1 tsp. white pepper
2 tbl. sage

1 pinch cayenne
2 tsp. black pepper
2 tsp. "quatre epices" (1 part nutmeg,
    cloves, ginger and 7 parts white
    pepper)
2 tbl. salt

Grind the pork butt, pork fat, ham and garlic on the large grind of a meat grinder. Place ground meat in a bowl and add spices, mixing thoroughly. You can sauté a small quantity of the mixture and taste for seasoning. You may want to add more spices, salt, pepper or garlic.

251

Next comes the nitty-gritty—stuffing the mixture into hog casing which you can get from your butcher. These casings are made from the intestines of hogs and must be kept in water or they will dry out. Take about 2 feet of the casings and tie a knot at one end. Slip the other end over the spout of a large funnel (½-inch spout), pushing the rest of the casing up onto the spout until you reach the knotted end. Now, place a large handful of the meat mixture into the cone and start pressing it down through the spout, using your fingers to get meat firmly through the spout into the casing. The meat will expand the casing to about ¾ of an inch thick, and the pressure of the meat will pull casing down off the spout as needed. Be sure not to tear the casing. If it should tear, you must tie another knot and start again.

Once you have stuffed all the meat into about 2 feet of casing, tie the other end and braid the sausages. This is done by carefully pinching the sausage at about 4- or 5-inch intervals and twisting to form each individual sausage. This recipe makes about six 4-inch sausages.

You can sauté the sausages over low heat with a little butter for 15 to 20 minutes, or poach in simmering liquid. You may grill them as well. Serve with cold beer.

VEGETABLES, GRAINS, POTATOES

FROM LES BLANK
Dottie's Spinach

2 pounds fresh spinach, steamed and chopped	¾ pound cheddar cheese, grated
2 white onions, diced	Bread crumbs
1 large head of garlic, minced or pressed	Cayenne pepper
	¼ pound butter

Melt the butter in a large frying pan. Cook the onions in the butter until transparent, but not brown. Add the garlic and cayenne pepper to taste. Add the spinach. Mix well and cook for five minutes. Add the grated cheese and when melted, put the mixture in a greased casserole. Cover the top with bread crumbs, dot with pieces of butter and bake at 350° for 30 to 40 minutes. Serves 6.

Onions Stuffed with Garlic

6 large onions	Salt and pepper
6 cloves garlic	Buttered bread crumbs
Olive oil	Toast

Peel and blanch onions and garlic cloves. Hollow out the centers of the onions. Pound the extracted pulp of the onions in a mortar with the garlic, salt, pepper and enough olive oil to make a workable paste which is stuffed back into the onion shells. Save some of the paste to serve as a spread for the toast. Place the stuffed onions in an oiled, ovenware dish. Sprinkle with buttered bread crumbs and set in a 400° oven for about 10 to 15 minutes. Serve with the toast and purée. Serves 6.

Cuban Style Rice

4 tbl. olive oil	1 cup white wine
4 cloves garlic, sliced	3 cups chicken broth
1 medium onion, chopped	½ tsp. coarse pepper
1 medium green pepper, chopped	2 cups uncooked white rice
1 pound shrimp	Parmesan cheese
½ cup tomato sauce	

Clean and cut shrimp into large pieces and sauté with garlic, onion, and green pepper in oil. When shrimp are pink and vegetables soft, add liquids and bring to boil. Add rice, stir and turn down to a simmer for ½ hour (with cover). Just before serving sprinkle with cheese. Serves 4-6.

Garlic Mashed Potatoes

2½ pounds baking potatoes	40 cloves garlic
4 tbl. softened butter	4 tbl. flour
Salt and white pepper	1 cup milk
3-4 tbl. whipping cream	¼ tsp. salt
4 tbl. minced parsley	Pinch of pepper

Peel garlic cloves or blanch first, then peel. Cook the garlics slowly in the butter in a covered sauce pan for 20 minutes or until very tender but not brown. Blend in flour and stir over low heat for 2 minutes without browning. Off the heat, beat in boiling milk and seasoning. Boil, stirring for 1 minute. Rub the sauce through a sieve or purée in an electric blender. Simmer for 2 minutes more.

The above can be done ahead of time. Do not mix with potatoes until the last minute. Peel and quarter potatoes and drop in boiling salted water; cover and boil until tender. Mash.

Reheat the purée in a sauce pan and beat with spatula or spoon for several minutes over moderate heat to evaporate moisture. Remove from heat and beat in the softened butter, small amounts at a time. Add salt and pepper to taste. Shortly before serving, beat the hot garlic sauce vigorously into the hot potatoes. Beat in the cream by spoonfuls but do not thin out the purée. Add parsley and correct the seasoning.

Serve with lamb, pork, goose or sausages. Serves 6 to 8.

Eggplant Chiu-Hwa

This is a delicious Chinese dish known also as Eggplant Pekinese. The ingredients include Chinese salted black beans which you can get in most markets or specialty shops.

1 eggplant (firm and dark)	½ tsp. sugar
8 cloves garlic	1½ cups chicken broth
1 tbl. Chinese black beans	Vegetable oil
2 tbl. soy sauce	

Cut eggplant into 2-inch cubes and leave unpeeled. Brown the eggplant in a heavy frying pan, adding a few drops of oil as is needed. You should start with a few pieces of the eggplant and continue adding pieces as you mix with a paste made of crushed garlic and black beans (about 2 tablespoons). Continue adding egg plant and oil as you mix in the soy sauce, sugar and chicken broth. Reduce heat and simmer with cover for 10 to 12 minutes.

Orak Orik

This is a delicious and *interesting* Javanese cabbage dish made with an Indonesian root, Laos, known also as Malaysian Ginger which it resembles in appearance. You can get this spice in specialty food shops.

1 large head green cabbage	Ginger, to taste
1 head garlic (7-10 cloves)	2 eggs
White pepper to taste	Vegetable or peanut oil
1 tsp. Laos or powdered ginger	

Shred cabbage very finely. Mash garlic with lots of white pepper, Laos and ginger to a paste. Heat oil in a wok and sauté the paste a few minutes. You can taste a dab to correct seasoning; it should be very spicy, but the ginger should not mask out the Laos. Add the cabbage and keep stirring over a high flame. Add eggs and continue stirring until the cabbage is soft and eggs cooked. You may add soy sauce at the table.

BRUCE AIDELLS'
Italian Vegetables

1 bunch broccoli (or zucchini,
    cauliflower, green beans, carrots)
½ cup fresh grated Parmesan or
    Romano cheese
2 tbl. garlic, finely chopped

½ cup olive oil
1 tbl. fresh sweet basil or other
    Fresh herbs or 2 tbl. parsley
2 tbl. lemon juice (opt.)
2 gallons salted water

Cut vegetables into florets or slices. Blanch or steam them, but blanching holds the color better. Broccoli takes about 5 minutes, zucchini about 3 minutes. Refresh the vegetable in cold water, drain, and dry.

Heat oil in a 10-12 inch skillet, add the garlic and fry for about 1 minute. Add blanched vegetable and toss with garlic for 1-2 minutes. Add the cheese, lemon juice and fresh herbs and serve.

This dish is a typical Italian method for garnishing vegetables, and it can be served as a side dish or placed over pasta as a more substantial main course. If you do this, double the amount of olive oil and cheese. Serves 4-6.

Carrot Casserole with Garlic

5½ cups carrots peeled and cut into
    ¼'' slices
1½ cups onions sliced
4 tbl. olive oil
5 cloves garlic, mashed
1 tbl. flour
¾ cup boiling brown stock, or
    bouillon

¾ cup boiling milk
Salt and pepper to taste
1 tsp. sugar
Pinch of nutmeg
2 egg yolks, blended with . . .
4 tbl. whipping cream
2 tbl. minced parsley

Cook the carrots and onions in olive oil slowly, tossing occasionally for 30 minutes. The vegetables should be tender but not brown. Add garlic for last 5 minutes. Toss the vegetables with flour and cook for 3 minutes.

Take pan off the heat and add the stock, milk and seasoning. Simmer uncovered for 20 minutes or until liquid reduces by ⅓. Just before serving, add egg yolks and cream, swirling the pan over a very low heat until thickened. Sprinkle with parsley in serving dish. Serves 6.

GARLIC TID-BITS

Tom's Feta Cheese Dip

This is a refreshing summer salad. Eat it with chips or pita bread.

½ pound feta cheese
1 large tomato (skinned)
3 tbl. olive oil

1-2 cloves garlic, pressed
1 tsp. oregano
2 tsp. chopped green onion (opt.)

Mash all together, but don't completely integrate ingredients. Refrigerate about 30 minutes before serving.

Garlic Croutons

1 long Italian bread (or French)
½ cup olive oil
2-4 cloves garlic, crushed

1 slice mozzarella cheese ½″ thick for
    each slice of bread

Cut bread into 1-inch slices and toast in moderate oven until dried out—about 5 minutes. Heat oil in frying pan and add crushed garlic and sauté for a few seconds, but do not brown. Take the bread out of the oven and dip the slices in the oil. Place a slice of cheese over the toast and return to oven for 5 minutes until cheese melts. Serve hot with soup poured over or cut into cubes and toss in salad.

Mock Boursin

This is an inexpensive but delicious imitation of the French cheese Boursin, a triple-cream cheese with herbs. The *Cheese Board* in Berkeley devised this creamy spread.

⅔ pound cream cheese (fresh with no gum)
⅓ pound bakers cheese
1 or 2 cloves garlic

Salt to taste
½ cup chives, minced
½ cup parsley, minced

Mash garlic, chives and parsley in a mortar and pestle. Add this paste to the cheese in a rotary beater. Great as a dip, or spread over broiled meats.

Garlic Stuffed Olives

Large, or medium pitted olives, or as many as you need per person for an hors d'oeuvre
Garlic cloves, as many small cloves as olives, or large cloves cut in half

Olive oil, enough to coat a pan large enough to hold the olives in one layer
Salt to taste

Place the individual cloves of garlic, unpeeled if you like, in a pot of boiling water. Blanch for a few minutes until cloves are soft when a knife is inserted. Drain and cool. Take off the skins if necessary.

Stuff a clove, or half of a large clove, into each olive. You can apply a little pressure to make sure garlic is packed into the space.

Heat the olive oil in a pan, and when hot, sauté the olives for about 15 minutes, or until they pucker up and begin to harden and shrink. Shake the pan to cook the olives on all sides. Towards the end, squeeze a few cloves of garlic through a press over the olives and continue to shake the olives about. When this purée starts to brown, take the pan off the fire, and let cool. Salt can be added along with the garlic purée.

Serve hot or cold with tooth picks.

Garlic Mango Chutney

This recipe comes from Barbados. Sealed in jars, the chutney will keep for two or three years and improve in flavor.

8 pounds mangoes	4 oz. garlic
2 tbl. salt	4 oz. red pepper
2 pounds raisins	8 oz. mustard seed
8 pounds sugar	4 pounds currents
1 pound green ginger, after peeling	8 pints cider vinegar

First day: Use mangoes that are not ripe but are full; peel and cut into long strips. To the fruit add 2 tablespoons of salt and leave for 24 hours.

Second day: Throw away the water that has drained from the mangoes and put them into 4 pints of vinegar in a non-aluminum pot. Bring to boil. Put the other 4 pints of vinegar on to boil with the sugar, removing any scum that rises. Remove from fire and add garlic, ginger and peppers. Stir well. Mix raisins, currants and mustard seed into mangoes and pour syrup over all. Let it simmer for ½ hour or until thickened. Allow to set at least 12-18 hours before bottling. Seal tightly in bottles.

Garlic Garbanzos

This garlicky snack kept some friends of mine hopping for a year in Italy.

2 tbl. butter	Sesame seeds
2 cloves garlic, chopped fine	Salt
1 cup cooked, dry garbanzo beans	

Melt the butter in a heavy pan and sauté the chopped garlic. Add the garbanzos and sauté until they are golden brown. They should be crunchy but still tender inside. Mix with sesame seeds and salt.

BEVERAGES

Sahag's Tahn

This is an Armenian drink served at the Juice Bar in Berkeley, California. A refreshing summer treat!

> Yogurt
> Water
> Garlic
> Mint

The ratio of yogurt to water is about 6 to 1. You need just enough water to liquefy the yogurt. For each serving you will want about ½ clove of garlic pressed and a pinch of mint. This mixture should be mixed thoroughly and chilled before serving.

Garlic Tomato Juice

This is a homemade V-8 cocktail juice. It can also be used as a Bloody Mary mix.

> Tomato juice
> Garlic
> Tabasco sauce
> Herbs of choice
> Lemon juice

For each serving of juice, use about 1 small clove of garlic, a few teaspoons of lemon juice, several drops of Tabasco and a pinch of herbs (dill is very good).

DESSERTS

BARBARA FLASKA'S
Holiday Garlic Ice Cream

After a spicy, rich dinner, this dessert is a refreshing climax. It should not be served after a bland, garlic-free meal as the slight hint of garlic will be extremely offensive to some. The strawberry or other fruit topping can be eliminated, along with the sugar, and the resulting mixture can be served with roast beef in lieu of horseradish sauce.

1-1½ tsp. gelatin	2 tbl. lemon juice
¼ cup cold water	2 cloves garlic, minced
2 cups milk	2 cups whipping cream
¾-1 cup sugar	Strawberry topping (or
⅛ tsp. salt	other fruit)

Soak the gelatin in cold water while you heat to a boil the milk, sugar and salt. Dissolve the gelatin in the hot milk. Cool, then add the lemon juice and garlic. Chill the mixture until slushy. Whip the cream until thick but not stiff and stir into the mixture. Freeze in a mold, or in a foil-covered tray.

Top portions with the fresh fruit topping. Serves 6-8.

Garlic Ice Cream Sundae LSR

1 pint honey
10-20 cloves garlic
2 tbl. chopped nuts, dates, raisins
1 quart vanilla ice cream

At least two weeks, but preferably one month prior to your garlic feast, place whole peeled cloves of garlic into one pint of honey. You can also add chopped dates, raisins and chopped, unsalted nuts (almonds, cashews, etc.).

Seal jar and set aside at room temperature.

Every few days, turn jar upside down and leave for several more days. This lets garlic and other ingredients mix with honey, as the dry ingredients tend to rise to the top. (Allow about ¼" between level of honey and lid.)

Taste honey the morning before the feast. It should have a very subtle garlic flavor and bouquet. If too strong, add more honey. If too weak, press a few cloves of garlic through a garlic press and mix thoroughly through the honey. This is best done by placing the jar of honey in a warm water bath until honey liquefies slightly. Repeat this process of liquefying honey prior to serving.

Scoop balls of vanilla or other lightly flavored ice cream into dishes and spoon honey over the top. Honey should be warm and slightly liquid to enhance bouquet and eatability. Serves 4-6.

Stewed Figs with Garlic

1 pound fresh figs	3 tbl. honey
2 cups red wine	1-2 cloves garlic slit length-wise
2 or 3 sprigs fresh thyme	½ pint creme fraiche or whipped cream
or ½ tsp. dry thyme	½ tsp. lavender

This recipe is Helen Gustafson's variation of Chez Panisse's variation of a Richard Olney recipe.

Place all ingredients in a saucepan and simmer covered for about 1 hour. Turn figs if not completely covered by the liquid. Remove figs to serving dish, discard thyme and garlic and reduce liquid over a high flame by ⅓. It should have the consistency of a light syrup. Chill figs in the syrup and serve with a dollop of creme. Serves 4-6.

GARLIC TIMES
RECIPE SUPPLEMENT

Border design by Freema Hillman of Oakland, CA.

From Bruce Aidells

Cold White Beans in Marinade

1 lb. small white beans
3 T garlic, finely chopped
1½ lemons
¼ C olive oil
2 T shallots
1 qt. rich chicken stock
1 bay leaf
2 sprigs thyme or 1 t dried thyme

Soak beans overnight. Cook beans in the stock with the thyme and bay leaf until just soft but so that the beans are still whole (1½-2 hours). Drain the beans and while they are still hot add the lemon juice and other ingredients. Mix in well and add about ¼ C of the stock. Let cool.

This dish makes an excellent appetizer or part of an antipasta tray. The beans can be sprinkled with parsley or fresh herbs.

Leeks in Garlic Vinaigrette

Serves 6

The leek is a marvelous vegetable, and a shamefully neglected relation to garlic. I recently served this recipe as a side dish with roast pork.

2 bunches leeks or about 6 large leeks.
1½ C garlic vinaigrette dressing (see recipe below)
Finely diced Italian salami (optional)

Simmer leeks in 2 gallons of salted water for 15-20 minutes or until soft. Refresh under cold water, then drain well by holding leeks upside-down and shaking off the water. Toss in the vinaigrette and refrigerate until cool. Serve with chopped parsley and sprinkle the optional diced salami over the top.

Garlic Vinaigrette

Makes 1½ cups

1 t garlic, crushed or pressed
2 t Dijon mustard
2 T white wine vinegar
1 T boiling water
6 T olive oil
salt and pepper to taste

Beat together mustard, vinegar, salt and pepper and then the water and garlic. Slowly beat in the oil until thick and creamy. This dressing is wonderful with all kinds of salads.

Bruce's Pesto Sauce

Serves 4

Pesto is usually served over fresh pasta, but can be served with fish dishes and soups.

3 C loosely packed fresh sweet basil
¼ C walnuts
½ C grated Parmesan or Romano cheese
¼ C parsley, loosely packed
1 t salt
½ t pepper
1-1½ C olive oil
1½ T garlic, chopped

1. If you have a large mortar and pestle add the salt and garlic and pound to a paste. Add nuts and continue to pound until pasty. Add basil and parsley one cup at a time, pounding the greens until all have been completely crushed. Add cheese, pepper and mix in the oil.

2. Finely chop parsley and basil together. Place in a mixing bowl. Chop nuts. Squeeze garlic through a press. Add to mixing bowl along with cheese, salt, pepper and beat in oil.

Pumpkin and White Bean Soup

Serves 8

2 lbs. fresh pumpkin, chopped
½ lb. Great Northern white beans
2 carrots, sliced
4 leeks, sliced
1 sprig celery, sliced
2 qts. chicken stock
3 T garlic, chopped
salt and pepper to taste
½ t marjoram
¼ t thyme
3 T bacon fat
1 lemon sliced

Soak beans overnight and simmer 1 hour in stock with the pumpkin. Sauté sliced vegetables in bacon fat and add to soup along with the herbs. Continue cooking for 1-1½ hours until the beans and pumpkin are soft.

Serve with slices of lemon.

Eggplant and Red Bell Peppers Sauté

Serves 4-6

1 large eggplant (1-2 lbs.)
2 red bell peppers
1 T garlic, chopped
2 T lemon juice
½ C olive oil
2 T parsley or fresh herbs

Slice eggplant into rounds ½" thick and dredge in salt. Let vegetable sweat for at least 30 minutes or as long as 4 hours. Wash off salt and pat dry.

Slice peppers in half and remove seeds. Place halves skin side up under a broiler and roast until skins are charred black. This takes 5-10 minutes if broiler has been preheated. Remove peppers, wrap in wet paper towel and place in a bag for 10 minutes. Remove as much of the charred skin as you can and slice into ½" wide strips.

Fry eggplant in oil until lightly browned and soft. Arrange slices on a platter and intersperse with strips of red pepper. Add the garlic to the remaining oil in the skillet and fry over low heat without browning for 1 minute. Add lemon juice parsley or fresh herbs to pan and pour over the platter of vegetables. Serve this dish hot or cold. I prefer it lukewarm.

Calve's Liver with Chorizo and Red Peppers

Serves 6

2 lbs. calve's liver
2 lemons
1 T garlic, crushed
½ lb. onions
1 green pepper
3 red peppers
¾ lbs. Spanish chorizo (you may substitute
    linguisa or pepperoni, but do not use
    Mexican chorizo)
¼ C olive oil
¼ t sage
⅛ t allspice
¼ t thyme
1 t salt
½ t pepper

Sauté the peppers cut in strips and the onions cut in thin rounds in hot olive oil until the peppers have just begun to lose their crispness (about 5 minutes). Remove and add sausage cut in ¼" rounds and sauté until just lightly brown. Remove and sauté the liver cut in ½" strips in the fat from the chorizo and the remaining olive oil. Liver should be browned but still pinkish on the inside. Add salt, pepper, spices, lemon juice, and toss all together. Add back the vegetables, chorizo and the garlic. Continue to toss 1 minute or so until all pieces are well coated.

This dish can be served hot or cold.

Kosher-Style Dill and Garlic Pickles

10 lbs. pickling cucumbers
¼ lb. salt
⅛ lb. kosher pickling spice
2 heads garlic (about 25 cloves)
1 gallon water
½ large bunch fresh dill, or 1 oz. dill seed

Wash each cucumber well with a vegetable brush. Pack cucumbers into crocks, or 1 gallon jars or large plastic tubs (10 pounds of cucumbers makes about 3 gallons of pickles).

Intersperse the cucumbers with dill and garlic cloves (peeled). Each gallon should have about a dozen garlic cloves and 1 sprig of dill or a teaspoon dill seed.

Add salt to the water and bring to a boil stirring to dissolve the salt. Add spices, then let brine cool. Pour the brine over the cucumbers making sure they are completely immersed. If necessary weight the cucumbers with a plate if using a crock, and close lids on glass or plastic containers. Leave at room temperature until done to your liking. It takes about a week at 60° F. and 3 to 4 days at 70° F. Store in a refrigerator.

The pickled garlics are very tasty and mild, and many people zero in on the garlics. Keeps 4-5 months in the fridge.

Fish du Sète

Serves 4

2 lb. fish steaks (halibut, snapper or rock cod)
1 head garlic (10-12 cloves) chopped
½ C olive oil
juice of ½ lemon or ½ C dry white wine
½ C parsley

Either poach or broil the fish steaks.

Heat the olive oil in a small skillet and add the garlic and parsley. Fry for 1-2 minutes over a moderate heat without letting the garlic brown. Add all the juice from the broiling pan or ½ C of the poaching liquid and either the lemon juice or the wine. Cook for another 2 minutes. Salt and pepper to taste and pour over the fish.

Nancy's Artichoke Pie

Serves 6

8 baby artichokes or 2 large ones or 1 can artichokes
2 onions finely chopped
3 cloves garlic chopped
½ C chopped parsley
1 lb. grated sharp cheddar, swiss or a combination (jack cheese is also OK)
10 eggs
½ C bread crumbs
½ C butter
2 T olive oil
1 t oregano
¼ C chopped scallions
½ C milk
8 drops Tabasco sauce
1 t salt
½ t pepper

If you are using baby artichokes, finely chop the whole vegetable. If you use large artichokes, chop only the bottom ¼″ of the large leaves, the whole heart and the inner tender leaves. If you use the canned variety quarter them and set aside.

Sauté the chopped artichoke with onions in the butter and oil. When these are soft add the garlic and cook for another minute. In a bowl mix the eggs, milk, bread crumbs, oregano, parsley, Tabasco, all but ¼ cup of the grated cheese, oregano, salt and pepper. Mix this well and add the sauteed vegetables. Pour into a roasting pan so that the pie will be at least ¼″ thick but no greater than

1½″. If you are using canned artichokes press each quartered piece into the egg-cheese mixture in the pan so that the pieces are evenly distributed. Sprinkle the top with the chopped scallions and the remaining grated cheese. Bake at 350° until a knife inserted comes out dry (about 30 minutes for the ½″ pie and 1 hour for the 1½″ pie).

Serve this dish hot or cold.

John Street Lamb Ragout

Serves 6

3-4 lbs. lamb shoulder
1 pt. sour cream
3 T olive oil
6 cloves garlic
5 leeks
1 t rosemary
½ t marjoram
½ lemon
2 C stock (beef) or 2 bouillon cubes in 2 C
    water
1 lb. mushrooms
1¼ C dry white wine
16 oz. tomato purée
salt and pepper

Salt and pepper the lamb chunks cut from a lamb shoulder. Brown in olive oil and remove. Brown the garlic and leeks that have been cut into slices. Add back the lamb, all but ¼ cup of white wine (dry sauterne is best), stock, tomato purée and water. Season with rosemary and marjoram and simmer covered 1 hour and uncovered for 2 hours. Add the mushrooms and cook down sauce till it just thickens and finish with ¼ cup white wine, juice from ½ lemon and the sour cream stirred in off the fire. Sprinkle with parsley and serve.

Veal Chops from the Youth Hostel of Angers

Serves 4

4 large veal chops, ½-¾ lbs. each
1 onion sliced thin
1 large tomato sliced into rounds
2 T garlic, chopped
1 C dry white wine
½ C heavy cream
¼ t taragon
¼ t thyme
2 T olive oil
2 T butter
1 t French mustard
salt and pepper to taste

Salt and pepper chops. Sauté chops in butter and oil until brown. Remove and sauté onions. Deglaze pan with white wine and add the garlic. Add back the chops and cover with the onion and slices of tomato. Sprinkle with the herbs. Cover pan and cook 30 minutes. Remove chops and arrange on a platter with tomato and onions on top. Reduce sauce to ¼ C and stir in the mustard and cream. Pour over chops and garnish with boiled new potatoes and slices of fresh tomatoes sprinkled with parsley.

Lamb Steaks

Serves 4

4¾ lb. shoulder lamb chops
3 cloves garlic, chopped
3 T olive oil
½ C red wine
1½ C beef stock or 1½ C water and 1
    bouillon cube
¾ t summer savory or rosemary
¼ C tomato purée
2 T chopped chives, parsley or green onion
salt and pepper to taste

Have a butcher cut the chops off a shoulder roast and use the rest for lamb stew. Salt and pepper each steak and sprinkle with the savory. Brown in olive oil. Remove lamb and add the garlic and sauté 1 minute. Then deglaze the pan with red wine and add the stock, ½ t savory and tomato paste. Mix well and add back the steaks and simmer covered in the sauce for 20-30 minutes depending on how done you like your meat. Remove steaks and cook sauce down till thickened (about ½ cup). Pour over the meat and sprinkle with chopped chives. (The sauce can also be enriched by adding sour cream right before serving).

From Margaret Spillane

Breizh-Provañs

(Bretagne-Provence)

This dish is the marriage of the crepe from Britanny and aioli from Provence. You already have an aioli recipe (see *The Book of Garlic* or *Garlic Times 1 & 2*). Now for the crepes:

2 C buckwheat flour (available in health
    food stores)
1 C white flour
3½ C water (approx.)
½ t salt

Combine flours and salt, and add the water slowly, stirring rapidly all the time: this will prevent lumps from forming. Once batter is completely smooth and the consistency of pancake batter, let it "rest" for at least an hour. Stir again before using.

Heat a skillet and brush it with oil. Pour in a small amount of batter and quickly tilt pan so that the batter spreads evenly. Cook until set: 1 or 2 minutes. Turn crepe and cook for another minute or so (until crisp). Slide onto a plate and top with a generous dose of aioli.

Kotriad

(Breton Bouillabaisse)

6 whole fishes (half firm-fleshed: mackerel,
    conger, eel, etc.; half soft-fleshed:
    sardine, skate, hake)
shellfish, assorted varieties
3 lbs. potatoes, peeled and quartered
10 big tomatoes, peeled and chopped
6 onions, sliced in rings
4 leeks, chopped
some shallots
6-12 cloves garlic, chopped
1 bunch celery, chopped
parsley
pinch saffron
herbs of your choice (bay leaf, rosemary,
    thyme)
salt and pepper
olive oil to taste, at least ½ cup

At your fish market, ask that the fish be cleaned, but that the heads be left on the smaller varieties. At home, cut those bigger fish into large chunks, and leave the small ones whole. Put the firm-fleshed varieties, as well as any crab or lobster, on a plate. On a second plate, place the softer fish plus any shrimp, mussels or clams. Boil the potatoes till soft in the biggest pot you can find (they use a cauldron here), then add all your vegetables, seasonings, olive oil, and the first plate of fish. Make sure there's enough water to completely cover the contents of the pot. Cover with a tight-fitting lid and let boil rapidly for 5 minutes. Then add the second plate of fish and let boil a few more minutes. Arrange the fish and vegetables on a warmed platter; fill a soup tureen with the bouillon. On each plate should be a slice of bread fried in olive oil, over which is spooned first the fish and vegetables, then the bouillon. A dry red wine goes best with Kotriad.

From Charles Perry

Sarimsok Palov
(Uzbekistan Garlic Pilaf)

½ lb. lamb
4 onions, diced
¾ lbs. carrots, sliced
5 heads garlic
4 T clarified butter
2 sticks butter
5 C rice
4 T salt
1-2 T cumin
10 C water
black or red pepper to taste

Cut the lamb into strips, about ¾″ wide, two inches long and ½″ thick. Brown in clarified butter. Separately brown the onions and carrots in clarified butter. Then simmer all together for ½ hour.

Take the heads of garlic intact and trim off the roots, pull out the stems and remove the outer layer of parchment. This can be done without breaking up the cloves. Cover the bottom of a casserole with half the rice and arrange the heads of garlic in a circle on the rice. Add the fried meat, carrots and onions, the salt, cumin and pepper. Cover with the rest of the rice.

Boil the water, at least part of it being boiled in the pan where the meat was cooked to pick up the pan juices. Melt the sticks of butter in the boiling water and pour into the casserole. Cook until the rice is done.

To serve, remove the heads of garlic, separate into cloves and peel. Serve a couple of cloves on top of each portion of pilaf.

Pollo à la Condesita
(Chicken with Garlic and Almonds)

1½ lbs. chicken breasts, boned and skinned
24 blanched almonds
6 large cloves garlic
7 T olive oil
juice of one lemon
¼ C dry sherry
1½ C stock (beef)

Freeze the chicken breasts, then partially thaw and slice into thin scaloppini, making about 12 equal slices. With a very sharp knife you can do this without freezing. Soak in the lemon juice and about half the olive oil.

Toast the almonds in the oven. Toast the garlic cloves one at a time over a flame, holding them about an inch above the flame with a skewer or fork until the clove is soft and the skin charred. Remove the burnt peels, mash the garlics and fry briefly in one tablespoon of olive oil. Grind the toasted almonds (or put through a food processor) with the sherry and the garlic, reserving the garlicky oil for frying the ckicken. Add the stock to the almond-garlic mixture.

Add the remaining olive oil to the garlic oil and fry the ckicken slices, two or three at a time, over high heat.

Add the sauce and simmer for ten minutes.

From LSR Members

Anzonini's Cauliflore Gitanno*

2 heads cauliflower
10-15 cloves garlic
½ C olive oil
juice of 2 lemons
salt and pepper to taste

Boil the cauliflower in water until very soft. Slice the garlic cloves lengthwise and fry in the olive oil until golden, but not burnt. Drain well, then mash the cauliflower. Mix the garlic and oil into the cauliflower, then sauté this mixture over medium heat for 10 minutes. Off heat, mix in the lemon juice, salt and pepper. Serve warm or cold, as a vegetable or hors d'oeuvre.

This recipe comes from famed gypsy Flamenco singer Anzonini del Puerto. His love of garlic is legendary. When he makes this dish, he burns the garlic slightly, which gives the dish a more pungent, but very delicious quality. The lyrics from one of Anzonini's songs go as follows: "If you want husbands content with their work/tell their women to put 5 heads of garlic in their meals." In Spanish, it rhymes.

Alice's Whole Baked Garlic*

4 whole heads garlic
4 T butter
¼ C olive oil
salt and pepper to taste

Remove the outer layer of skins from the heads, exposing the cloves. Place them in a baking dish and pour the oil and butter over the bulbs. Bake, uncovered, in a 200° oven for about half an hour. You can continue to baste the bulbs with additional fat if desired.

Add ½ cup water to the dish, cover, and bake another 1½ hours, or until bulbs are soft. Serve with French bread and a creamy goat cheese.

This recipe was originally served at the Chez Panisse Garlic Festival.

Garlic Corn Squares

6 T yellow corn meal
1 T ground sesame seeds
2 T sunflower seeds
2 T grated Parmesan-Romano cheese
1 T soy flour
2 T toasted wheat germ
1 T raw wheat bran
1 T oil
2-5 cloves garlic, crushed

Combine the crushed garlic and oil in ⅓ cup hot water. Stir a little and set aside. In a separate bowl, mix together all the dry ingredients. Add the garlic-water to the dry ingredients and mix. Take small clumps of the batter (the size of a golf ball) and form into very thin patties (⅛ inch thick) on an oiled 9″ × 13″ pan. The patties must be thin, and the thinner the better. Cover the entire surface of the pan, then take a metal spatula and divide into six even squares. Bake in a preheated 325° oven until patties are golden brown (20-25 minutes). Turn over and bake about 5 more minutes. The patties will not brown evenly, so you will have to make adjustments. Cool on a wire rack before eating.

The patties should be thoroughly crisp. If they are not, then the oven temperature was too high, or the patties not thin enough. They should have the texture of a cracker.

—*Chris Kushner*

Jim's Garlic Olives

1 can large unpitted California black olives
4 cloves garlic sliced
½ C red wine vinegar
½ C water
2 T red wine
1 t lemon juice
1 t soy sauce
pinch dill
pinch salt

Drain and rinse olives, then slit them lengthwise with a sharp knife. Mix the other ingredients in a bowl. Taste the mixture. If you find it too tart, add some red wine. Put the olives in an 18 ounce jar and pour in the mixture. Keep the lid tight.

Try an olive each day and observe the change in taste. If the taste is becoming too strong, simply drain the olives and refrigerate until serving. Ordinarily, the taste will stabilize after 3-4 days and the olives need not be drained.

—*Jim and Laticia Wiley, Berkeley*

Tzatziki

(Greek yogurt and garlic salad)

3-4 cloves garlic
½ cucumber, peeled
1 C plain yogurt
juice of ½ lemon
salt and pepper to taste
2 T olive oil

Grate cucumber corsely, mince the garlic fine, and combine with the yogurt and lemon juice. Add salt and pepper, stir and refrigerate. Before serving, drizzle olive oil over the chilled sauce. Serve over meatballs, rice or as a side dish or appetizer.

—*Jerna and Petros Verrios,*
Moraga, CA

Midge's Spanish Garlic Soup

(Sopa de Ajo)

Rich chicken stock (2 cups per person)
olive oil
4 cloves garlic per person
French bread, cubed
Parmesan cheese, grated
paprika, about a ¼ tsp. per person

Make a chicken broth using any good recipe—the better the stock the better the soup. Then sauté garlic in olive oil until the cloves just start to turn color. Then transfer the garlic to the broth.

In the same olive oil, fry the cubes of bread until crisp and brown. Set aside on a paper bag to drain.

In an ungreased frying pan, toast the paprika and put into the soup. In a casserole, place the soup, the bread and the cheese sprinkled on top. Bake in a 350° oven for 20 minutes or until cheese melts and starts to bubble.

—*Mica Grana, Berkeley*

Chilled South American Garlic Soup

½ loaf French bread
½ C water
½ C shelled, peeled almonds
3 garlic cloves
3 T olive oil
2 T vinegar
1 t salt
1 pint ice water or 1 C water and 1 C chicken broth

Remove and discard crust from bread. Soak bread in water. In a blender pulverize the almonds. Add the bread, garlic, oil, vinegar, salt and blend. Add the pint of liquid and blend again. Serve chilled.

—*Jo Anne Chrisman,*
The Folderol Restaurant, Westtown, N.Y.

Hattye's Pitzbah
(Rumanian appetizer)

6 large chicken wings
3 eggs
⅓ C vinegar
pinch salt
3 cloves garlic, crushed

Boil the wings like for a soup. Remove from liquid and refrigerate overnight. Next day: In a sauce pan over a low heat, place the beaten eggs, vinegar, salt and garlic. Stir until it comes to a custard thickness.

Separate each wing into three parts and place in a shallow serving dish. Pour sauce over wings and let stand for a few hours to cool before serving.

—*Betty Slosberg, Los Angeles*

From the Garlic Growers

Bagna Cauda
(Hot Dip)

6 large cloves garlic
1 C sweet butter
¼ C olive oil
2 T chopped anchovies
Vegetables and bread sticks for dipping

Peel garlic. Mince or put through garlic press. Melt butter in small saucepan. Add garlic and oil. Cook over very low heat 5 minutes until garlic is softened but not browned. Add anchovies and continue cooking 5 minutes. Transfer to flame-proof container and keep warm while serving. Serve as a dip for raw or lightly blanched vegetables such as cucumbers, fresh mushrooms, celery, zucchini, carrots, cauliflower, green pepper and green onions, and bread sticks. Makes a generous 1 cup.

Variation: Blend 1 C whipping cream and a generous dash or two freshly ground pepper into garlic-butter mixture. Simmer 2 or 3 minutes.

Sopa De Albondigas or Meatball Soup
Serves 4

4 large cloves garlic
½ pound ground beef
1 large egg, beaten
1½ t salt, pinch pepper
2 T uncooked rice
¼ C finely chopped parsley
½ C chopped onion
1 T oil
2 cans (10½ oz. each) condensed beef broth
2 C water
1 C carrots, cut in 2 x ¼ inch strips
1 C celery, cut in 2 x ¼ inch strips
1 can (8¾ oz.) garbanzos, undrained
1 can (1 lb.) tomatoes
Cheese-Butter

Peel garlic. Mash, or put through garlic press, 1 clove garlic. Combine with beef, egg, ½ t salt, pepper, rice and 2 T parsley. Shape mixture into 20 small meatballs and set aside. Chop remaining 3 cloves garlic or mash. Cook garlic with onion in oil, over medium heat until soft but not browned in covered 3 quart saucepan. Add remaining 1 t salt, broth, water, carrots, and celery. Bring to boiling. Drop in meatballs and simmer 20 minutes. Add undrained garbanzos, tomatoes and remaining chopped parsley. Continue cooking 10 minutes longer. Ladle into large soup bowls and serve with a spoonful of Cheese-Butter.

Cheese-Butter: Blend together ½ C softened butter with ½ t pressed garlic, 2 T grated Parmesan cheese and 1 T minced parsley. Makes about ½ cup.

AFTERWORD

I FEEL I must explain how it is I came to write *The Book of Garlic*. I am embarrassed whenever people ask this question. Not that I don't have an answer: It's just that the answer is another book—and even more "personal" than the garlic book. I will try to outline this book about a book as briefly as I can.

While certain cultural movements were leading me inexorably towards this book (a new Nature-consciousness, the death of nature . . . and other contradictory movements), certain personal-emotional events have recently conspired to bring me to this task. In the last several years I have been searching for my lost Jewishness (not that I've ever had it). Having never been Bar Mitzvahed, I've always looked for substitute ways of enjoining myself to the Faith of my Fathers. Before starting on this book I attempted to write a script for a Jewish cooking show (The Jewish Schef) . . . sort of a spoof on Julia Child and the cooking show fad; but at the same time a show rich in the aura and aroma of an old world sabbath meal. This scheme never came off. The idea developed into a treatise on "Garlic and the Jew," garlic seeming to symbolize my notion of bridging the gap between piety and levity, which is characteristic of Jewish consciousness.

My early research into garlic yielded so much international Garliciana, though, that I was soon launched into a more encyclopedic adventure. But I began to feel as if the whole world, symbolized by one of its smallest and most pungent particles of Creation, was falling down upon my shoulders. The amount of information on garlic tucked away in the infinite corners of libraries, bookstores, and people's minds was staggering, and I felt as if I was being consumed in a phantasmagoria of cross references. But if I ever needed proof that "in every thing . . . Everything", I had it now. The humble garlic, herb of gods, witches, peasants, physicians, artists, poets and herbalists proved to be a vital agent in the mysterious machinations of Existence throughout recorded time.

So the initial fancy that led me to garlic became a serious attempt at scholarship. Months of research followed, and the futility of *this* approach became obvious; it was clear that I could spend five years traveling around the world and still not unveil all the latent garliciana. I then returned to my initial vision of the book as a bridge between spoof and scholarship, fantasy and history. There were several more switches back and forth between these seemingly opposing attitudes, and if I tend to forget which side of the bridge (or see-saw) I'm on at any given point, I am sure that the reader will forgive me. Like the wandering Jews in the Sinai, I have been wandering on this bridge for a long, long time.

If my attempt to rekindle my Jewish faith through garlic has failed, I pray that my obsessional attachment to garlic has meant *something*. It would be reward enough that just as my father always remembered beans as the Musical Fruit (the more you eat the more you toot), garlic may be remembered with the help of this book as the Comical Herb (the more you eat, the more you burb (p)...) and the Philosophers' Rose — the more you eat the more you *nose*.

Shindet and Bon Garlique!
L.J. Harris

THE AUTHOR STUFFED WITH GARLIC

FOOTNOTES

PART ONE–A SERIOUS HISTORY

1. Strubing, "Garlic in Ancient Times", p.595
2. Mendelsohn, *A Salute to Onions*, Adelaide: Rigby Limited, 1965, p. 30
3. Strubing, p.591. A valuable source of garlic-lore unavailable in English until now.
4. Ibid., p.590
5. Boettcher, *Wonder Drugs.*
6. Binding, *Everything You Wanted to Know About Garlic*, p.29. Mr. Binding gives very few sources for his material and no bibliography, so whenever possible I have found his sources and used those instead.
7. Strubing, p.595
8. Ibid., p.599
9. Ibid., pp.600-601. German researchers are today using garlic to treat menstrual disturbances and the problems involved with menopause. None of this work has been translated into English as yet.
10. Boettcher.
11. *The Bible*, Numbers 11.5
12. Trachtenberg, *Jewish Magic and Mysticism.* See his index under "garlic".
13. Ibid.
14. Ibid.
15. Ginzberg, *The Legends and Myths of the Jews.*
16. Boettcher.
17. Ginzberg, p.44, v.6
18. Boettcher, p.66
19. Crowfoot, *From Cedar to Hyssop.*
20. Burton, *A Pilgrimage to Al-Madinah and Mecca*, p.32
21. Binding, p.30
22. Lawson, *Modern Greek Folklore.*
23. Ibid.
24. *Svenska Folksgner*, 1972. Thanks to Agneta Schipper for translating this folk tale.
25. Strubing, p.606
26. Ibid., p.607
27. Hehn, *The Wanderings of Plants and Animals.*
28. Strubing, p.592

29. Pliny, *Natural History*. Translation by Bertock and Riley. Vol. IV, Book XX, p. 225
30. Strubing, p. 593-4
31. Ibid., p. 611
32. Dastur, *Medicinal Plants of India and Pakistan*, pp. 23-5
33. Polo, *Travels*.
34. *Journal of Science, Food and Agriculture*, V. 22, pp. 96-98, 1971
35. Smith, *Chinese Materia Medica*. See his index under "garlic".
36. Krutch, *Herbal*.
37. Folkard, *Plant-lore, Legend and Lyrics*.
38. Ibid.
39. Krutch.
40. Ibid., p. 34
41. Culpepper, *The British Herbal*.
42. Reed, *A Short History of the Plant Sciences*.
43. Lucas, *Nature's Medicines*, pp. 40-58. See his chapter on "The Bulb with Miracle Healing Powers".
44. Ibid.
45. Browne, *Works*, V. 2.
46. Binding, p. 33
47. Ibid., p. 34
48. Masters, *The Natural History of Vampires*.
50. Ibid.
51. Ibid.
52. Zimmels, *Magicians, Theologians and Doctors*, p. 45
53. Curtin.
54. Vogel, *American Indian Medicine*, p. 102
55. Ibid.,
56. Note: Nanos Valaoritis was kind enough to supply these artworks through his connection with The Garlic Museum in Alburria.
57. Hehn; see his index under "garlic".
58. Friend, *Flowers and Flower Lore*, p. 544. Another verse follows: "Such savory deities must sure be good, which serve at once for worship and for food."
59. Hehn.
60. Ibid.
61. Mazza, *Herbs for the Kitchen*, p. 303
62. Hehn.
63. Ibid.
64. Binding, p. 35
65. Mazza, p. 309
66. Leighton, *Early American Gardens*, p. 307
67. Fletcher, *Herbs*.

68. Grieve, *Modern Herbal.*
69. *Newsweek,* August 15, 1936, p.31
70. *Alan Watts Journal,* October, 1970
71. Humpfrey, *Spices, Seasonings and Herbs.*
72. This remedy courtesy of Jeanne Rose.

PART TWO–MEDICAL

1. Quoted in Hartwell, "Garlic in Cancer Therapy."
2. Westlake, *The Pattern of Health,* p.172
3. Inglis, *The Case for Unorthodox Medicine.* This is an excellent and very readable study of the relationships between orthodox and unorthodox (fringe) medicine.
4. Ellacombe, *Plant Lore and Garden Craft of Shakespeare.* See his index.
5. Quisumbing, *Medical Plants of the Philippines*, p.158. It has been noted that the allyl sulphides of garlic are about .2% of the raw garlic.
6. Kato, *Garlic, The Unknown Miracle Worker*
7. Pensky and Weisenberg, *Science,* V.126, pp.1112-4, November, 1957
8. Kato.
9. George and Amonkar, *Chemo-Biological Interactions,* pp.169-75
10. *Prevention,* November, 1972, p.83
11. Weiss, *Medical Record,* pp.404-8
12. Damsau, *Medical Record,* pp.249-51
13. In Strubing, "Garlic in Ancient Times", *Ernahrunsforschung.* p.589
14. Stoll, *Advances in Enzymology,* V.7, pp.377-400
15. Kimura, *GANN,* V.55, pp.325-9
16. Fujiwara, *Nature,* V.216, p.83
17. *San Francisco Chronicle,* December 2, 1973
18. An article by Jack Anderson appeared in *The Los Angeles Free Press* (Feb. 1, 1974) outlining Senator Gaylord Nelson's investigations into "Antibiotic Killers". Statistics show that 100,000 Americans die each year from drug-resistant bacteria. This can be caused by administration of the wrong drugs or by overdoses of very dangerous antibiotics such as chloromysetin which has been found to cause fatal aplastic anemia.
19. Stoll, pp.377-400
20. Lucas, *Nature's Medicine.* See index. It has been found, however, that powdered garlic retains from 50-100% of its effectiveness for up to three years when stored in an air-tight container in a cool environment. This also indicates the reason for garlic's preservative effect on fresh meats.
21. Tynecka, *Acta Microbiologica Polanica,* V.5, pp.51-62
22. *Organic Gardening,* September, 1972

23. Ibid.
24. George, *Chemo-Biological Interactions*, pp. 169-75
25. Westlake, p. xiv
26. *Time Magazine*, March, 1974. This issue presented an interesting review of the recent literature covering areas of meta-science.
27. Lucas, p. 162
28. Tompkins, *Secret Life of Plants*.

PART FOUR – THE GARLIC GALA

1. Humphrey, Sylvia, *Spices, Seasonings and Herbs*.
2. Lonacker, *The Green Thumb of Thales*, p. 140
3. Fields, *All Manner of Food*.
4. Tannehill, *Food in History*.
5. Ibid., p. 172

BIBLIOGRAPHY

BOOKS:

Arber, Agnus, *Herbals: Their Origin and Evolution.* Cambridge: The Syndics of Cambridge University Press, 1953.

Bauer, W.W., *Potions, Remedies and Old Wives' Tales.* New York: Doubleday Co., 1969.

Binding, G.J. *Everything You Wanted to Know About Garlic.* New York: Pyramid Books, 1970. A short and often simplistic overview that I might have written had I not read it first.

Boettcher, Helmuth M., *Wonder Drugs.* New York: J.B. Lippincott Co., 1964.

Browne, Sir Thomas, *Pseudoxia Epidemica.* From the *Works of Sir Thomas Browne,* Volume 2, edited by Charles Sayle. Edinburgh: John Grant Publishing, 1912.

Burtis, C. Edward, *Nature's Miracle Medicine Chest.* New York: Arco Publishing Co., 1974.

Candolle, Alphonse de, *The Origin of Cultivated Plants.* New York: D. Appleton Co., 1908.

Chopra, R.N., *Glossary of Indian Medicinal Plants.* New Delhi: Council of Science and Industry Research, 1956.

Clark, Linda, *Get Well Naturally.* New York: ABC Books, 1965.

Crowfoot, Grace M., and Balensperger, Louise, *From Cedar to Hyssop.* London: The Sheldon Press, 1932.

Culpepper, Nicholas, *The British Herbal.* Halifax: Nicholson Co.

Dastur, J.F., *Medicinal Plants of India and Pakistan.* Bombay: D.B. Taraporevala Sons Co., 1962.

Dyer, T.F. Thiselton, *The Folklore of Plants*. New York: 1889.

Ellacombe, H.N., *Plantlore and Garden Craft of Shakespeare*. London: 1884.

Elwood, Catharyn, *Feel Like a Million*. New York: Devin-Adair, 1954.

Fletcher, H.L.V., *Herbs*. New York: Drake Publishers, Inc., 1972. This gives a very British account of herbs, excluding of course any favorable mention of Allium Sativum.

Folkard, Richard, *Plant Lore, Legend and Lyrics*. London: Sampson Low, 1884.

Ford, Ford Madox *Provence*. New York: J.B. Lippincott.

Friend, Reverend Hilderic, *Flowers and Flower Lore*. New York: Columbia Publishing Co., 1891.

Gerard, John, *The Herbal*. Edited by Marcus Woodward. London: Gerald Howe Publishers, 1927.

Ginzberg, Louis, *The Legends and Myths of the Jews*. Philadelphia: Jewish Publication Society of America, 1911.

Grieve, Maud, *A Modern Herbal*. New York: Harcourt Brace, 1931. One of the best recent herbals; recently reprinted in two volumes, paperback.

Hehn, Victor, *The Wanderings of Plants and Animals*. London: Swan Sonnenschein and Co., 1888. Full of wonderful stories.

Inglis, Brian, *The Case for Unorthodox Medicine*. New York: G.P. Putnam, 1965.

Kato, Yoshio, *Garlic: The Unknown Miracle Worker*. Amagasaki: Oyima Garlic Laboratory, 1973.

Kourennoff, Paul M., and St. George, George, *Russian Folk Medicine*. New York: Pyramid Publications, 1971.

Krutch, Joseph Wood, *Herbal*. New York: Putnam, 1965.

Landry, Robert, *The Gentle Art of Flavoring*. Translated by Bruce Axler. New York: Abelard-Shuman, 1970.

Law, Dr. Donald, *Herbs for Cooking and Healing*. Los Angeles: Wilshire Books.

Lawson, John Cuthbert, *Modern Greek Folklore*. New York: University Books, 1964.

Leighton, Ann, *Early American Gardens: For Meat or Medicine.* Boston: Houghton Mifflin Co., 1970.

Lonacker, Irving, *The Green Thumb of Thales.* Unpublished manuscript. Mr. Lonacker has kindly allowed me to quote from his book, which may someday get the attention it deserves.

Lucas, Richard, *The Magic of Herbs in Daily Living.* Parker Publishers, 1972.

Lucas, Richard, *Nature's Medicine.* New York: Universal-Award House, Inc., 1966. An excellent chapter on garlic, although lacking any mention of research conducted after 1957.

Masters, Antony, *The Natural History of the Vampire.* London: Granada Publishers Ltd., 1972.

Mazza, Irma Goodrich, *Herbs for the Kitchen.* New York: Arco Publishing Co., 1973.

Muramoto, Naboru, *Healing Ourselves.* New York: Avon, 1973.

Palos, Stephan, *The Chinese Art of Healing.* New York: Bantam Books, 1972.

Parry, John W., *Spices.* New York: Chemical Publishing Co., 1969.

Polo, Marco, *Travels.* Translated by Ronald Catham, 1958,1968.

Quelch, Mary T., *Herbal Remedies.*

Quisumbing, Eduardo, *Medicinal Plants of the Philippines.* Manila: Bureau of Printing, 1951.

Reed, Howard S., *A Short History of the Plant Sciences.* New York: The Ronald Press Co., 1942.

Rodale, Robert (editor), *The Basic Book of Organic Gardening.* New York: Ballantine Books, 1971.

Rose, Jeanne, *Kitchen Cosmetics.* S.F. Pan/Aris, 1977.

Samuels, Mike, and Bennet, Hal, *Well Body Book.* New York: Random House, 1973.

Savage, F.G., *The Flora and Folklore of Shakespeare.* London: Ed. J. Burrow Co., 1923.

Scully, Virginia, *A Treasury of American Indian Herbs.* New York: Crown Publishing Co., 1970.

Skinner, Charles M., *Myth and Legends of Flowers, Trees, Fruits and Plants.* New York: J.B. Lippincott Co., 1913.

Spoerri, Daniel, *The Mythological Travels.* New York: Something Else Press, Inc., 1970.

Tannahill, Reay, *Food in History.* New York: Stein and Day, 1973.

Tompkins, Peter, and Bird, Christopher, *The Secret Life of Plants.* New York: Harper and Row, 1973.

Trachtenberg, Joshua, *Jewish Magic and Mysticism.* New York: Meridian Books, 1961. Jewish Book House, Inc., 1939.

Trager, James, *The Food Book.* New York: Grossman Publishers, 1970.

Vogel, Virgil J., *American Indian Medicine.* New York: Ballantine Books, 1973.

Watanabe Tadashi, *Garlic Therapy.* Japan Publications, 1974.

Westlake, Aubrey T., *The Pattern of Health.* Berkeley and London: Shambala, 1973.

Zimmels, J.J., *Magicians, Theologians and Doctors.* London: Edward Goldston and Son, Ltd., 1952.

SCIENTIFIC-MEDICAL JOURNALS:

Abdo, J., "Biological Activities of Allium Sativum," *Japanese Journal of Pharmacology.* 19:1-4, March, 1969.

Amonkar, S.V., Banerji, A., "Isolation and Characterization of Larvicidal Principle of Garlic," *Science.* 174:1343, December, 1971.

Amonkar, S.V., et. al., "Mosquito Control with Active Principle of Garlic," *Journal of Economic Entomology.* 63:1172-5, August, 1970.

Bastidas, G.J., "Effect of Garlic," *American Journal of Tropical Medicine.* 18:920-3, November, 1969.

Bordia, Arun, and Bansal, H.C., "Essential Oil of Garlic in Prevention of Arteriosclerosis," *Lancet.* December 29, 1973. (p.1491).

Cavallito, C.J., "Allicin, the Antibacterial Principle of Allium Sativum," *Journal of the American Chemical Society*. 66: 1950-1, 1944.

Chaudhury, D.S., et. al., "Garlic and Leprosy," *Journal of the Indian Medical Association*. 39:517-20, November 1962.

Chemical Pharmaceutical Bulletin, "Studies on the Biologically Active Component in Garlic," 17:2193-7, November, 1969.

"Isolation of Various Substances in Allium Sativum," 12:1114-5, September, 1964.

Damsau, Frederic, "The Use of Garlic Concentrate in Vascular Hypertension," *Medical Record*. 153:249-51, April, 1941.

Fujiwara, M., and Natata, T., "Induction of Tumor Immunity with Tumor Cells Treated with Extract of Garlic," *Nature*. 216:83, October, 1967.

George, K.C., and Amonkar, S.V., et. al., "Effect of Garlic Oil on Incorporation of Amino Acids into Proteins of Culex Pipiens Quinquefasciatus Say Larvae," *Chemo-Biological Interactions*. 6:169-75, 1973.

Hartwell, "Garlic in Cancer Therapy," *Cancer Chemotherapy Reports*. May, 1960.

Jain, R.C., et. al., "Hypoglycaemic Action of Onion and Garlic," *Lancet*. December 29, 1973. (p. 1491).

Johnson, M.G., and Vaughn, R.H., "Death of Salmonella typhimurium and Escherichia coli in the Presence of Freshly Reconstituted Dehydrated Garlic and Onion," *Applied Microbiology*. 17:903-5, June, 1969.

Kimura, Y., and Yamamoto, K., "Cytological Effect of Chemicals in Tumors: Influence of Crude Extracts from Garlic and some Related Species on MTK-Sarcoma III," *GANN*. 55:325-29, February, 1964.

Kotin, E., and Klein, D., *New York Physician*. September, 1937.

Marcovici, E.E., "Garlic Therapy for Digestive Disorders," *Medical Record*. 153:63-65, January, 1941.

Rao, R., "Investigations on Plant Antibiotics," *Journal of Scientific Industrial Resources*. 5:131, 1946.

Snell, S.B., "Garlic on the Baby's Breath," *Lancet*. 819:43, July 7, 1973.

Speenivasamurthy, V., et. al., "Studies on the Stability of Allicin and Alliin," *Journal of Scientific Industrial Resources.* 20c:292-5, October, 1961.

Stoll, Arthur, and Seebeck Ewald, "Chemical Investigations on Alliin, the Specific Principle of Garlic," *Advances in Enzymology.* VII:377-400, 1951.

Strubing, E. von, "Garlic in Ancient Times: A Contribution to the Dietetics and Nutrition of Man," *Ernahrunsforschung.* 12:585-623, 1967. (German)

Tynecka, Zofia, and Gos, Zofia, "The Inhibitory Action of Garlic on Growth and Respiration of Some Microorganisms," *Acta Microbiologica Polonica.* 5:51-62, 1973.

Utsumi, "Allicin and Proteins," *Journal of Vitamins.* 10:855-6, 1964.

Weiss, Emil, "A Clinical Study of the Effects of Desicated Garlic in Intestinal Flora," *Medical Record.* 153:404-8, June, 1941.

Willis, E.D., "Enzyme Inhibition by Allicin, the Active Principle of Garlic," *Biochemical Journal.* 63:514, 1956.

Yanovitch, T.D., *Comptes Rendus de l'Academie des Sciences de l'USSR.* 48:number 7, 1945.

PERIODICALS:

American Magazine. "Kissable Garlic," 159:51, February, 1955.

Colliers. "Garlic Lovers," 137:20-3, January 20, 1956.

-------"Don't Neglect Garlic," 97:26, April 11, 1936.

Field, Michael, "All About Garlic," *Holiday.* 39:24, June, 1966.

McCabe, Charles, "Garlic Country" and "Romance and Garlic," *San Francisco Chronicle.* August 1 and July 11, 1973.

Organic Gardening and Farming. "Will Garlic Replace DDT?" Lawrence D. Hills, 19:46, September, 1972.

-------"Growing Great Garlic," 19:97, June, 1972.

-------"Nature's Secret Life," Robert Rodale, 21:36   May, 1974.

Podolsky, Edward, M.D., "Medical Virtues of Garlic,"*American Cookery.* 36:508, February, 1932.

Prevention. "Garlic for Intestinal Disorder," November, 1958.

    -------"Stop that Cold with Garlic," March, 1959.

    -------"Garlic Triumphs Over Indigestion," May, 1960.

    -------"Experiments with Garlic and Cancer," June, 1958.

    -------Testimony on Garlic and Cancer," March 1960.

    -------"Garlic is a Potent Health Aid," November, 1972.

    -------"Discovery. Garlic Oil for Healthier Arteries," Harald J. Taub. April, 1974.

Reay, Devon, "Garlic," *Horticulture.* 41:228, April, 1963.

    -------, "Green Garlic," *Horticulture.* 50:65, May, 1972.

Rice, Louise, "Garlic, The Vegetable of the Poets," *The Delineator* 83:37, August, 1913.

Watts, Alan, *Alan Watts Journal.* 1:October, 1970.

THIRD EDITION:

Appleton, Judith A., and Tansey, Michael R., "Inhibition of Growth of Zoopathogenic Fungi by Garlic Extract," *Mycologia.* 67: 882-885, July-Aug., 1975

Barone, Frank E., and Tansey, Michael R., "Isolation . . . of the Anticandidal Component of Allium Sativum, and a Hypothesis for its Mode of Action," *Mycologia.* 69:793-825, July-Aug., 1977.

Jain, R. C., "Onion and Garlic in Experimental Cholesterol Induced Atherosclerosis," *Indian Journal of Medical Reserach.* 74,10: 1509-1515, October, 1976.

Jain, R. C., "Effect of alcoholic extract of garlic in atherosclerosis (letter)," *American Journal of Clinical Nutrition.* 31:198-203, November, 1978.

Jain, R. C., and Konar, D. B., "Effect of Garlic Oil in Experimental Cholesterol Atherosclerosis," *Atherosclerosis.* 29:125-129, February, 1978.

ACKNOWLEDGEMENTS

I wish to gratefully acknowledge the following publishers, galleries, and persons for permission to reprint material from their works. Any errors or omissions that may have inadvertently occurred will be corrected in any subsequent printings.

From *Travels* by Marco Polo, translated by Ronald Latham. Copyright © Penguin Books Ltd., 1958, 1968. From *Wonderful Food of Provence* by Jean-Noel Escudier and Peta J. Fuller. Copyright © 1968 by Robert Rebstock and Peta J. Fuller. Reprinted by permission of Houghton Mifflin Company. Macmillan London Ltd. "Burnt Norton," from *Four Quartets* by T.S. Eliot. Harcourt Brace Jovanovich, Inc. Reprinted by permission of Faber and Faber Ltd. From *Provence* by Ford Madox Ford. Copyright 1935 by Ford Madox Ford. Copyright © renewed 1963 by Janice Biala Brustlein. Reprinted by permission of J.B. Lippincott Company. "If Garlic Be the Food of Love," from *Stiff Upper Lip* by Lawrence Durrell. Copyright © 1959 by Lawrence Durrell. Published by E.P. Dutton & Co., Inc. and used with their permission. Faber and Faber Ltd. From *Russian Folk Medicine* by George St. George and Paul Kourennoff, Pyramid Publications © 1970. Reprinted by permission of Georges Borchardt, Inc. "Roasted Garlic" from *La Cuisine* by Raymond Olivier. Tudor Publishing Company. "Garlic Country" and "Romance and Garlic" by Charles McCabe. Copyright © Chronicle Publishing Co., 1973. Letter from Roman Polanski to author dated April 1, 1974. Letter by S.B. Snell, *The Lancet*, 1973, ii, 43 and from the letter by Bordia and Bansal in *The Lancet*, 1973, ii, 1491. From "Will Garlic Replace DDT" by Lawrence Hills, *Organic Gardening and Farming*. September, 1972, Rodale Press, Inc., Emmaus, Pennsylvania. From "Garlic Oil for Healthier Arteries" by Harald J. Taub, *Prevention*, April 1974. © 1974 by Rodale Press, Inc., Emmaus, Pennsylvania. Reprinted by special permission. From "Cytological Effect of Chemicals and Tumors. XXIII. Influence of Crude Extracts from Garlic and Some Related Species on MTK-Sarcoma III" by Y. Kimura and K. Yamamoto, *Gann*, Vol. 55, No. 4, pp. 325-329, 1964. Reprinted from *Gann* by permission of the copyright owner, the Japanese Cancer Association. From "Induction of Tumor Immunity with Tumor Cells Treated with Extract of Garlic" by Dr. M. Fujiwara and T. Natata. *Nature*, October, 1967. From "The Breath that Kills," *Newsweek*, March 30, 1970. Copyright Newsweek Inc., 1970. Reprinted by permission. From "Arthur Koestler: Neoplatonism Rides Again," by Martin Gardner, *World*, August 1, 1972. Also reprinted by permission from *Time*, "Boom Times on the Psychic Frontier," March 2, 1974 © Time Inc. From *Garlic, The Unknown Miracle Worker* by Yoshio Kato. Reprinted by permission of Oyama Garlic Laboratory. Copyright © 1973. Amagasaki, Japan. From "Knoblauch in alten Zeiten. Zur Diätetik und Ernahrung der Menschen," by E. Strübing, *Ernahrungsforschung* Band 12, pp. 585-623, 1967. By permission of Akademie Der Wissenschaften Der DDR, Berlin. *Saint Jerome in His Study* by Durer, courtesy of the Nelson Gallery, Atkins Museum, Kansas City, Missouri (gift of Mr. Robert B. Fizzell). From "Where Garlic Wins," by Macleod, in *Harpers Weekly*, Part 1, 54:34 Feb. 5, 1910. From "Introduction to the Pebble," in *Things* by Francis Ponge, Grossman Publishers. Copyright 1971, by Mushinsha Ltd. From a letter "A Dog's Recovery," from the *Morning Post*, London, December 12, 1922. From "The Book of Songs," in *Anthology of Chinese Literature*, Vol. 1. Reprinted by permission of Grove Press, Inc. © 1965 by Grove Press, Inc. "Consciousness-Raising Cuisine" by Susan Efros. © 1975. By permission of author. "Symiotic Keftedes," in *The Mythological Travels* by Daniel Spoerri. Reprinted by permission of the author. Copyright © 1970, Something Else Press, Inc.

Special Thanks To:

Nanos Valaoritis for his help in collecting the Garlic Papers, and for his contribution of raw garlic for several of the collages

Sahag and Elizabeth Avedisian, Berkeley collectivist entrepreneurs of the soul

Chester Aaron, literary contact, raconteur and co-gossip

Daniel Spoerri, for conceptual inspiration and permission to use material from his *Mythological Travels*

Patricia Darrow, for her support and contributions

Cookbooks from Aris Books
Garlic lovers will enjoy these related books from Aris, all full of garlicky recipes.

Ginger East to West by Bruce Cost. A celebration of ginger with recipes and information from China to California. 192 pages, cloth $17.95, paper $9.95

The California Seafood Cookbook by Isaac Cronin, Jay Harlow and Paul Johnson. The definitive recipe and reference guide to fish and shellfish of the Pacific. It includes 150 recipes, magnificent fish illustrations, important information and more. "... *one of the best manuals I have ever read* ..." —M.F.K. Fisher. 288 pages, cloth $20.00, paper $11.95

The Feast of the Olive: Cooking with Olives and Olive Oil by Maggie Blyth Klein. A complete recipe and reference guide to using fine olive oils and a variety of cured olives. 223 pages, cloth $16.95, paper $9.95

The Art of Filo Cookbook by Marti Sousanis. International entrées, appetizers and desserts wrapped in flaky pastry. 144 pages, paper $8.95

To receive the above titles, send a check or money order made out to Aris Books for the amount of the book plus $1.50 postage and handling for the first title, and 75¢ for each additional title. To receive our current catalogue of new titles, send your name and address plus 50¢ for postage and handling.

Aris Books, 1621 Fifth Street, Berkeley, CA 94710